IMAGES
of America

BERWICK

I0806246

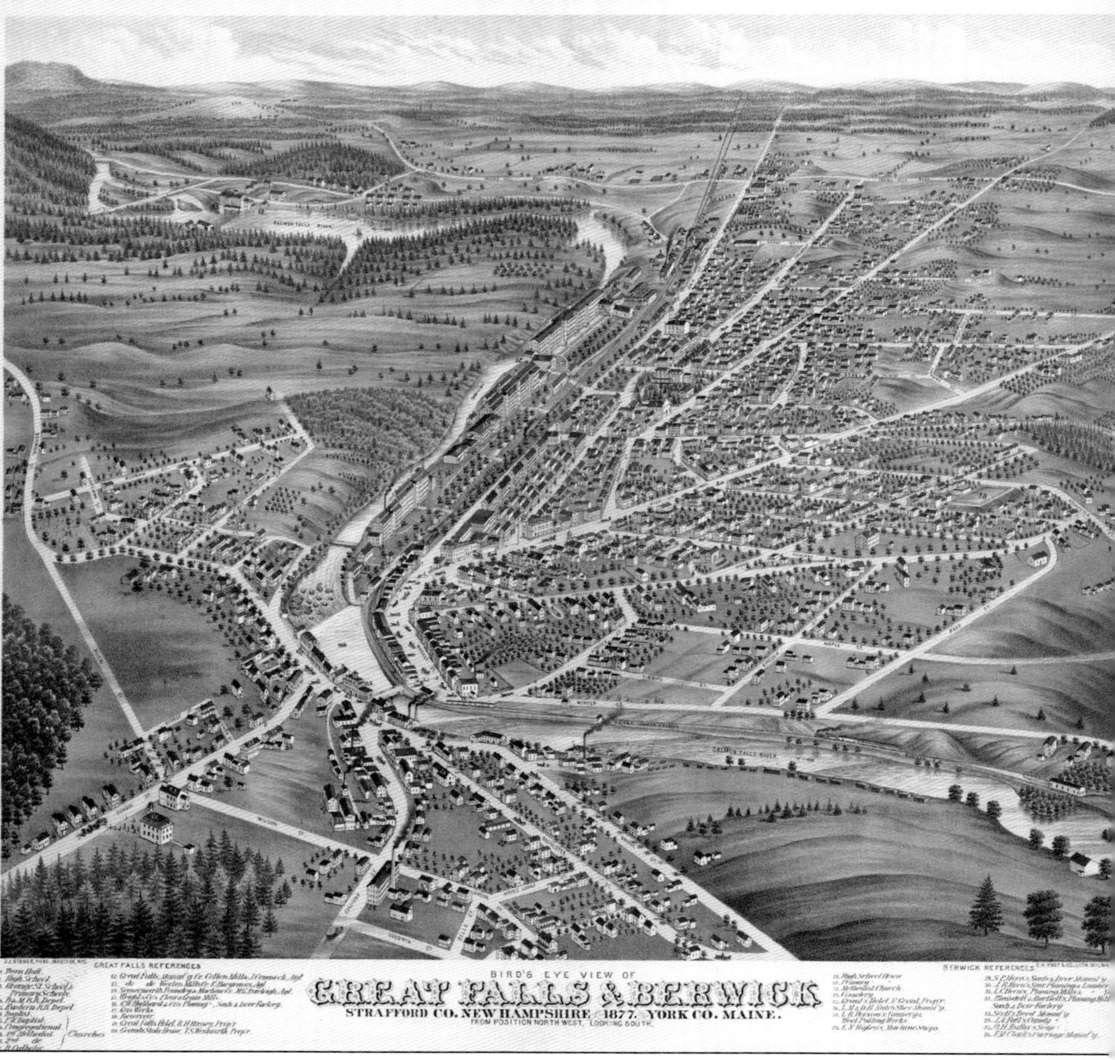

This hand-drawn map of Berwick, Maine, and Somersworth, New Hampshire, depicts a bird's-eye view of the two towns. Dated 1877, the map shows the relationship that early businesses had with the Salmon Falls River and the railroad. (Courtesy of Lynn Rouff.)

On the Cover: This photograph, thought to be taken around 1910, shows the businesses along the Salmon Falls River. This location, known as "the harbor" by the locals, was a place of recreation, freshwater fishing, and boat rentals during the late 19th century and the early 20th century. The Sweetser, once a wholesale confectioners shop, is the current location of the Summit Church, at 1 Sullivan Square. (Courtesy of the Berwick Historical Society.)

IMAGES
of America

BERWICK

Jessie Taylor

ARCADIA
PUBLISHING

ISBN 978-1-4671-2225-2

Published by Arcadia Publishing
Charleston, South Carolina

Printed in the United States of America

Library of Congress Control Number: 2014932354

For all general information, please contact Arcadia Publishing:
Telephone 843-853-2070
Fax 843-853-0044
E-mail sales@arcadiapublishing.com
For customer service and orders:
Toll-Free 1-888-313-2665

Visit us on the Internet at www.arcadiapublishing.com

Dedicated to the Berwick Historical Society, the Berwick Public Library, and the families of Berwick.

CONTENTS

ACKNOWLEDGMENTS

A special thank-you is given to the Berwick Historical Society, Berwick Public Library, and Berwick Town Hall. Gratitude is extended especially to Eleanor Murphy, who lent her time to ensure, to the best of her abilities, that the information included within this book was factual. Eleanor was able to fill in many gaps of what may have otherwise been lost history. Brian Cincotta was also instrumental in the completion of this book. Without his knowledge and willingness to provide access to numerous photographs, this book would not exist. Thank you to Lisa Huestis for connecting me with the people I needed to make this book a reality. Lisa, you were the key to the success of this book. Thank you to Lyn Rouff and Sharon Hall for always being ready with the magnifying glass. I enjoyed our time playing trivia and history detectives! Thank you to Dawn Milbury for digging through all those boxes of family photographs and sharing the priceless stories that accompanied many of them. Many thanks are extended to Pat and Paul Boisvert for their assistance in collecting and identifying photographs. Thank you to Ann Smith and Nancy Fulton for contributing some very important pieces of Berwick's farming history. Nancy, please rest easy knowing that as long as copies of this book exist, your photographs will never be missed again by anyone.

Unless otherwise noted, the images in this book were provided by the Berwick Historical Society. Courtesy lines have been included for those photographs that were acquired privately through Berwick residents who stepped forward to assist in the promotion of the book. Thank you!

Thank you to my editor, Caitrin Cunningham, for her patience and guidance through the process of compiling what at times felt like an overwhelming amount of information. And, lastly, thank you to my family and friends for believing in me even when I had lost faith in myself.

INTRODUCTION

Situated on the banks of the Salmon Falls River, Berwick originally offered an ideal location for Native American tribes that relied on the natural elements to survive. It is the general consensus among most historians that, in 1631, Ambrose Gibbens was the first white settler in Berwick. At this time, Berwick was still considered part of Kittery and was called Kittery Commons or Kittery North Parish. Not long after his arrival, Gibbens started a trading post with his wife and daughter. The store was reported to sell ammunition for protection from some of the Native American tribes that were unfriendly toward the white men.

One of the attractions that brought many other settlers to the area was the outstanding growth of pine covering the area. As a result of these pines, the first sawmill in America was set up at the Great Works Falls. This was popularly referred to as Gibbens' Mill. The number of sawmills quickly rose, to as many as 18, and Native Americans began referring to the area as "the place of great works." This was the start of a thriving community that was born at the head of the Piscataqua River, now known as South Berwick.

With a prosperous trading post, boat building, fishing, busy sawmills, and hunting, the population of the community grew quickly. When the town had 200 inhabitants, a meetinghouse was erected.

A short time later, the town adopted the name Unity, after the ship that transported Scot prisoners of war from the Battle of Dunbar in 1650 to the colonies. Landing in Massachusetts, the royalist soldiers were sold as indentured servants, many of whom went to work at the Great Works Saw Mill. They worked at mills until they were able to pay for their freedom.

In 1675, the town endured the first of many Native American raids during what was known as King Philip's War. Between 1690 and 1691, the village was burned to the ground by an attack from a hostile Indian tribe, fighting for the king. The raid would later be known as the Raid on Salmon Falls. The band of Canadian Natives attacked the town in three locations, killing 30 men and capturing another 50. The attack was so severe that it caused the town to be abandoned altogether.

However, the lure of prosperity was so great that settlers would not stay away for long. In 1703, the town was resettled once again, and it adopted a new name, Newichawannock. The name came from the Abernaki tribe, who were friendly to the settlers and assisted them in rebuilding the town.

It was around the early part of the 18th century that Newichawannock cast off its name once again and adopted the name Barwick (later translated to Berwick), after England's Berwick-Upon-Tweed.

The Sullivans were a prominent family in town during the 1700s, and today, many landmarks and schools bear the name. James Sullivan, born in 1744, was a lawyer and politician in Massachusetts. He was an early associate justice of the Massachusetts Supreme Judicial Court and served as the state's attorney general for many years. In 1807, he became the seventh governor of Massachusetts.

Sullivan had been born and raised in Berwick, Maine, which was still a part of Massachusetts at the time. He studied law with his brother John, who was known for his time serving as a general in the American Revolution, a delegate in Congress, and the governor of New Hampshire.

In 1712, the town of Kittery requested that it be divided into two or more parts. This request was not well received by Berwick. However, regardless of Berwick's position on the matter, on June 9, 1713, Berwick became the state's ninth incorporated town. At this time, Berwick was the most inland town nearest to Canada, which put the community in a constant state of fear of Indian raids.

As the town grew, a second community began to thrive on Blackberry Hill. In 1749, it was voted to divide the town into two parishes. The south end was known as Old Fields, and the north end adopted the name Blackberry Hill. That same year, the town voted to build a second meetinghouse on Blackberry Hill.

Berwick's first church was erected in 1755 on Blackberry Hill, when a parish meeting in Old Fields released some of its members to form a new church. This can be considered the origin of the area now known as Berwick. The church remained open until 1848, when meetings stopped because of the growth and development at Great Falls, now downtown Berwick, where another congregational church had been built.

Around 1765, the tensions between the New World and Great Britain were escalating. Initially, town records indicated a fierce loyalty toward the crown, but relations were quickly dissolving as dissatisfaction regarding the management of the colonies grew. In 1776, the town voted to support the colonies in the Declaration of Independence.

In 1783, the Second Treaty of Paris was signed, ending the Revolutionary War. The community of Berwick shifted its focus back to development and manufacturing. Between 1783 and 1839, one or more shipyards were built, and roadways were made to connect Boston and Portland.

By 1814, the town had expanded so much that South Berwick petitioned the Massachusetts Court to become its own town. This petition was granted and, soon after, in 1831, North Berwick also became its own town.

The Salmon Falls River continued to be a valuable asset to Berwick residents through the 19th and 20th centuries. Lumbering, the primary industry in the early part of the 19th century, relied heavily on the falls to power the mills where the lumber was processed. In the mid-19th century, the introduction of the railroad in Berwick made meeting the demands for lumber and other goods more obtainable, and Berwick became less reliant on the river for transportation and power. Toward the end of the 19th century and the beginning of the 20th century, factories were becoming more popular. Nute's Shoe Factory came to Berwick in the 1870s, and others soon followed. Prime Tanning came to Berwick in the 1930s; at one time, it was the country's leading leather manufacturer.

Prime Tanning closed its doors for good just after the turn of the 21st century, leaving the town to rediscover itself and adopt a new identity. Today, the town that once turned its back on the Salmon Falls River in the days of industrialism is now preparing to turn and face it again in a new light. No longer do Berwick residents see the river as a means of power or transportation, but instead as a place where people can gather and enjoy its beauty and recreational potential.

One

Landmarks and Landscapes

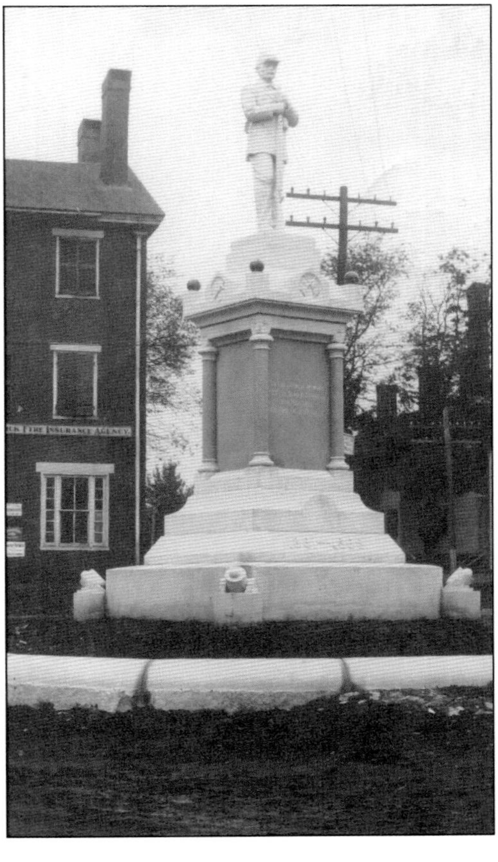

In 1911, the Soldiers' Monument was erected in Sullivan Square, where, 50 years earlier, more than 150 men and boys gathered to go forth to fight in the Civil War. As part of the presentation and dedication of the monument, a procession was started from the GAR Hall in Somersworth, New Hampshire, to the monument site in Berwick.

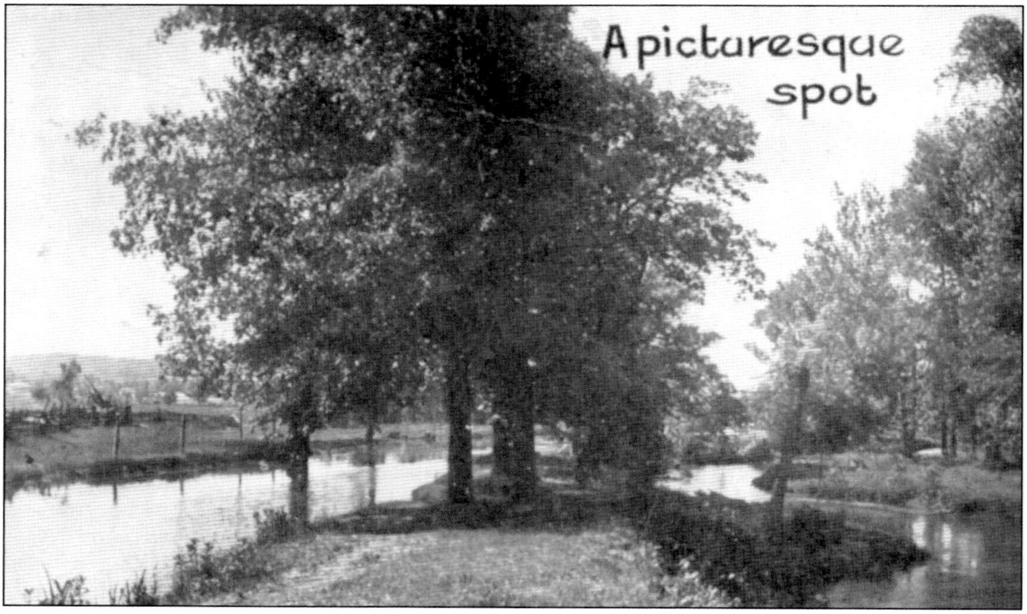

These postcards, dated 1914, show a view of Salmon Falls River from an area located off Bridge Street in Berwick. The Salmon Falls River is an arm of the Piscataqua River, which runs through Maine and New Hampshire. It rises at Great East Lake and flows south-southeast for approximately 38 miles, serving as a natural border between Maine and New Hampshire. It is known for providing hydroelectric power in the New Hampshire towns of Milton, North Rochester, and Rollinsford and the Maine towns of Berwick and South Berwick. The final three miles of the river, running from South Berwick to the Piscataqua, are tidal.

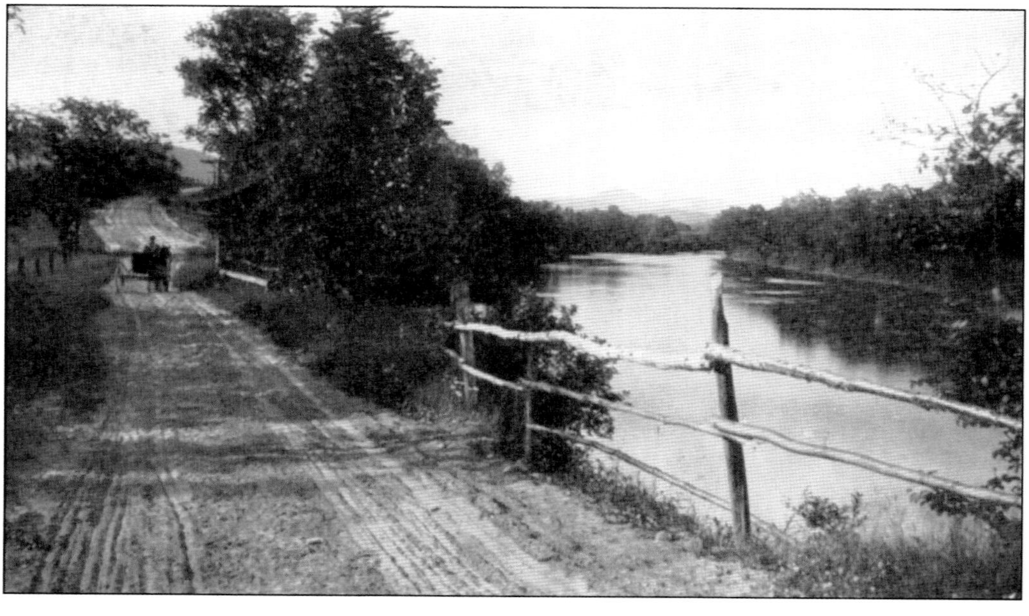

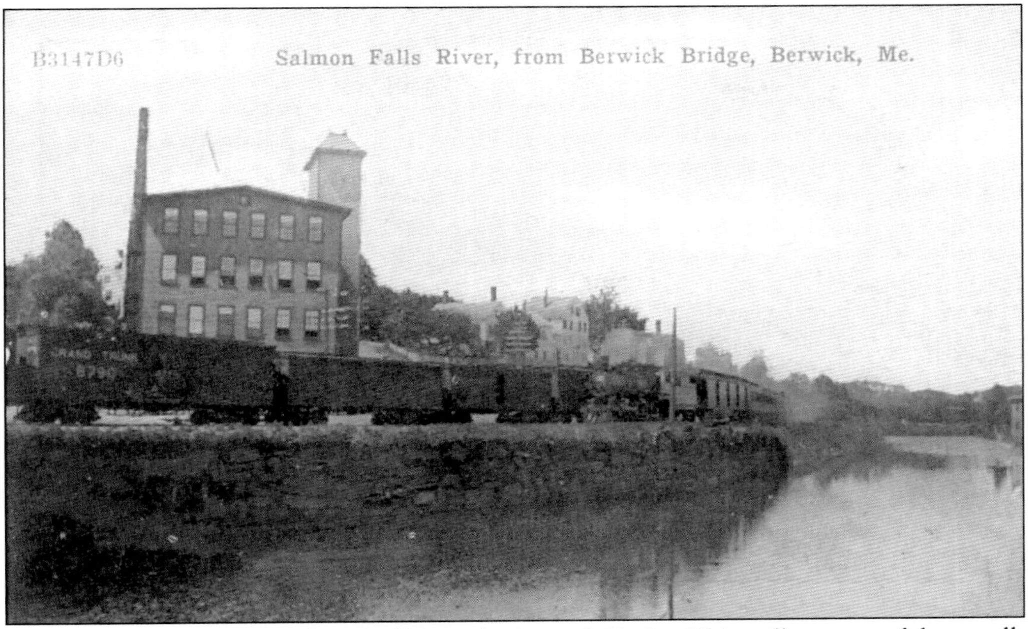

This postcard shows Queensbury Mill from the Berwick Bridge. This mill was one of three well-known mills used for spinning threads and weaving cotton and woolen fabric. A train runs on the tracks beside the Salmon Falls River. The Boston & Maine Railroad came to Berwick in 1843. These tracks still serve as a major transportation route between Portland and Boston.

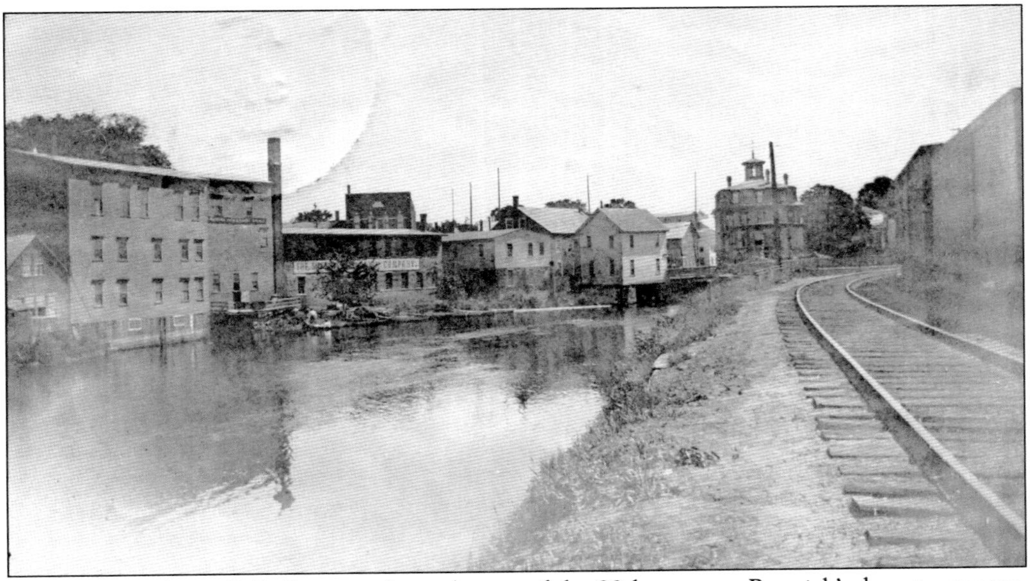

Looking up Salmon Falls River in the early part of the 20th century, Berwick's downtown area, including the Grant's Hotel, is clearly visible. Note the men tying up their boat in front of the building with a smokestack. It was common to rent a boat at this location for convenient transportation into New Hampshire. This postcard is dated August 20, 1906.

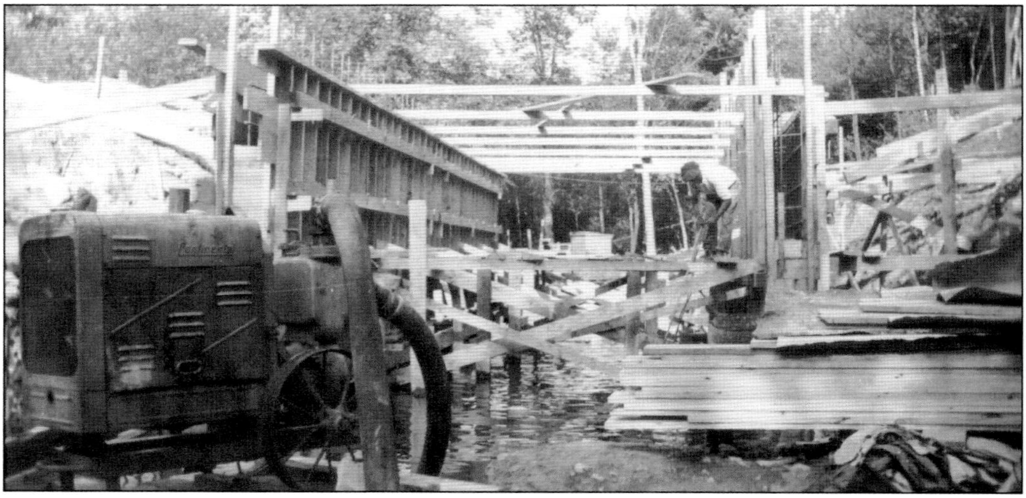

The Worster Bridge, located on Blackberry Hill Road, crosses over the Worster Brook. The brook was named after Moses Worster, who built a sawmill there with Timothy Wentworth in 1709. Born in 1643, Worster was known as "Old Contrary" and lived to at least age 88. He first farmed for many years on 200 acres in present-day Eliot near Sturgeon Creek. However, at the age of 66, he built his mill on the creek at Berwick. The Worster Brook flows into the nearby Salmon Falls River, which eventually meets with the Piscataqua River. Historically, the brook marks the scene of a Native American attack on the settlements of the Salmon Falls during the King William's War in the late 1600s. Settlers whose family members had been taken captive made an unsuccessful effort to recover the hostages before they were taken to Canada.

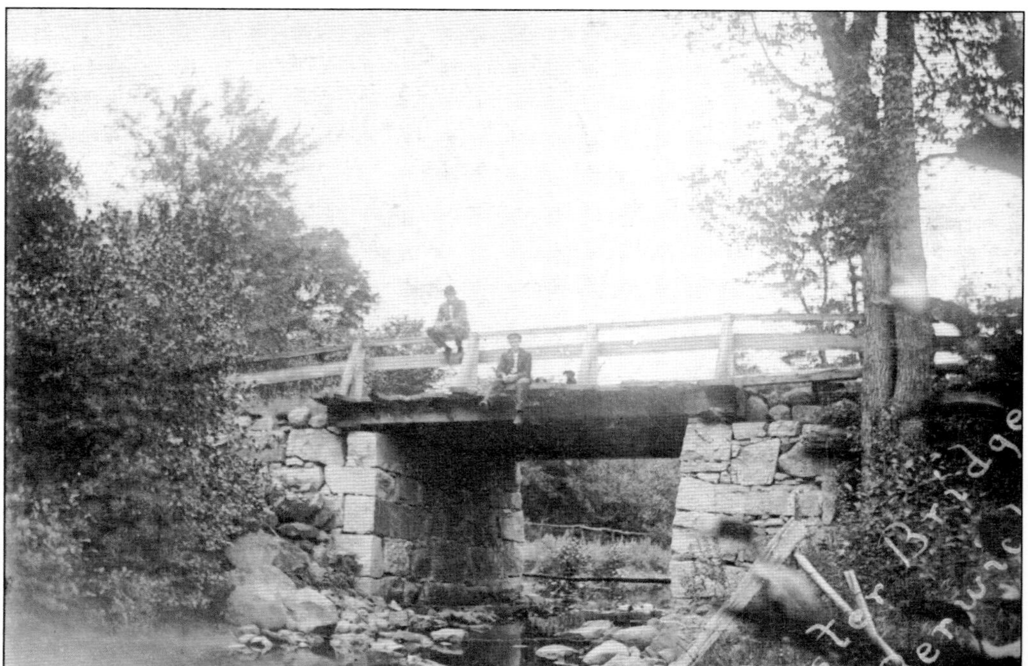

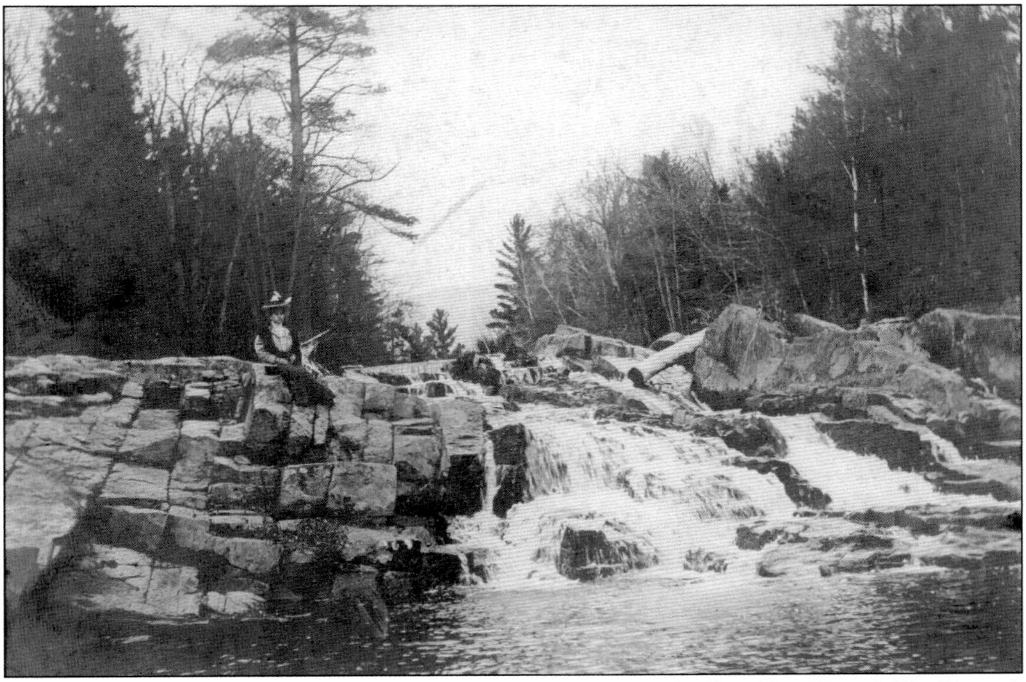

Martha Litchfield sits on the rocks at Horne's Mill Dam, located off Hubbard Road. The Horne's Mill, built in 1872, was equipped with machinery for all types of woodwork. During that period, building dams was a common way to create waterpower for sawmills and gristmills.

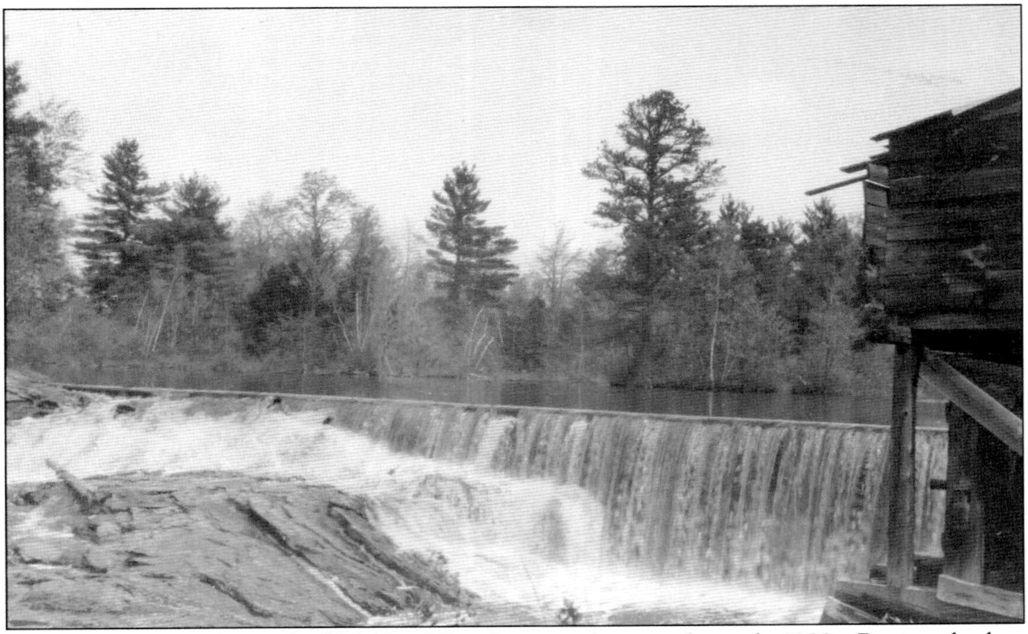

Horne's Mill Dam, located off Hubbard Road, is seen here in the early 1900s. During the late 1800s and early 1900s, America adopted an aggressive dam-building philosophy. Beginning in the early 19th century, dams were built mostly to power the mills of the industrial revolution. These dams were considered symbols of power, innovation, and technical progress.

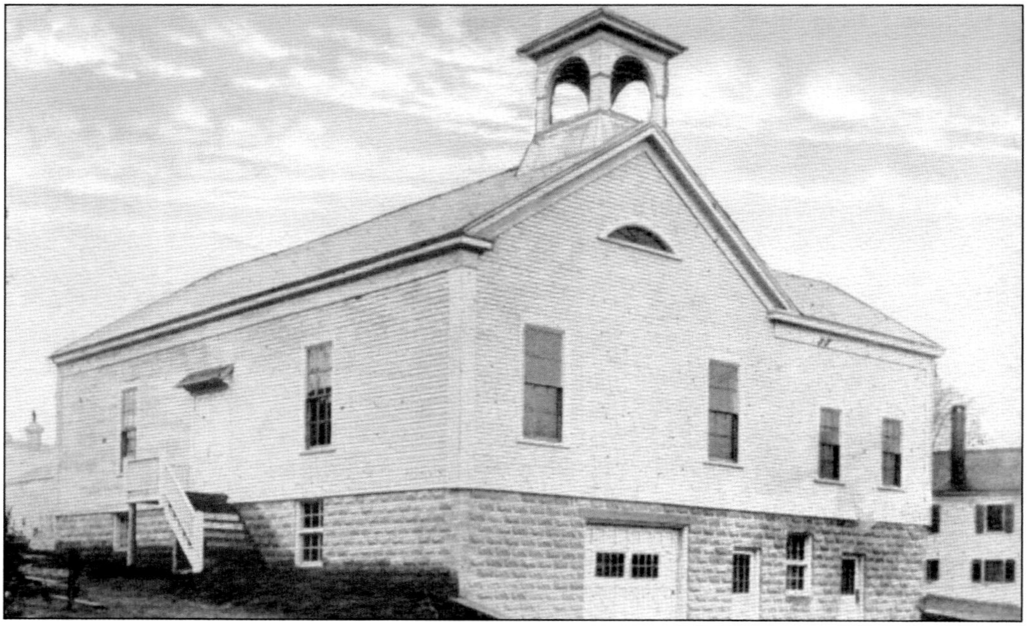

These postcards shows Berwick's first town hall, when it was located on School Street. This town hall was used until 1938, when the new town hall was built. After 1938, it served as a school for grades three and four. It was demolished in July 1966 to make way for the fire station. As of 2013, its bell is on display adjacent to the Berwick Fire Department.

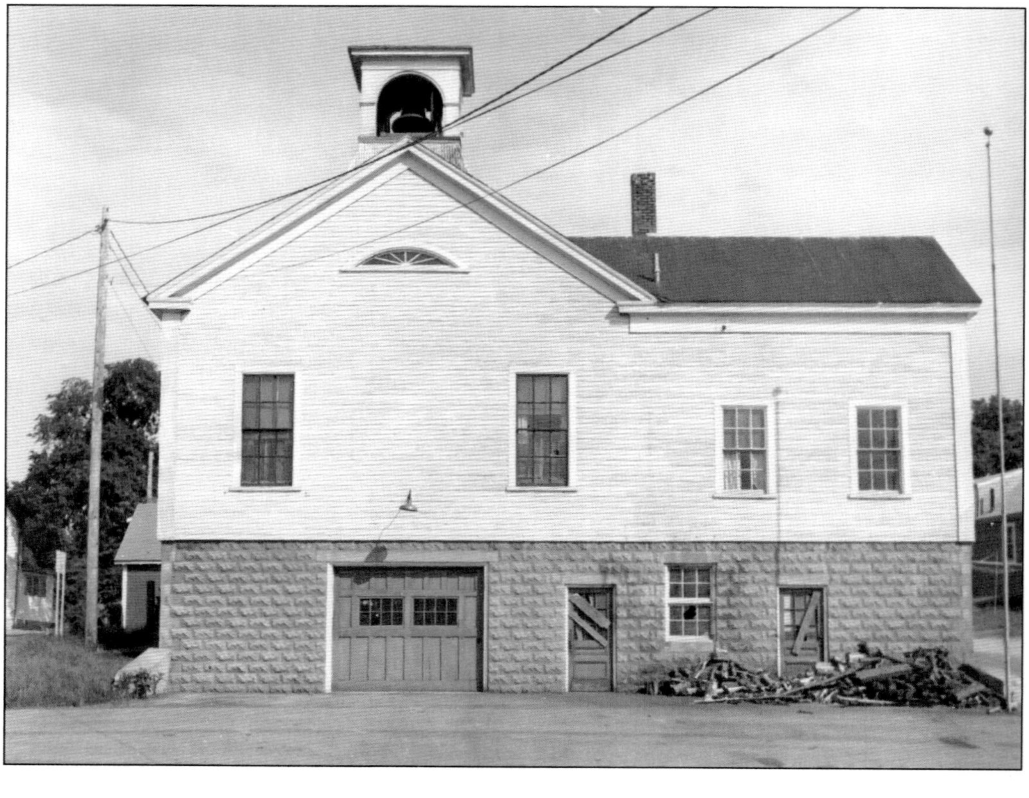

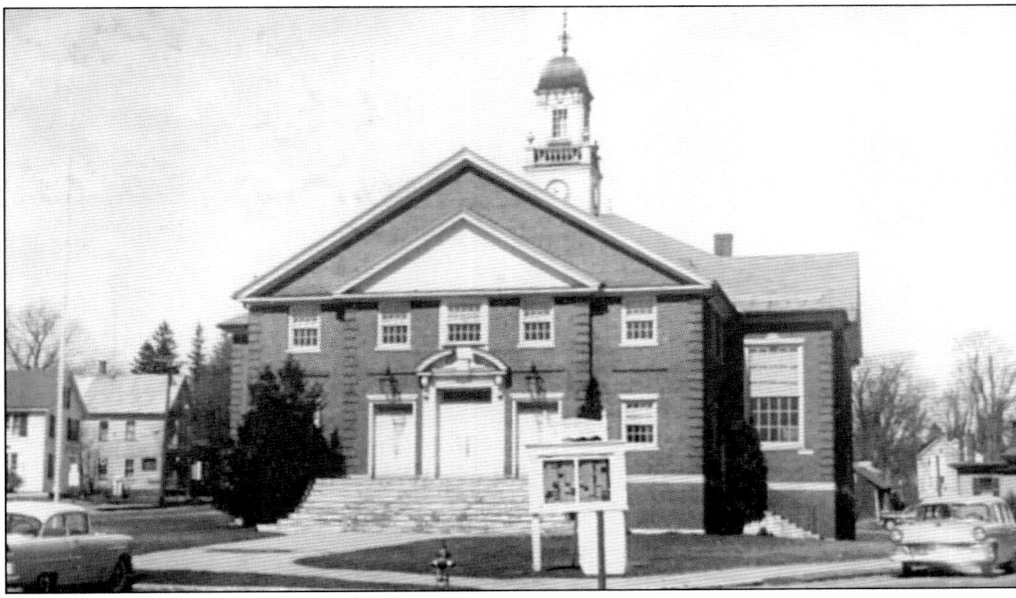

These postcards shows Berwick's second town hall, built in 1939. Plans for the building were in the making for nearly a decade before its completion. Plans started in 1928 with a donation from Lena Clark in the amount of several thousand dollars. Interest was allowed to collect on her donation until 1937, when a committee was formed to oversee the building of the new town hall. Several properties were acquired for the building, including the Casper Marshall property, the site of Manchester Rendering Company, Butler Stable Lots, and the Clarence Butler homestead. This large area of land was situated between Sullivan and Rochester Streets. The total coast of the project was $85,000. The Federal Public Works Department contributed 45 percent of the cost.

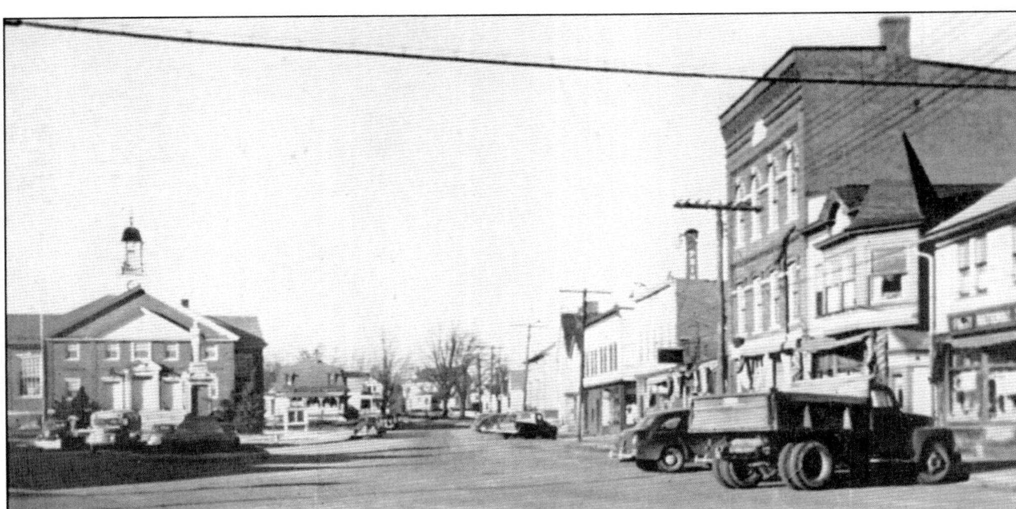

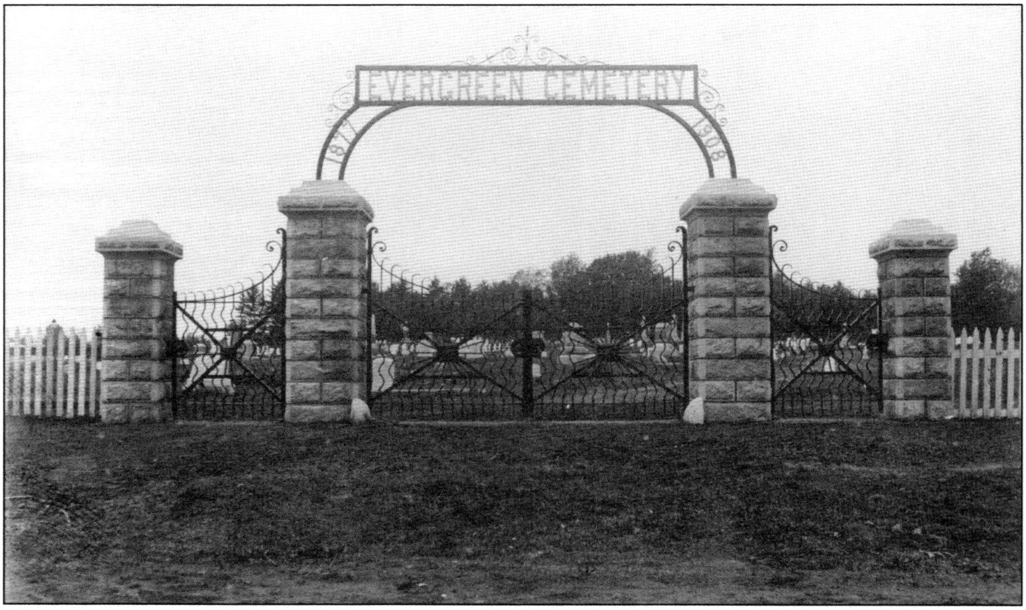

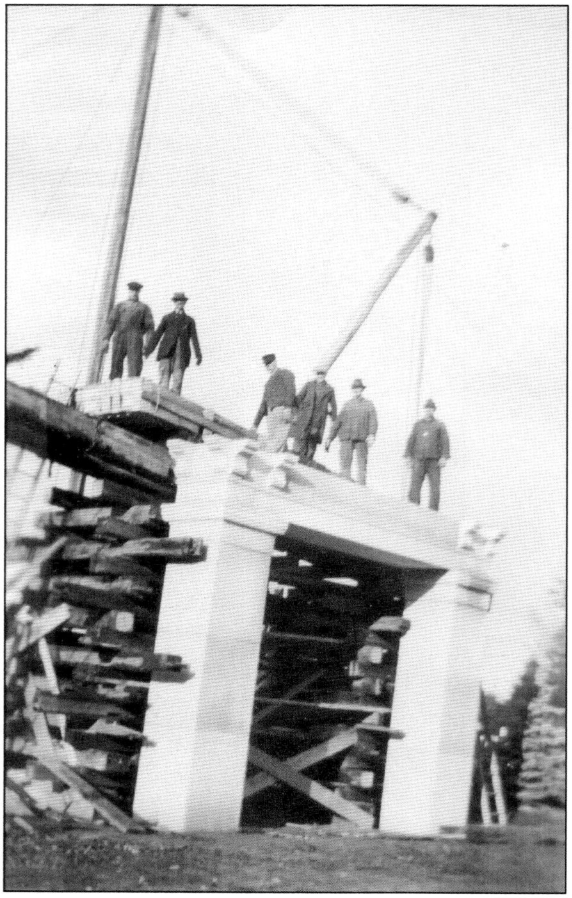

Prior to 1877, the town had no official burial grounds. Instead, the deceased were placed in private family cemeteries scattered throughout town. When the Evergreen Cemetery was built, many of the deceased that had been placed in private burial grounds were moved here. It is located on Cemetery Road, which is a crossroad from Pine Hill and Cranberry Meadow Road. The gate shown in the above photograph displays two dates: 1877, marking the opening of the cemetery, and 1908, marking the installation of the new gate. This gate was unable to stand the test of time and, within a few decades, was in need of replacement, as shown at left.

This postcard of Our Lady of Peace Church depicts the church in the beginning of the 20th century, shortly after it opened. Located on Saw Mill Hill, it was the first Catholic church in Berwick. Prior to its opening, Berwick Catholics attended services in Somersworth, New Hampshire, and then later in South Berwick. In 1924, Father Fitzpatrick purchased the Lord property on Saw Mill Hill, which later became the site of Our Lady of Peace Church. Today, the church sits abandoned, awaiting purchase.

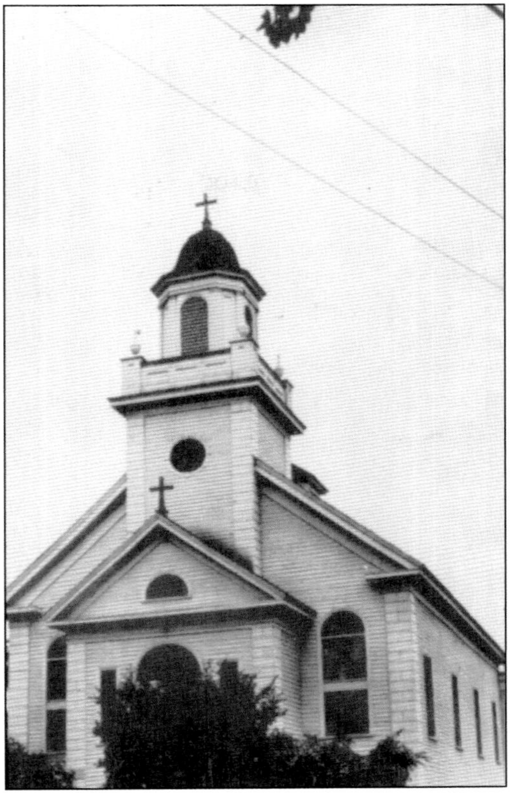

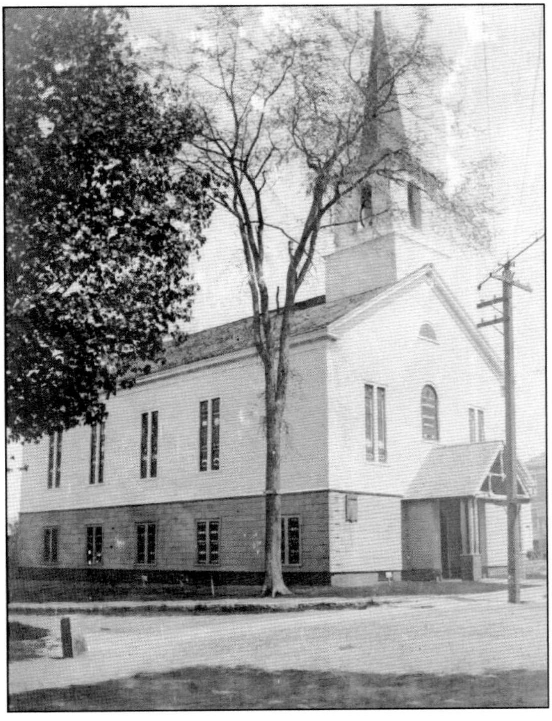

Built in 1877, the Methodist Episcopal Church is located on School Street. It was originally located on Cranberry Meadow Road but was moved in two sections in the late 1800s to its present location. Once situated, a third section was added in the middle, as well as an additional window. In March 1910, the church was significantly damaged in two separate fires. It was not until December of that year that a virtually whole new church was rebuilt. The church continues to hold services and is a showcase of period craftsmanship, found in the detailed ceilings and traditional balcony.

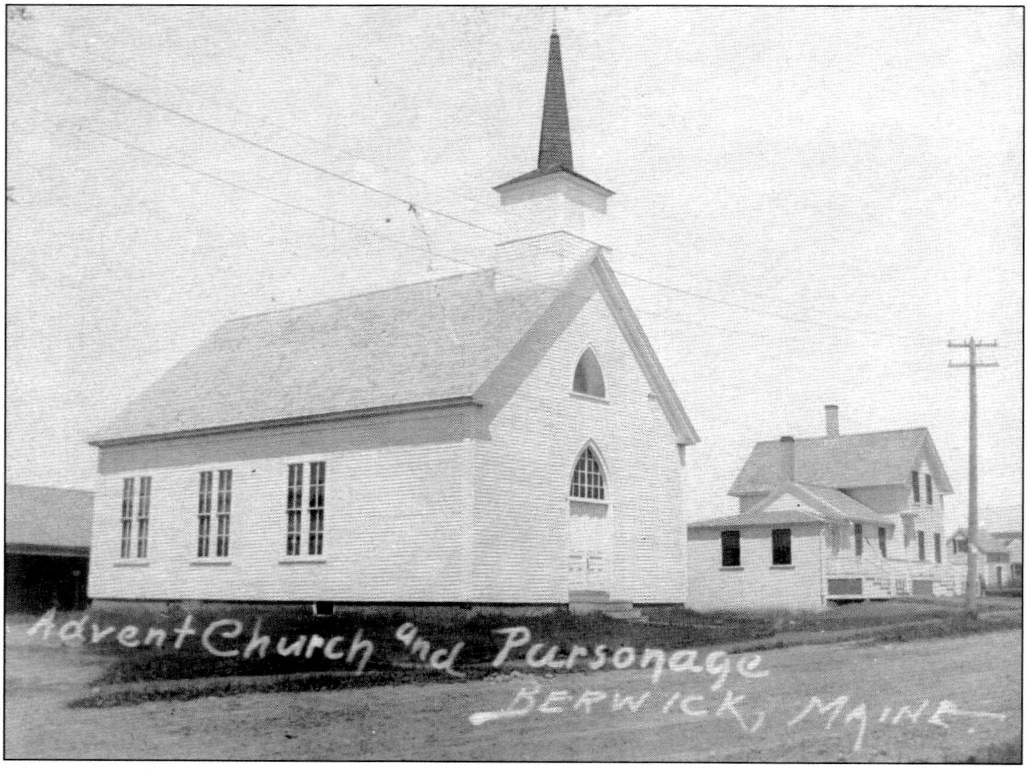

This postcard of "Advent Church and Parsonage" is dated October 6, 1905. The Advent Church is located on Sullivan Street. The house next to the church served as the parsonage. Active as early as 1880, the church continued to hold services until about 1948. The buildings are presently privately owned.

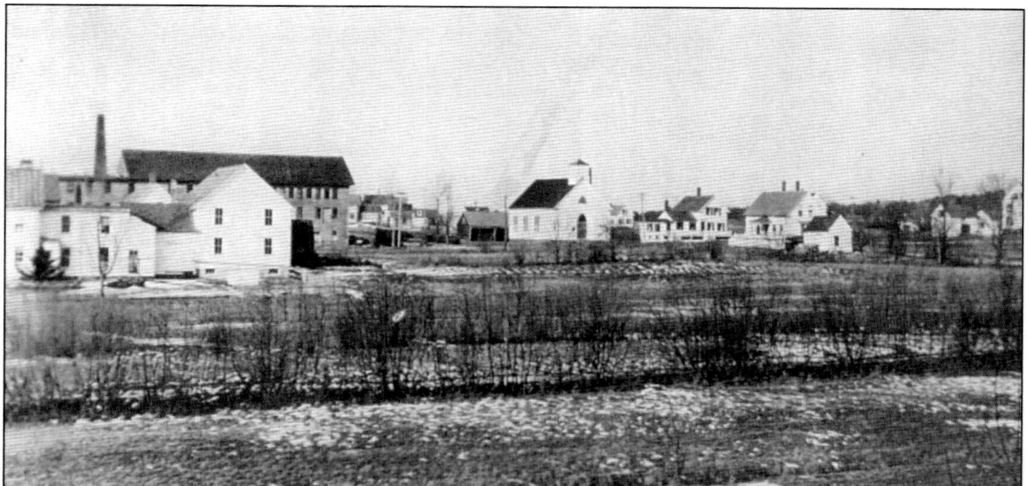

This photograph of downtown Berwick shows the Advent Christian Church in the center of this image of Sullivan Street. The house to the right of the church was known as the Chase property during that time. The building on the far left with a smokestack was Nute's Shoe Factory.

Two

SULLIVAN SQUARE

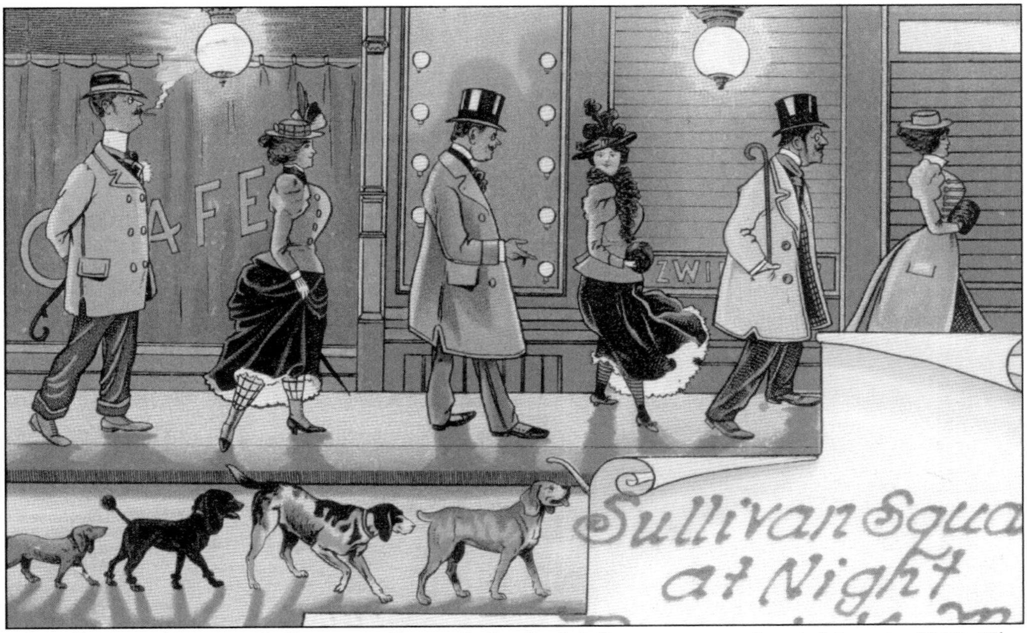

This illustrated postcard, depicting Berwick "night life," was sent to Annie Nute in 1909. The town at that time was known as a successful, bustling mill town. Nute was a prominent name in Berwick; the family was known for ownership of the Nute Shoe Factory, which stood on the corner of Sullivan and Jordan Streets in the late 19th century.

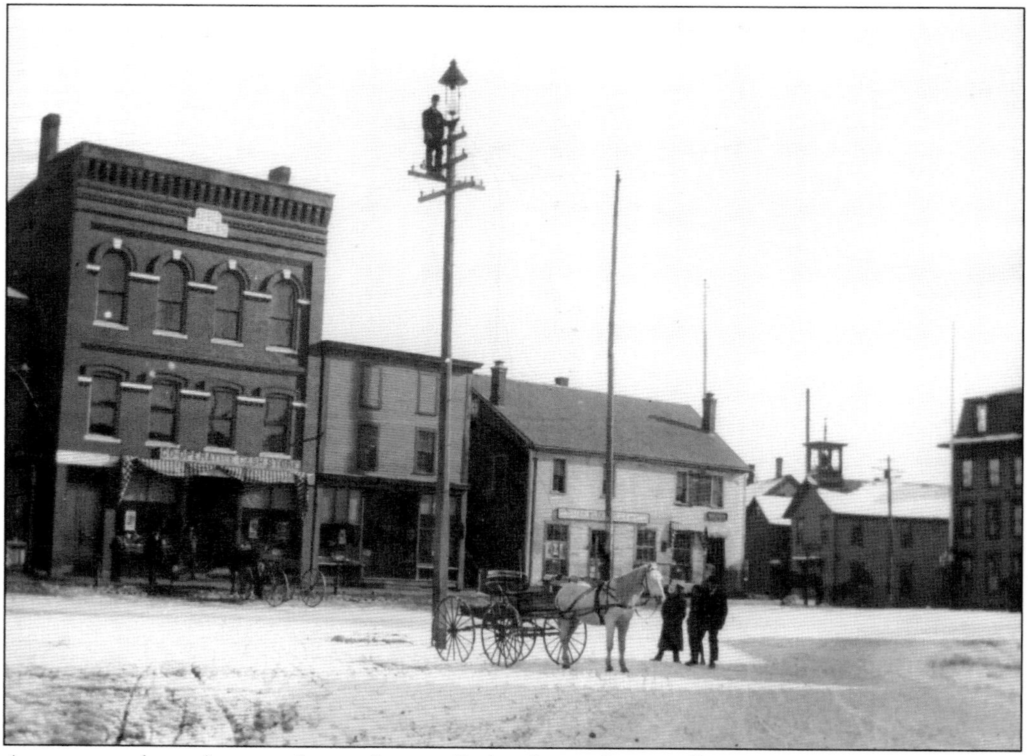

A man stands at the top of a newly installed utility pole in Sullivan Square. Directly behind him is the Co-operative Cash Store, which sold ammunition, tools, clothing, feed for stock, and groceries. The word "cash" in the title, not uncommon at the time, indicated that the store did not allow purchases on credit.

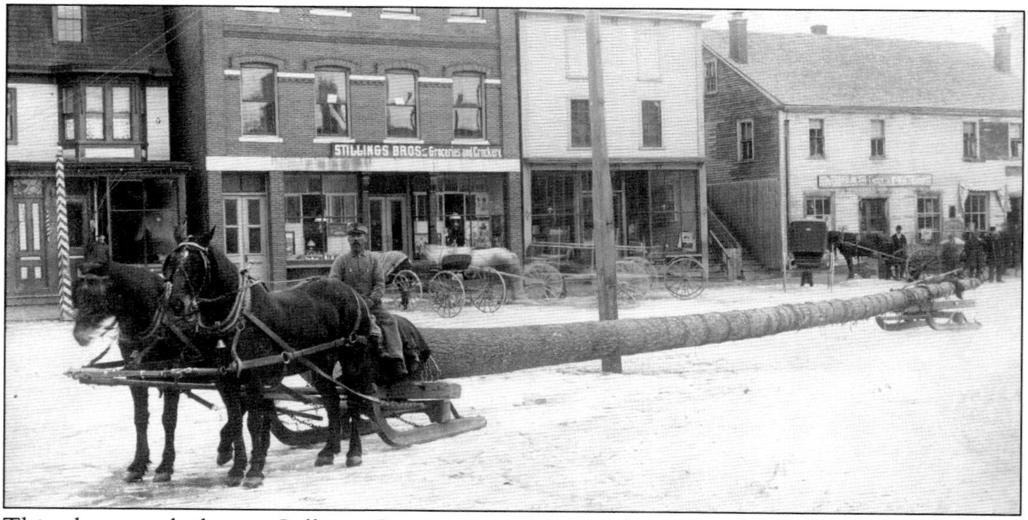

This photograph depicts Sullivan Square around 1890. The horse is pulling a log that will be used for a utility pole. In the background are storefronts of the downtown area. At the far left is a barbershop, and next to it are two merchandise stores. The building on the right later became Berwick's first post office.

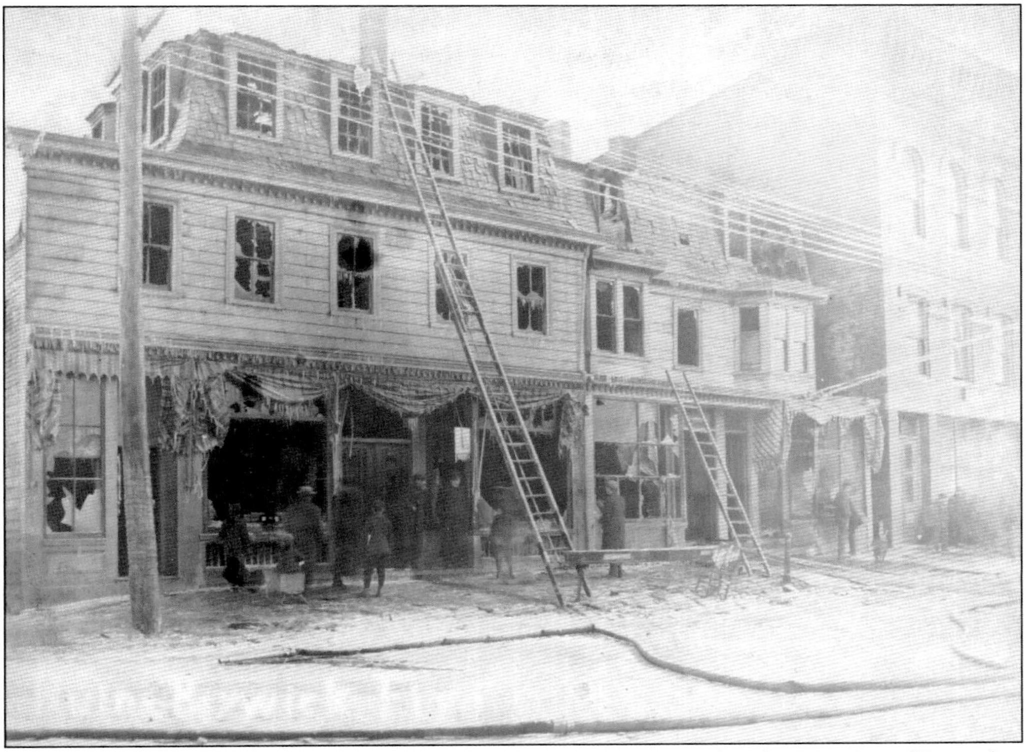

The photographs for these postcards were taken by Maurice Austin after the great fire of December 1906. The Sullivan Square fire of the Spencer Lord Block took place at 4:15 on the morning of December, 15, 1907. This fire claimed the entire block up to the Odd Fellow building. The Stillings Brothers store and burned-out storefronts can be seen in these photographs. The Stilling Brothers store was located inside the brick building on the far right of the above photograph. It was a grocery store established in 1874 by the Sovereigns of Industry. J.H. Stillings was the agent who ran the store.

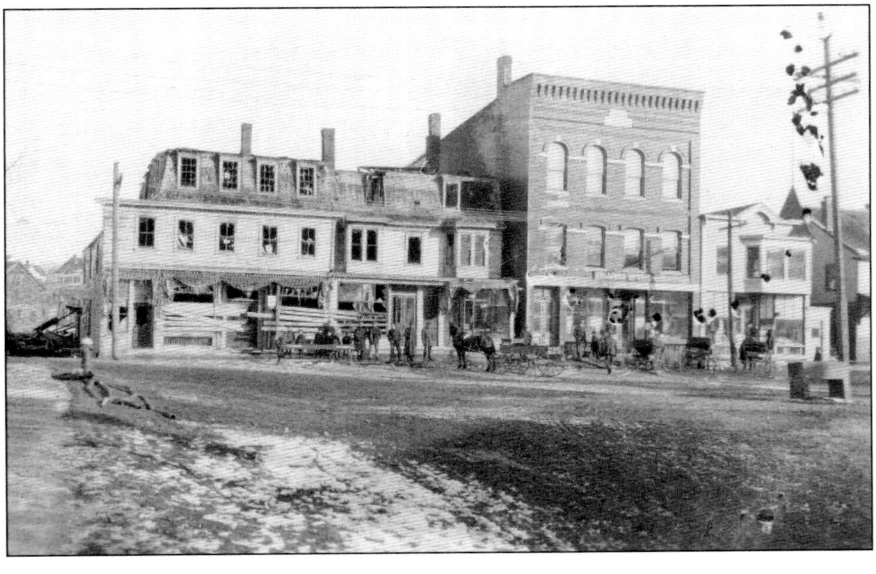

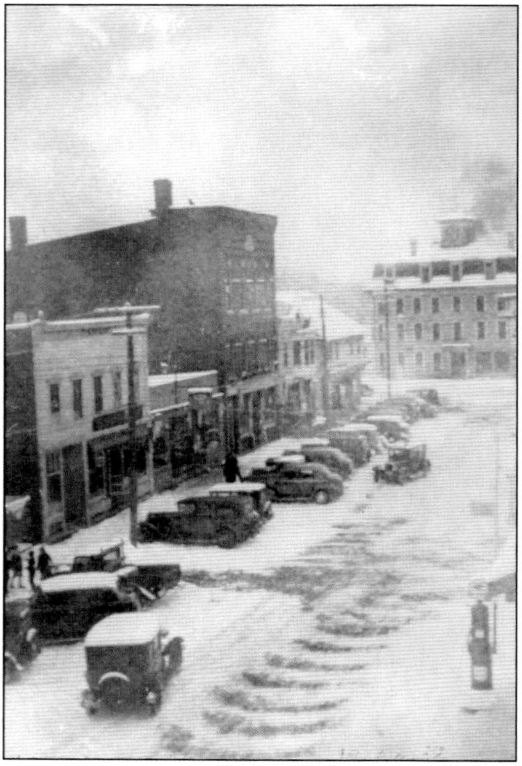

This photograph, taken by Meredith Clement, shows a bird's-eye view of Sullivan Square between 1936 and 1937. This was before the new town hall was built. Among the businesses seen here are Grant's Hotel (background) and the Odd Fellow Block, encompassing a grocery store and Berwick Fire Agency.

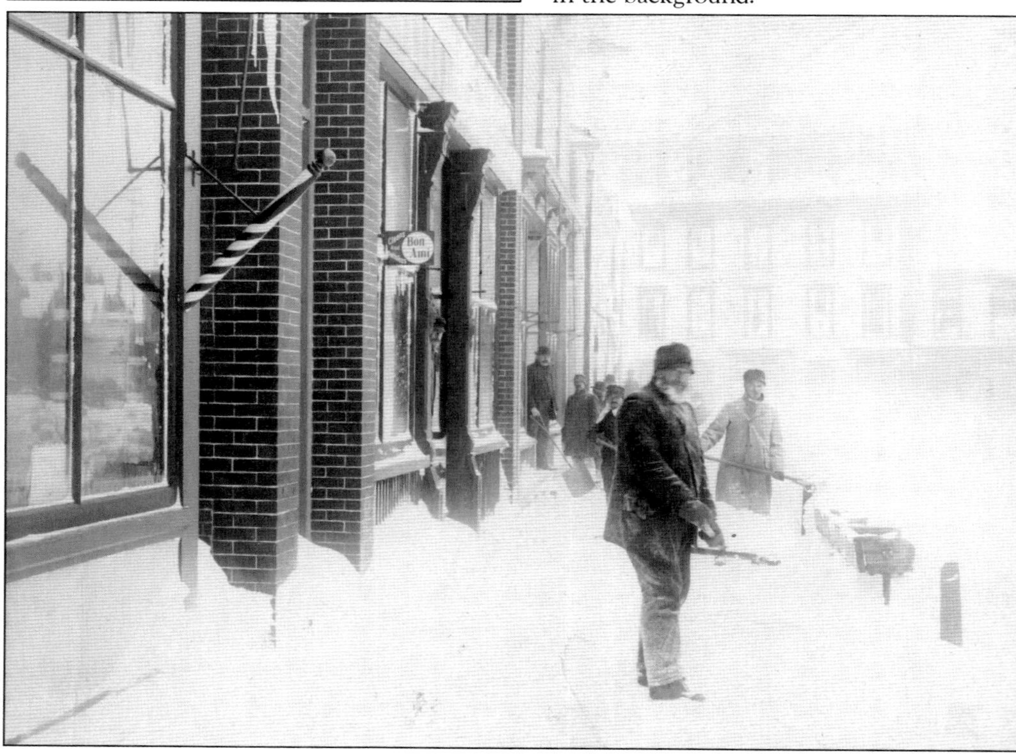

Here, local business owners attempt to clear the sidewalks in front of their Sullivan Square storefronts during the storm of 1898. The man in the foreground is standing in front of one of Berwick's first barbershops. The Grant's Hotel can be seen in the background.

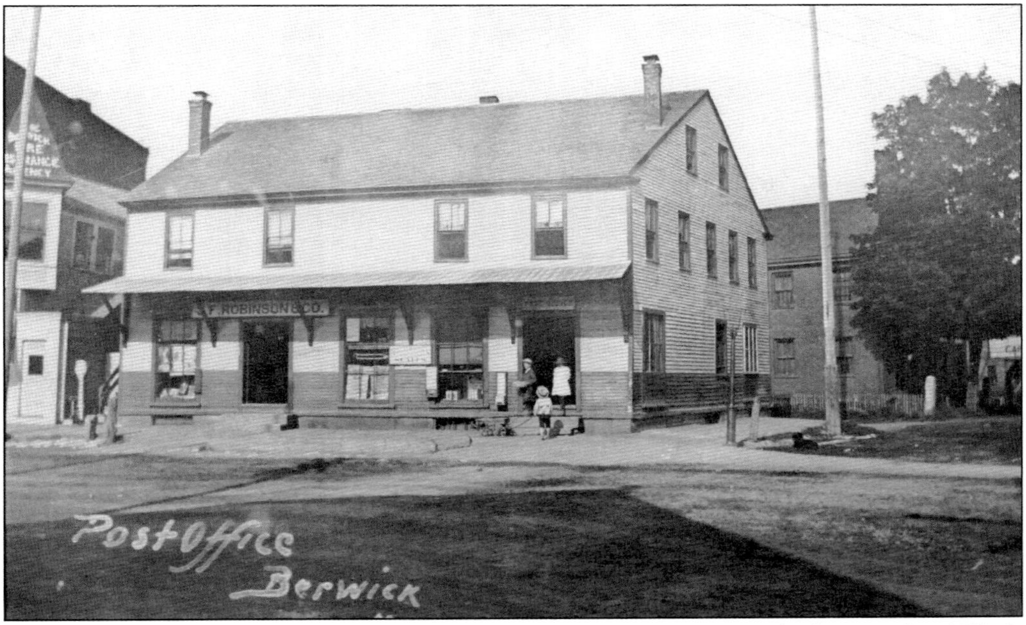

These photographs are of Berwick's first post office in Sullivan Square, which opened in 1871. It was one of the earliest buildings in the business district. Crossing the bridge from Somersworth, New Hampshire, into Berwick in the 1870s, it was one of the first buildings that could be seen. The post office, built by Park & Harris, remained at this location until the 1960s. After that, the site became home to a market. After a short period of time following the days of the market, it became an apartment house and was then destroyed by fire. Today, it is the site of a park. The brick building in the background was once known as Bell's Hardware store. It was demolished in the 1930s when Prime Tanning expanded.

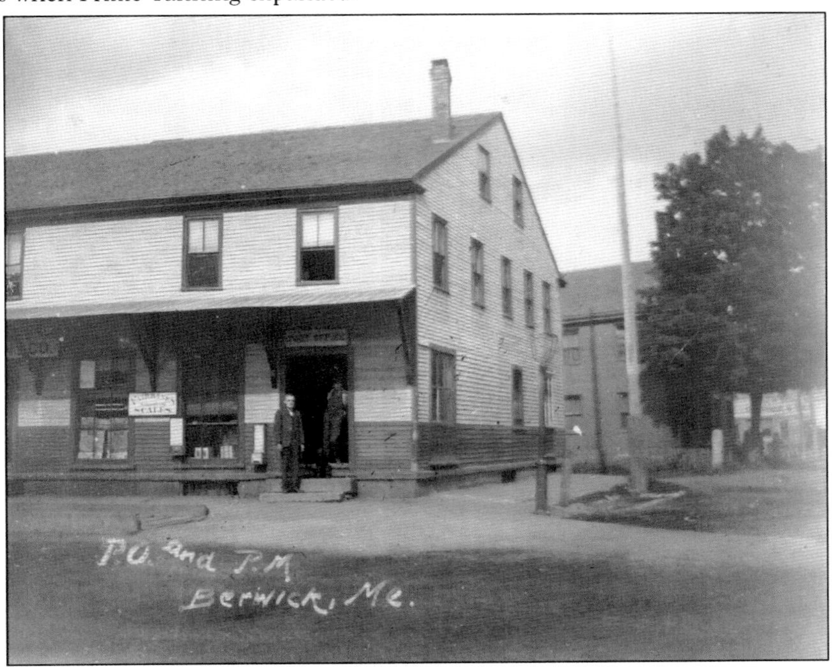

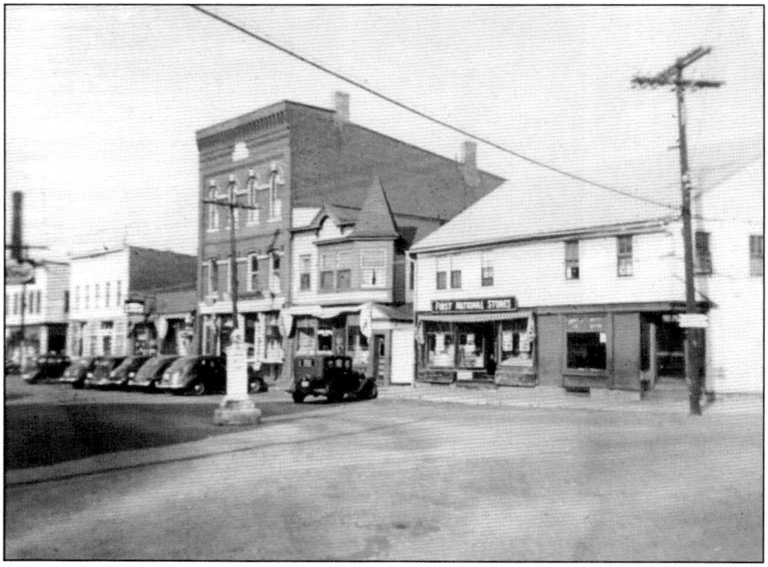

In this 1940 photograph, the Prime Tanning smokestack is at far left. Other businesses shown here are, from right to left, Garvin & Armstrong, Dru & Bill's Convenience Store, Odd Fellow building, grocery store, First National Stores, and the Berwick Post Office.

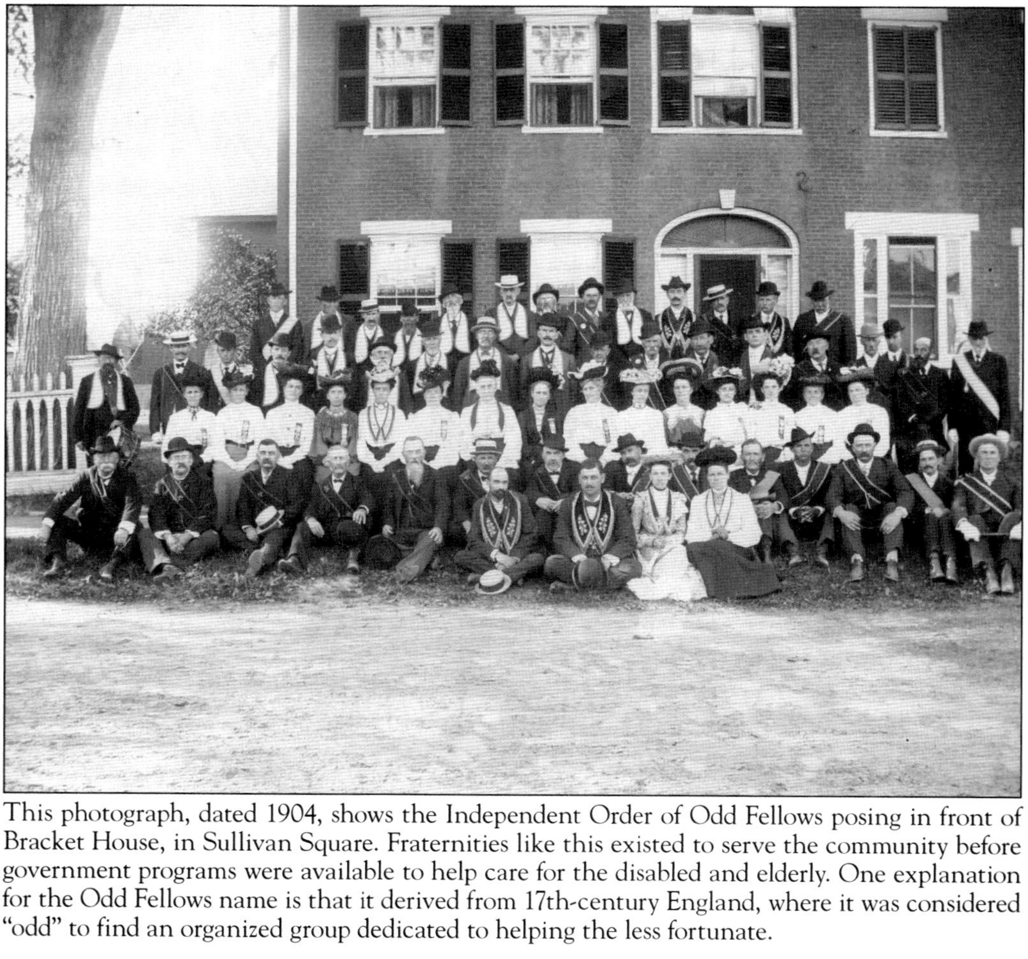

This photograph, dated 1904, shows the Independent Order of Odd Fellows posing in front of Bracket House, in Sullivan Square. Fraternities like this existed to serve the community before government programs were available to help care for the disabled and elderly. One explanation for the Odd Fellows name is that it derived from 17th-century England, where it was considered "odd" to find an organized group dedicated to helping the less fortunate.

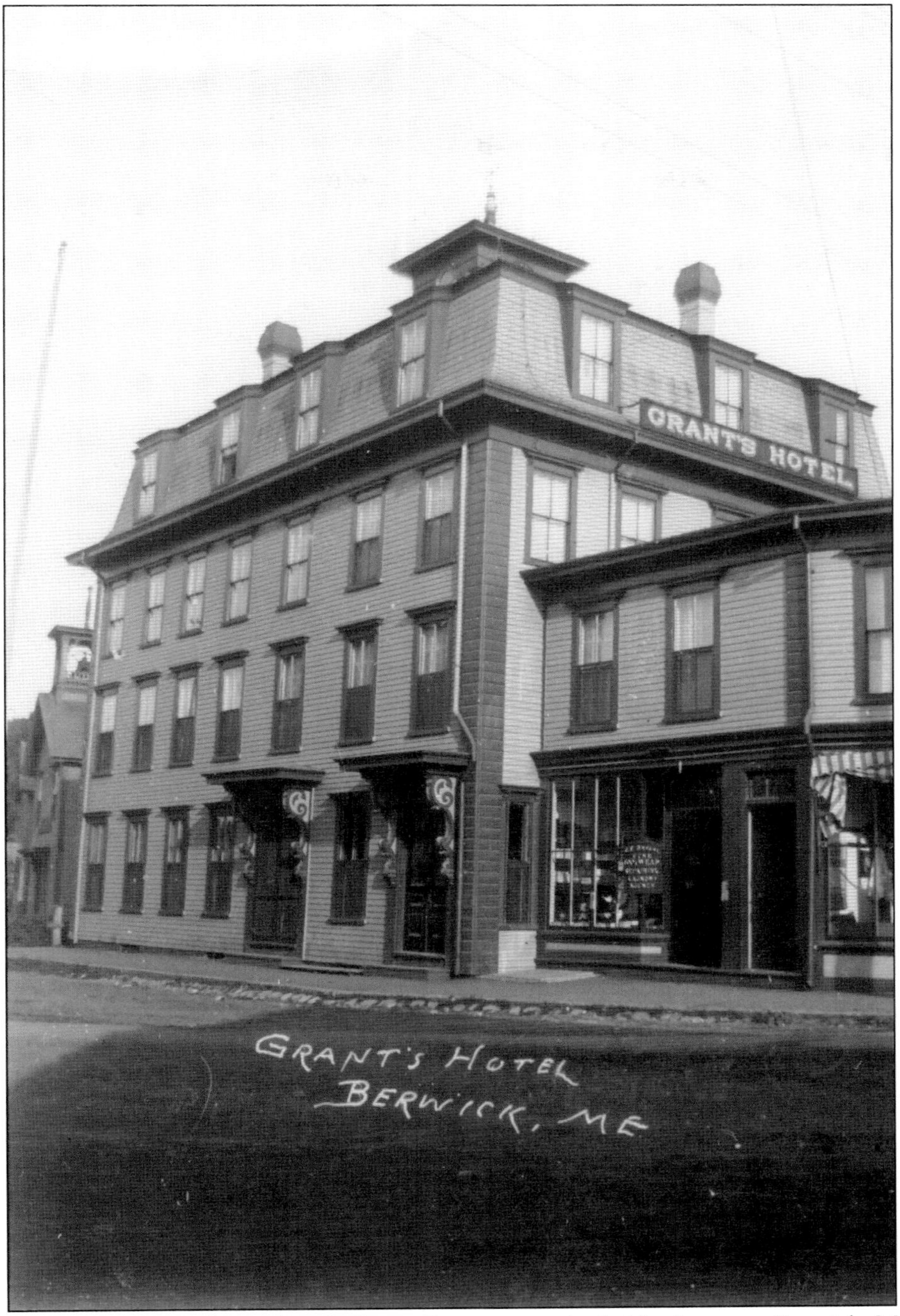

The Grant's Hotel was located in Sullivan Square near the bridge between Berwick, Maine, and Somersworth, New Hampshire. It was built in 1874 and continued to serve residents and tourists well into the 20th century. However, it was destroyed by fire shortly before World War II, in the 1940s. The hotel, consisting of four floors, had steam heat. Its location was convenient for railroad passengers traveling between Boston, Massachusetts, and Portland, Maine, as well as many other places.

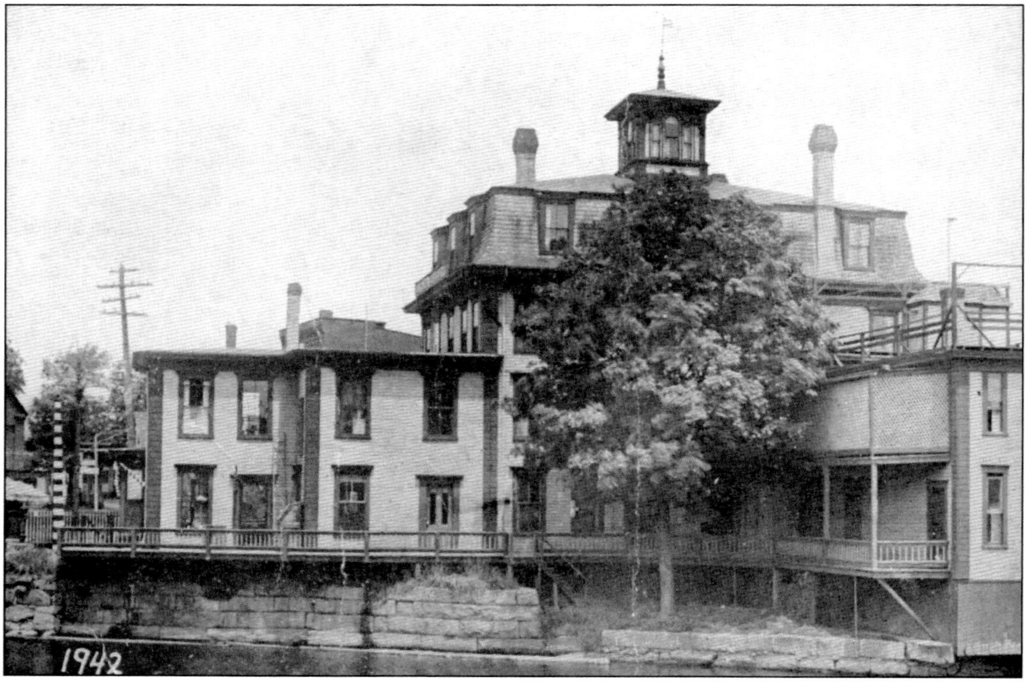

This photograph offers a unique view of the Grant's Hotel, on the edge of the Salmon Falls River. The photograph was taken from across the bridge in Somersworth, New Hampshire.

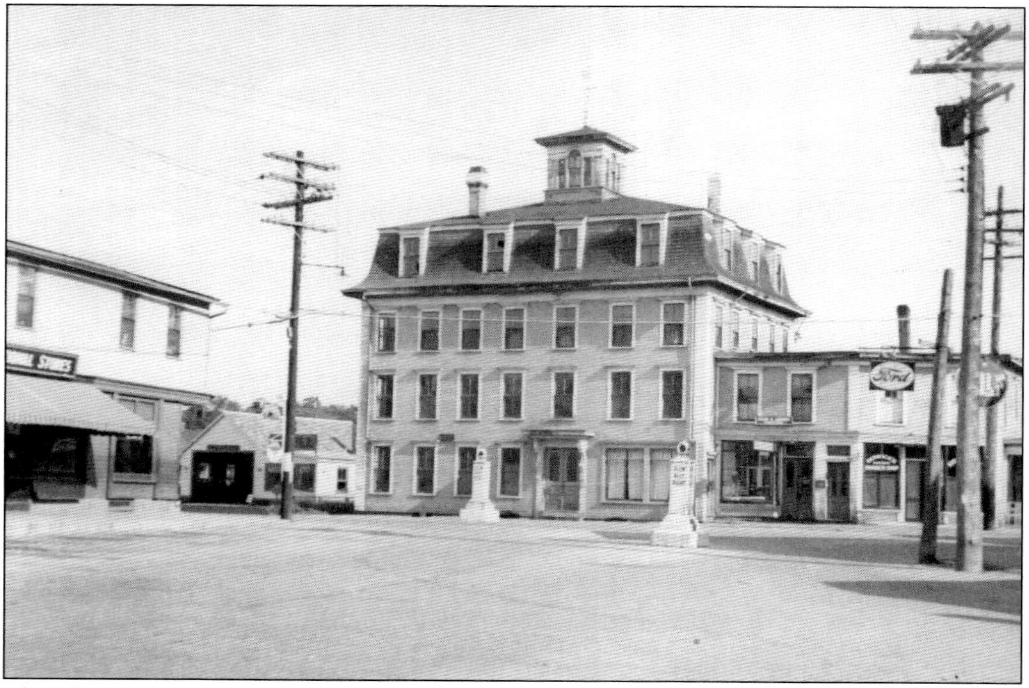

This photograph of the Grant's Hotel also shows, at far left, the First National Store and, beside that, the post office. To the left of the Grant's Hotel is a gas station, and to the right is a Ford station. In front of the hotel are two traffic stations with lights on their tops.

This photograph depicts New York Life Insurance, occupying the Brackett House. This Federal-style brick home, located in Sullivan Square, was built in the 1800s with three stories. The right side of the building was reserved for businesses, which changed various times; living quarters were located on the left. The Brackett House was demolished in 1938 to make way for the new town hall.

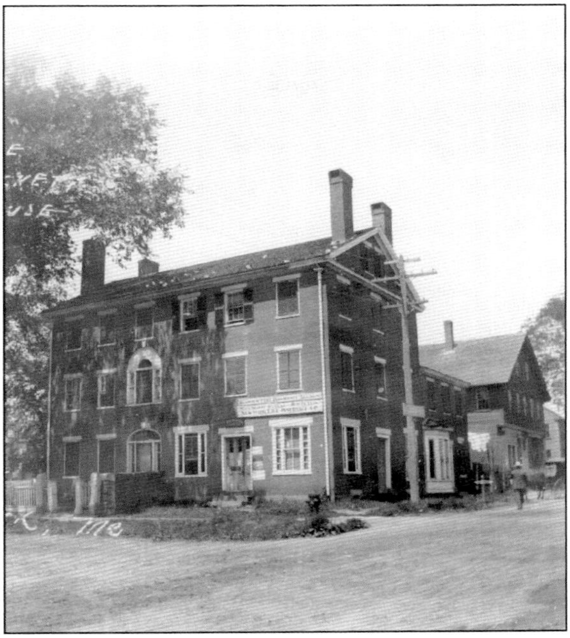

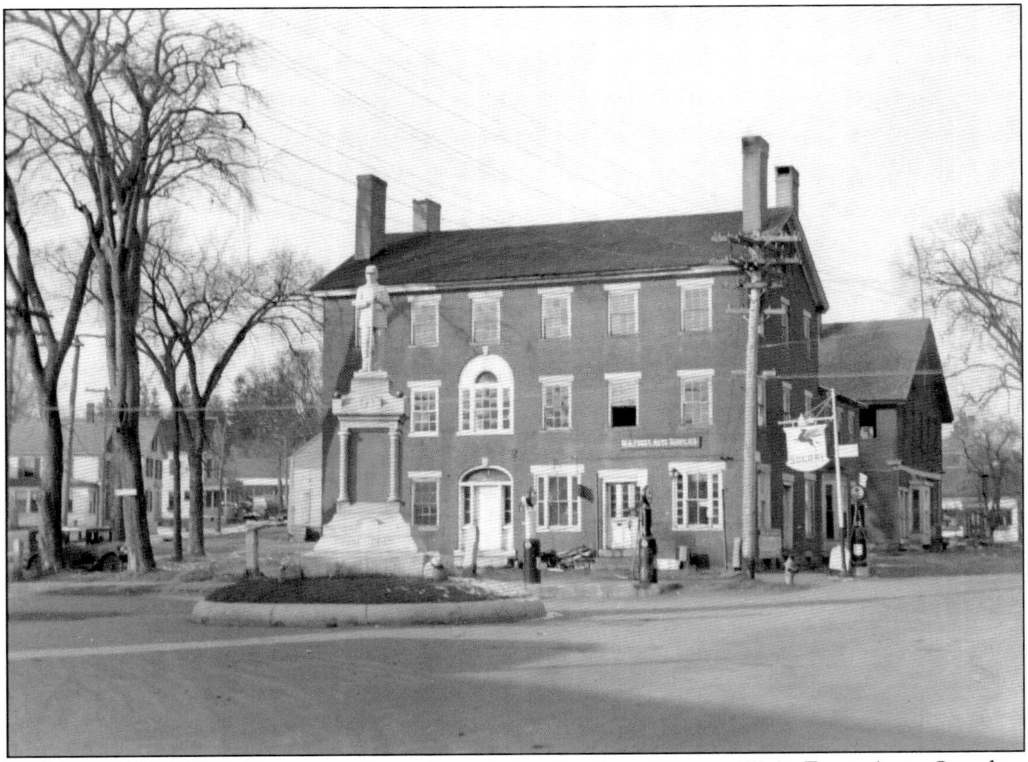

This postcard offers a more modern view of the Brackett House. W.A. Frost Auto Supplies replaced New York Life Insurance, and a gas station was added. In this photograph, the Soldiers' Monument, erected by the Women's Relief Corps in 1911, can be seen. The gas pumps belong to the Socony station. At that time, gas was about 20¢ per gallon.

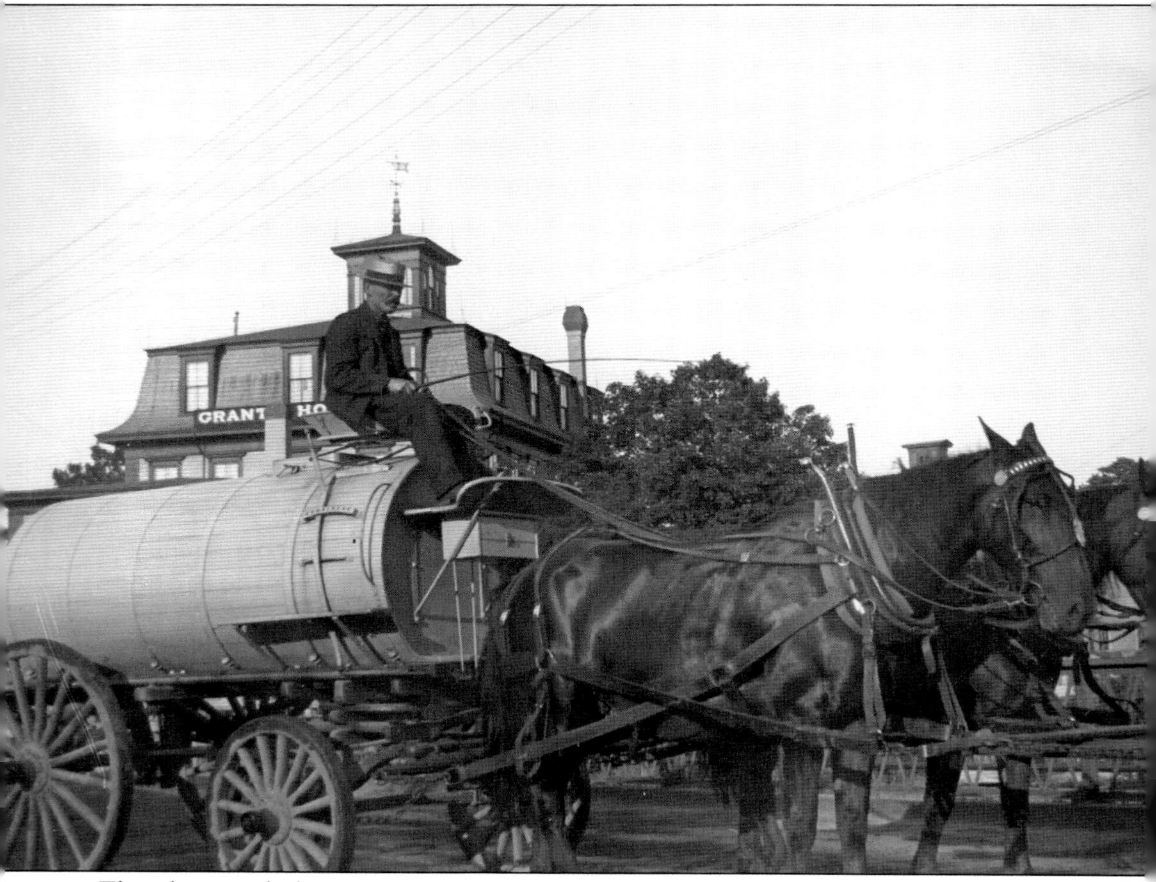

This photograph demonstrates an example of early road maintenance. The passage of wagons, buggies, and horses caused the rise of dust, which would enter homes and businesses along the roadway. In the spring and summer months, a man was hired to sprinkle the streets with water to control the dust. If the town did not tax for the water sprinkler, it was the responsibility of the individual property owner to hire the street sprinkler. The Grant's Hotel can be seen in the background.

Three

Firehouses

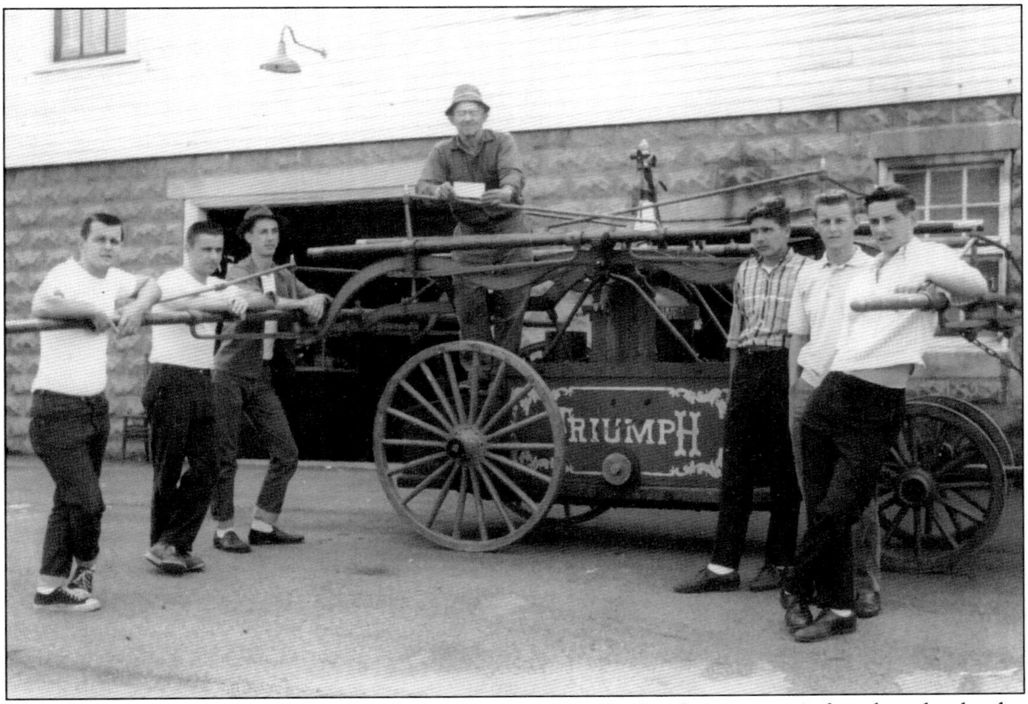

Berwick firemen stand outside the fire department with the department's first hand tub, the Triumph. The Triumph, manufactured in 1848, was purchased from the town of Biddeford. It is said that there is only one other like it in the country. The Triumph's best record stands at 257 feet, 11.75 inches, made during a muster competition held at Portsmouth, New Hampshire, in 1925. According to the official muster records, this put Berwick third best in the country for hand-tub competitions.

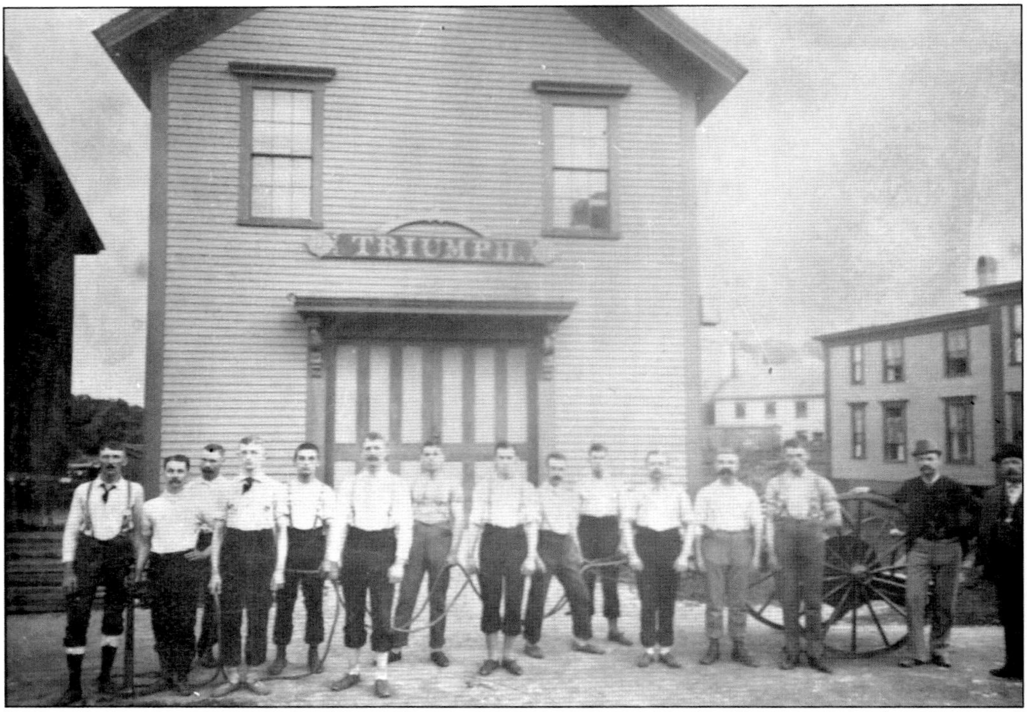

The crew of the Triumph hand tub poses outside the Berwick Fire Station. The Triumph Hose Company was formed at the schoolhouse on Rochester Street in 1873. Andrew G. Bracy was the first foreman, followed by William Rich, who served for many years thereafter. This photograph was taken near the Grant's Hotel. Somersworth, New Hampshire, can be seen in the background.

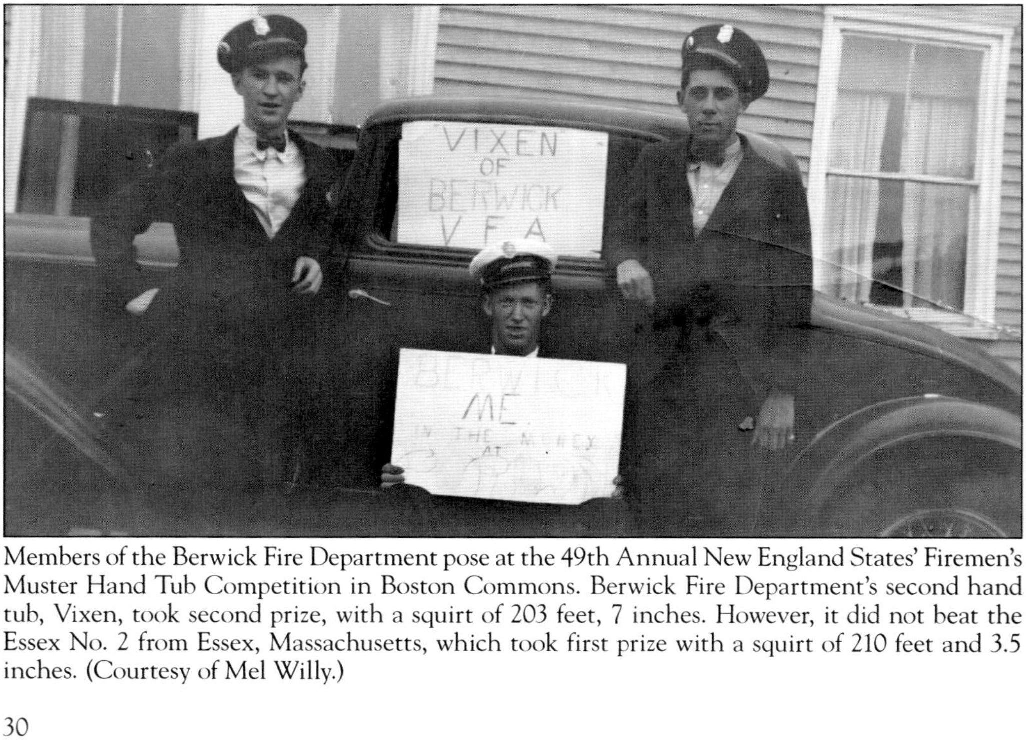

Members of the Berwick Fire Department pose at the 49th Annual New England States' Firemen's Muster Hand Tub Competition in Boston Commons. Berwick Fire Department's second hand tub, Vixen, took second prize, with a squirt of 203 feet, 7 inches. However, it did not beat the Essex No. 2 from Essex, Massachusetts, which took first prize with a squirt of 210 feet and 3.5 inches. (Courtesy of Mel Willy.)

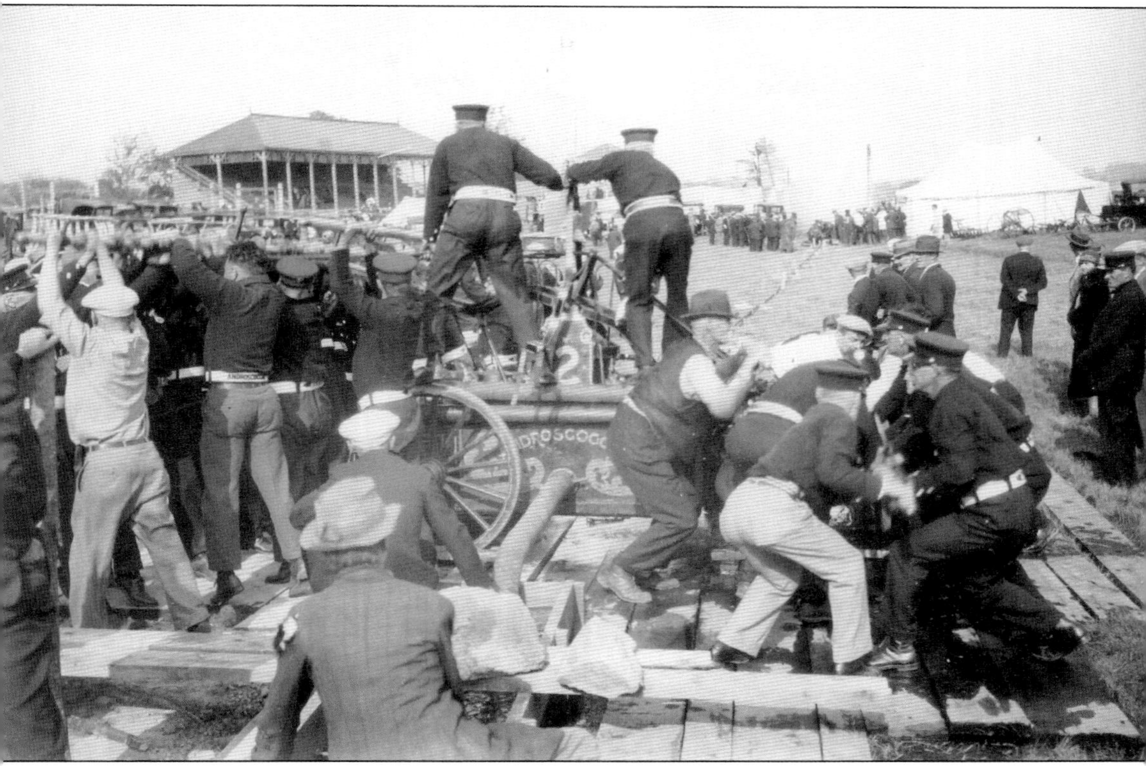

This is a New England States' Firemen's Muster Hand Tub Competition from the 1930s. Fire departments from various New England states would gather with their hand tub, some of which dated to the Civil War, to compete for the longest stream of water. The streams would be measured on long rolls of paper, which would be replaced after each hand tub competed.

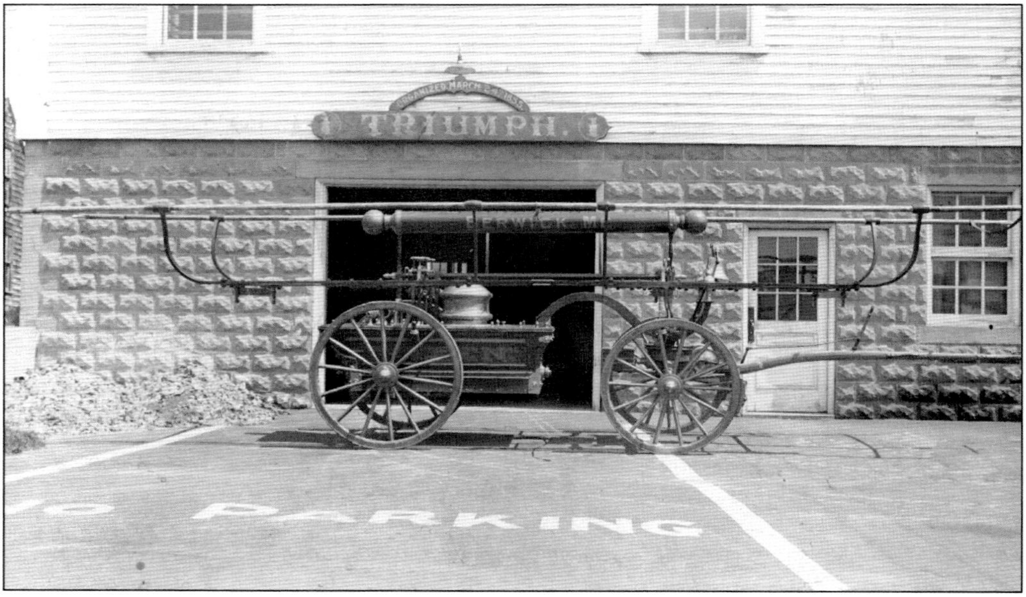

In 1908, Somersworth, New Hampshire, sold the Vixen hand tub to Berwick. The powerful machine won its first of five championships in 1926 in Salem, Massachusetts. The engine would go on to win the New England League Championship again in 1931, 1935, 1938, and 1946. The best record for the Vixen was 236 feet, 6.25 inches. This record was made in Portsmouth, New Hampshire, at the 47th Annual Official Muster of the New England States Veteran Fireman's League in 1938. Both the Vixen and the Triumph were famous during their time and were ranked among the best throughout the country. Together, they won many competitions and earned $10,000 in prizes.

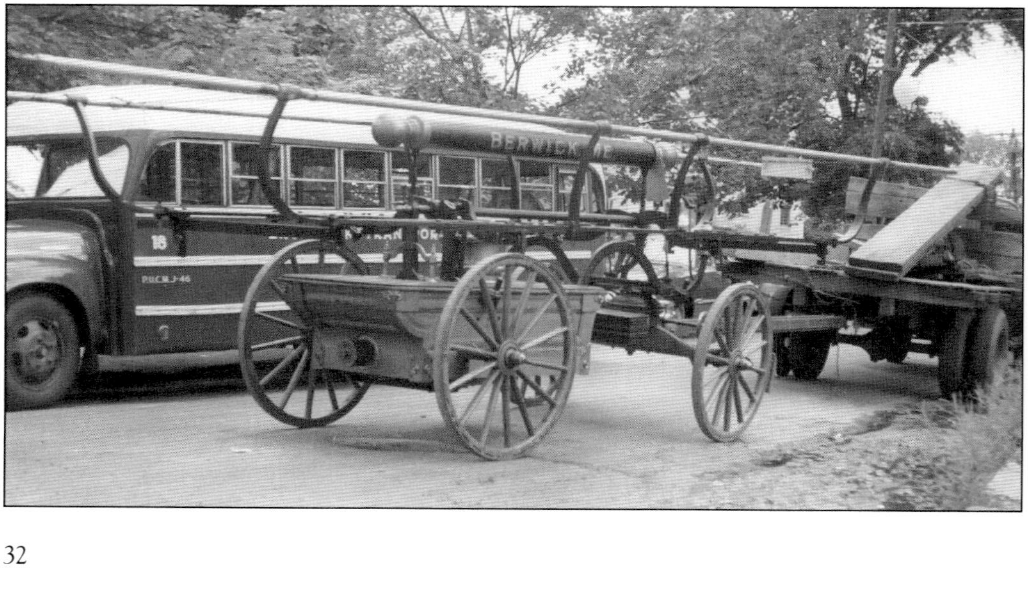

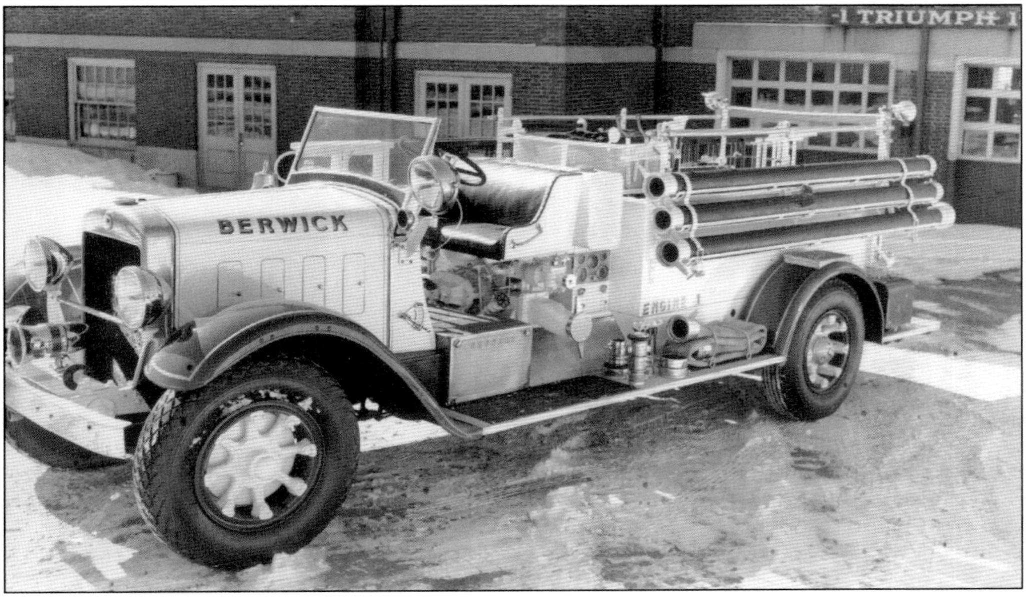

These photographs show Berwick's first motorized fire engine. Purchased between 1925 and 1935, this engine replaced the days of the hand tubs, when men had to manually maneuver a fire apparatus. In the 1930s, buildings began to grow taller, making it necessary for the engines to carry ladders. The first pumper using a single engine for pumping and propulsion was a steam pumper manufactured in the United States in 1907. By 1925, the steam pumper had been completely replaced by motorized pumpers. Additionally, the engines were equipped with a water tank for the initial attack on a fire while firefighters connected the pump to hydrants and for areas where no water supply was available. In rural areas, pumpers carried a suction hose to draw water from rivers and ponds.

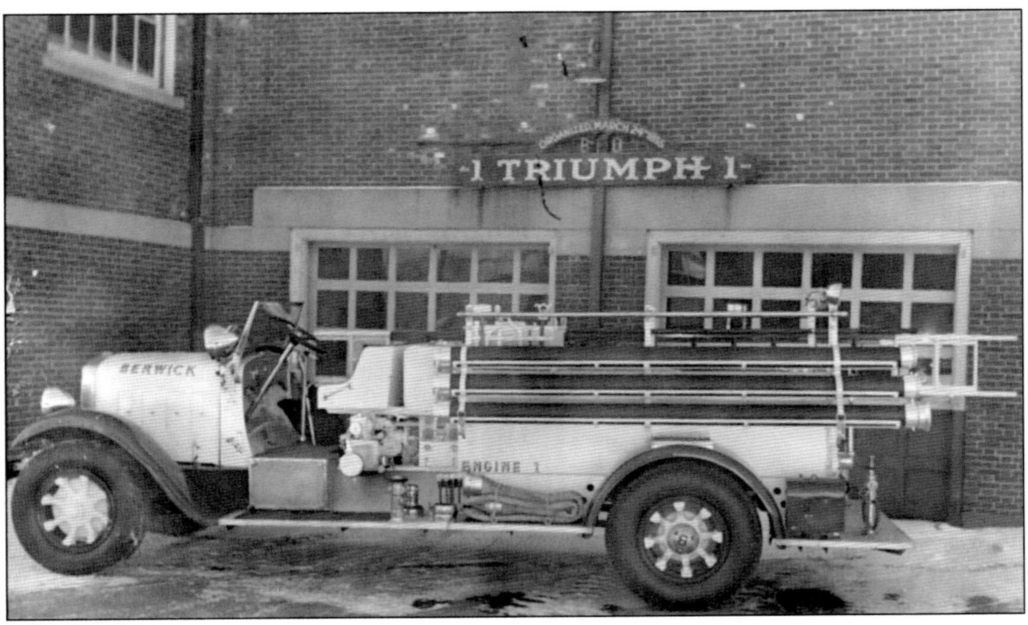

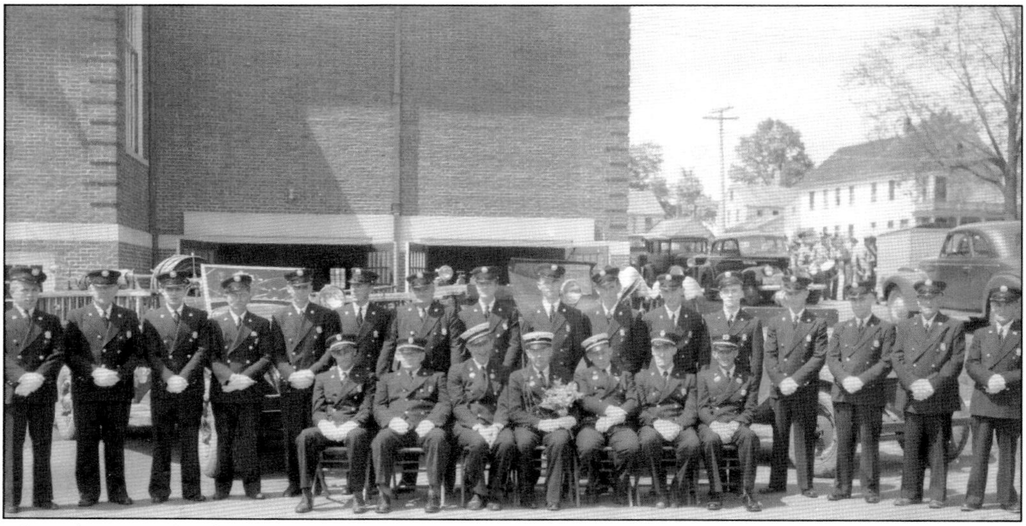

This photograph of Berwick firefighters was taken in May 1940. Shown here are, from left to right, (seated) Maurice Bragdon, George Guptil, Evret Rendall, Jim Butler, Murton Burrill, Ronald Straford, and Linsay Leach; (standing) Norman Matthews, Arthur Brooks, Let Matthews, Frestram Fall, Richard Cate, Lester Bragdon, Raymond Brown, Forrest Varney, Vern Kindell, Vern Brooks, Horace Moulton, Gerald Mason, Joel Moulton, Henry Folson, and Harry McIntyre. (Courtesy of Sharon Hall.)

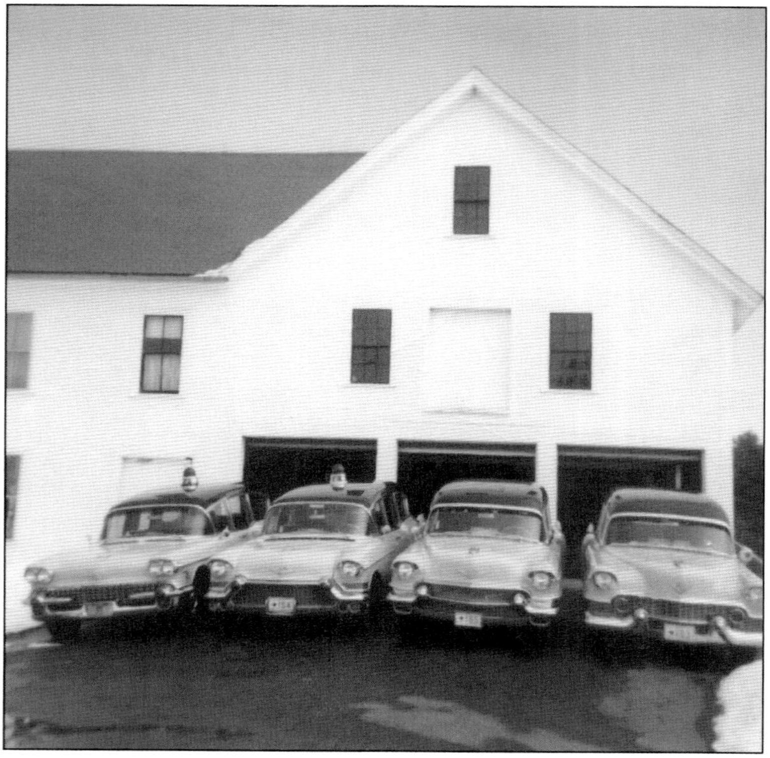

Berwick's first ambulance service was started by Walter Hall, at Hall's Pond, located on Old Pine Hill Road. The town's undertaker, Lester Lang, drove one of the ambulances when the service first started in the early 1950s. Evolving from the days of horse-drawn ambulances, the passenger-based ambulances, like the ones shown here, played an important role in the emergency medical care for most of the 20th century. Cadillac produced the last ambulance car in 1979.

Four

Businesses

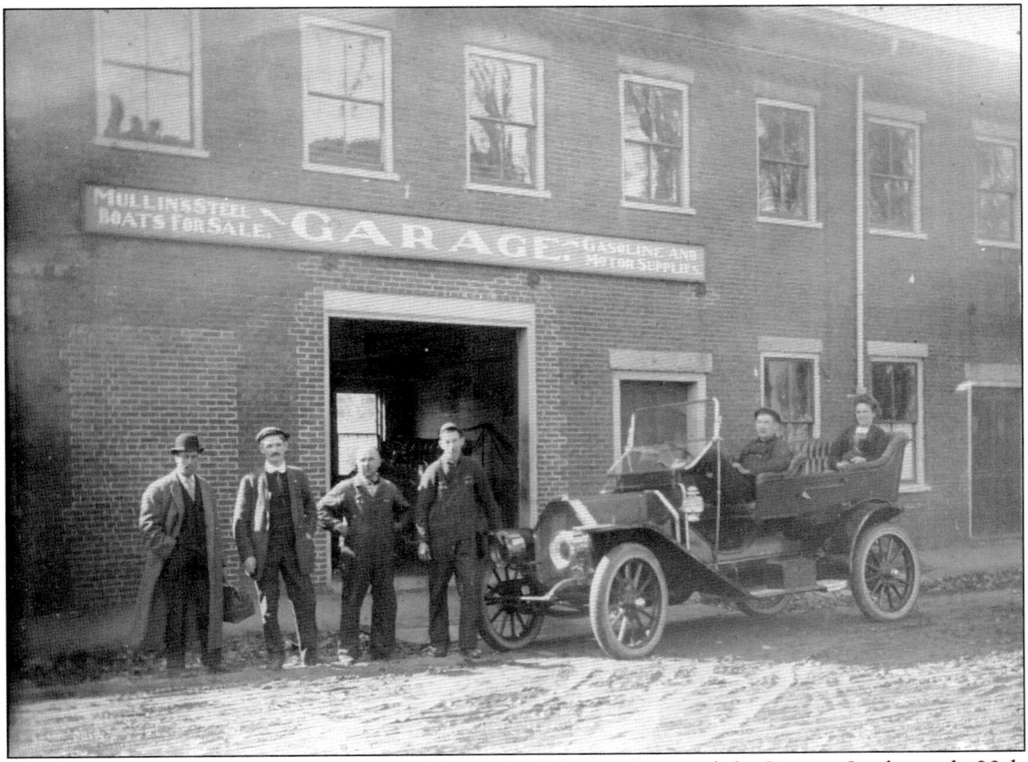

Here, locals visit with the mechanics of the School Street Automobile Garage. In the early 20th century, residents went here for automobile and boat repairs. The business also sold gasoline and other motor supplies to locals and those just passing through town.

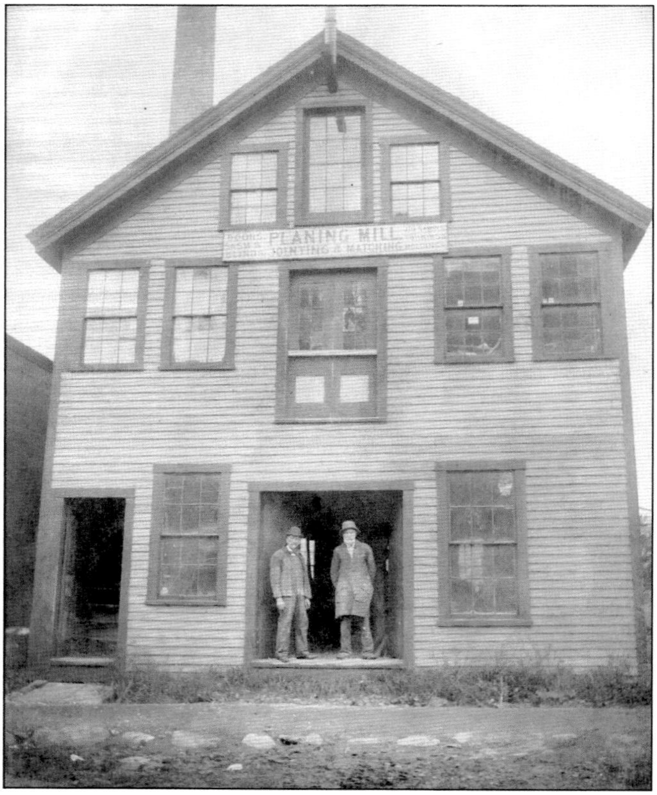

Mark Chase (left) and Samuel Horne (right) stand in the doorway of their planing mill. This was an extension of the J.R. Horne Mill, built in 1870. Both businesses were located on Berwick Street. Cut and seasoned boards from a local sawmill were turned into finished dimensional lumber at this facility.

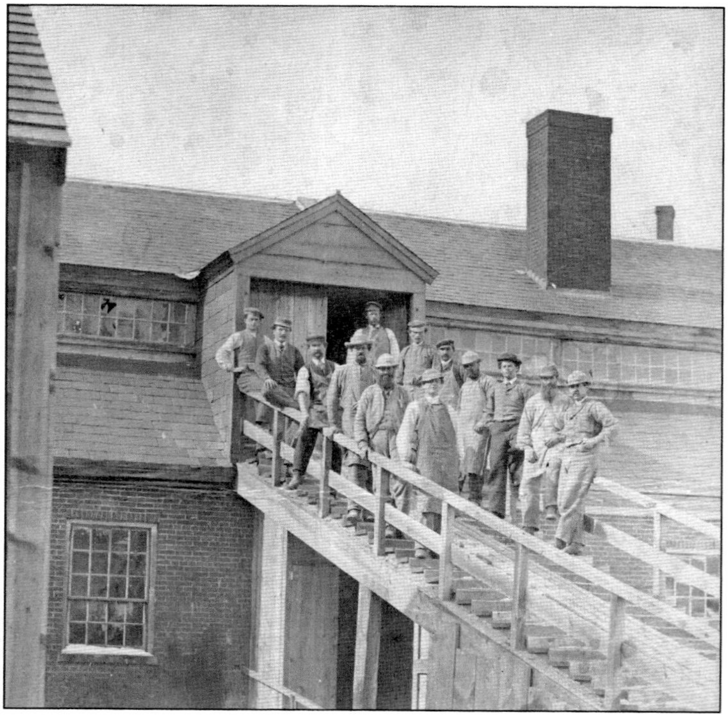

The E.N. Higley's Machine Shop, located on Berwick Street, was in operation for 40 years. This business specialized in farm machinery in the late 20th century and the beginning of the 21st century. It supplied local farmers with the equipment they needed to keep up with the growing demand for produce.

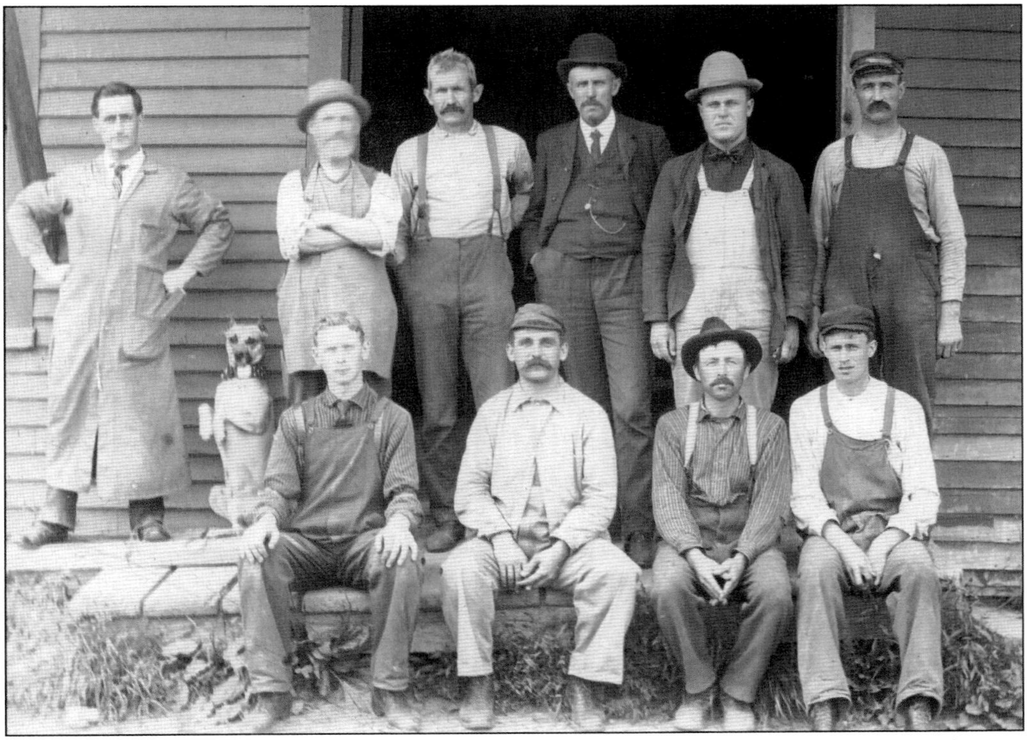

This is a photograph of 19th-century millworkers. Sam Mathews, owner of Mathews Brothers, is standing, third from left. His company later became known as Normand's Mill. Standing fourth from left is his brother John Mathews. The Mathews Brothers firm, established in 1899, specialized in manufacturing all kinds of building materials.

Oxen carrying firewood pause in front of A.H. Winn Wholesale Confectioner, which was one of the many businesses operating out of the Brackett House. The building, once located on Sullivan Street, was demolished in 1938 to accommodate the construction of the new town hall.

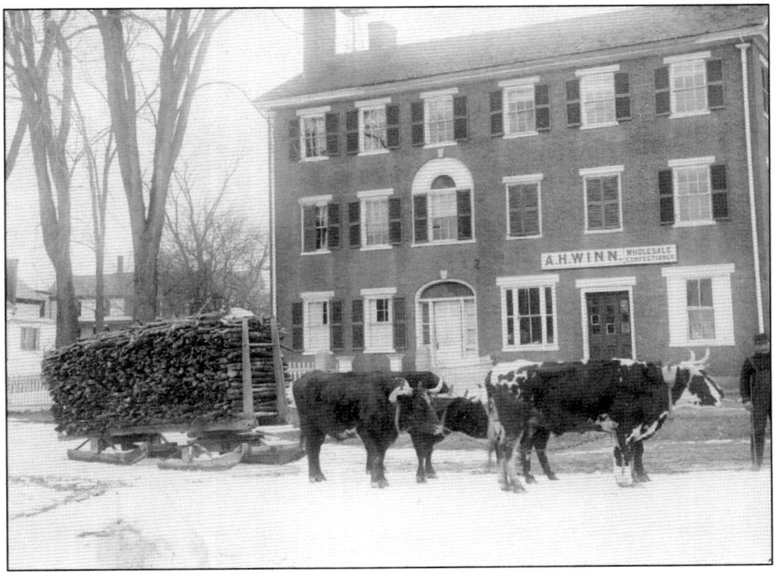

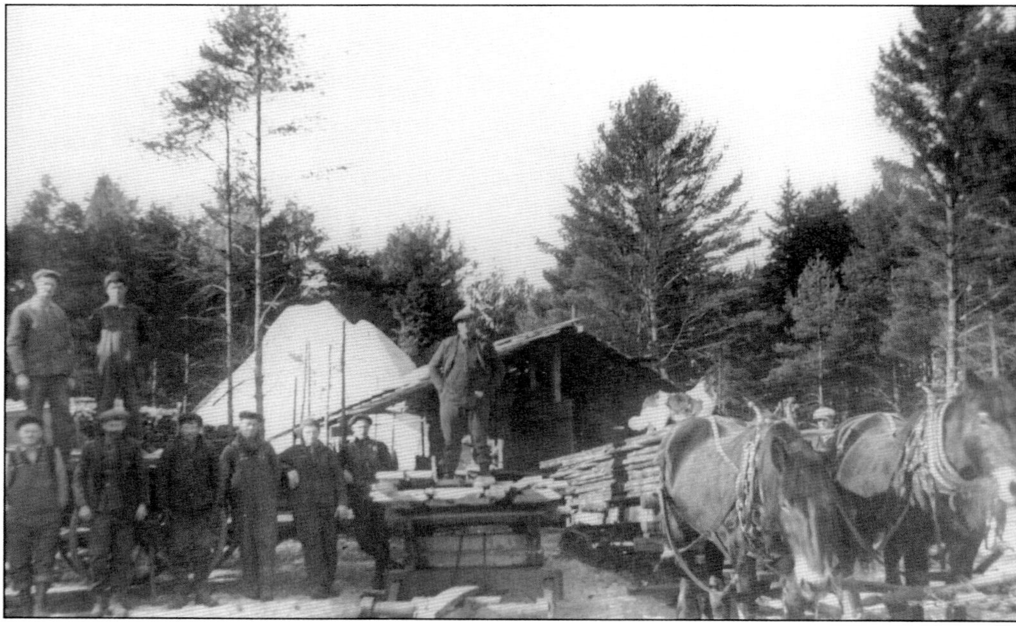

Harry Knox stands on his wagon in the early 1920s, surrounded by his sawmill crew. This site was formerly known as Hanscom Lot, located on Pine Hill Road. The demand for lumber products grew as the nation expanded in the 19th century and well into the 20th century. A wide range of skills were needed for the success of the industry: surveyors to identify trees, lumbermen to cut timber, teamsters and their draft animals to haul logs, scalers to measure the timber's worth, and river drivers to float logs to the mills.

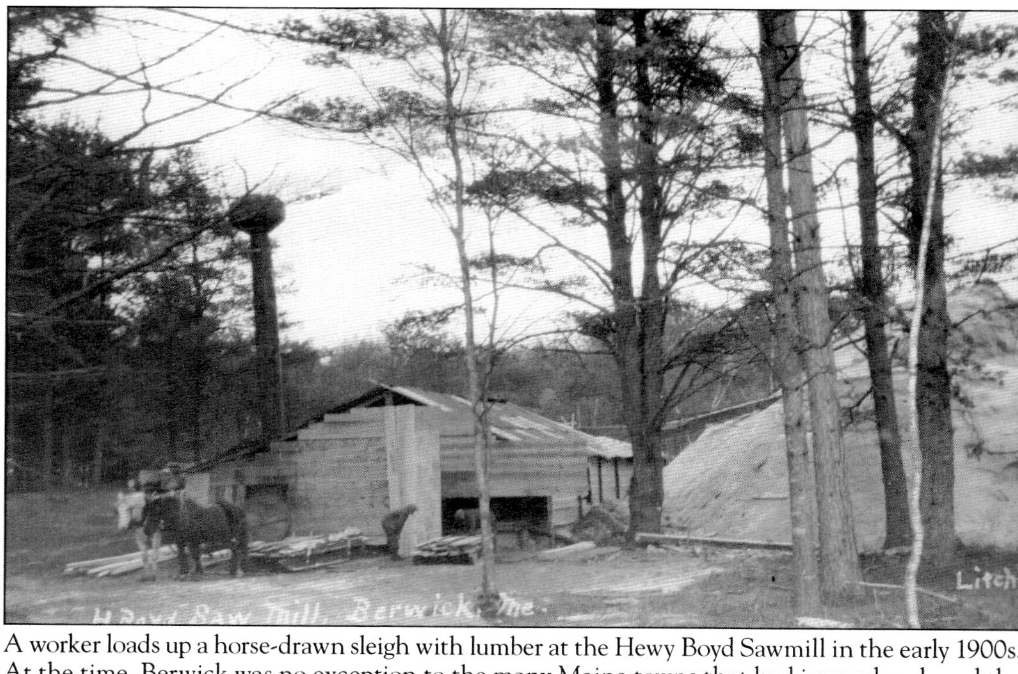

A worker loads up a horse-drawn sleigh with lumber at the Hewy Boyd Sawmill in the early 1900s. At the time, Berwick was no exception to the many Maine towns that had jumped on board the lumber industry, making the state the nation's leading lumber producer.

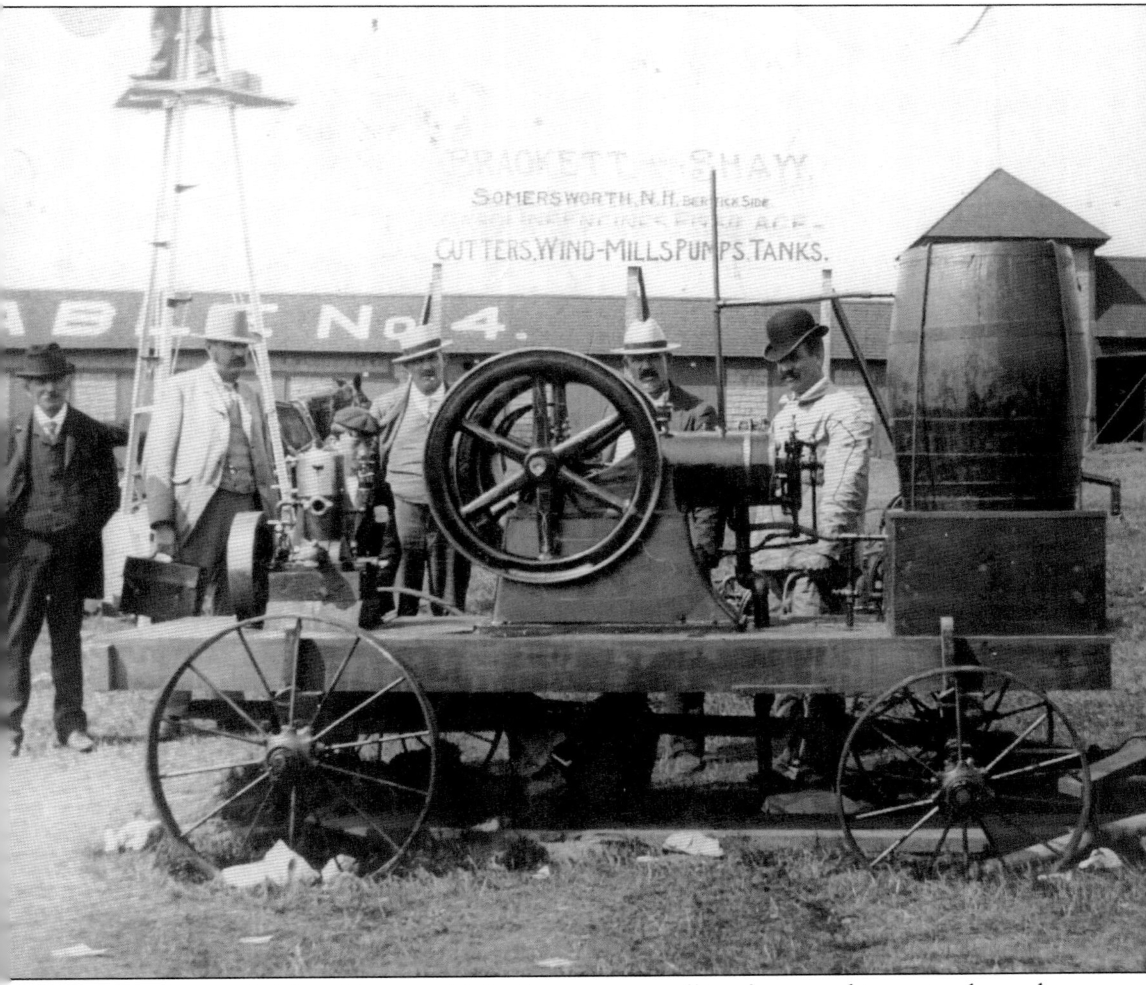

Joseph Brackett and Julian Shaw established a company selling farm machinery in the early 1900s. They are shown here, at the beginning of their long business relationship, demonstrating the installation of windmills to pump water for farmers. At one point, Brackett and Shaw had all of New England and parts of New York in their sales territory. Their business started on Saw Mill Hill and later moved to Bridge Street.

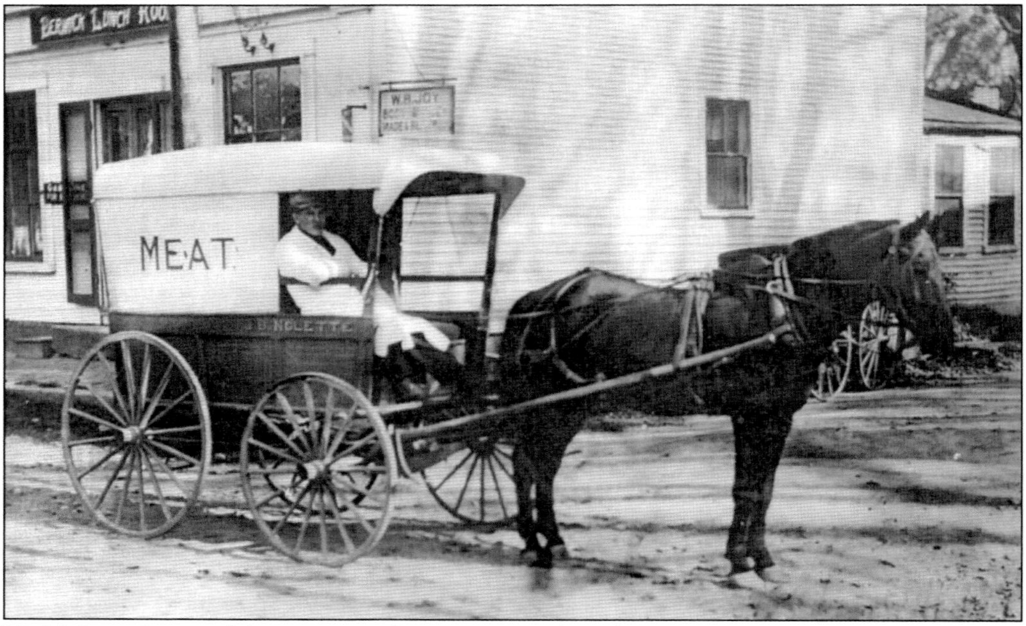

J.B. Nolette drives a delivery wagon for groceries and meals. Beginning in the late 19th century, it was common for farmers to sell their produce from their wagons. Large amounts of produce were sold this way, along with chickens, pigs, goats, and eggs. The Berwick Lunch Room and a store for boats are visible in the background.

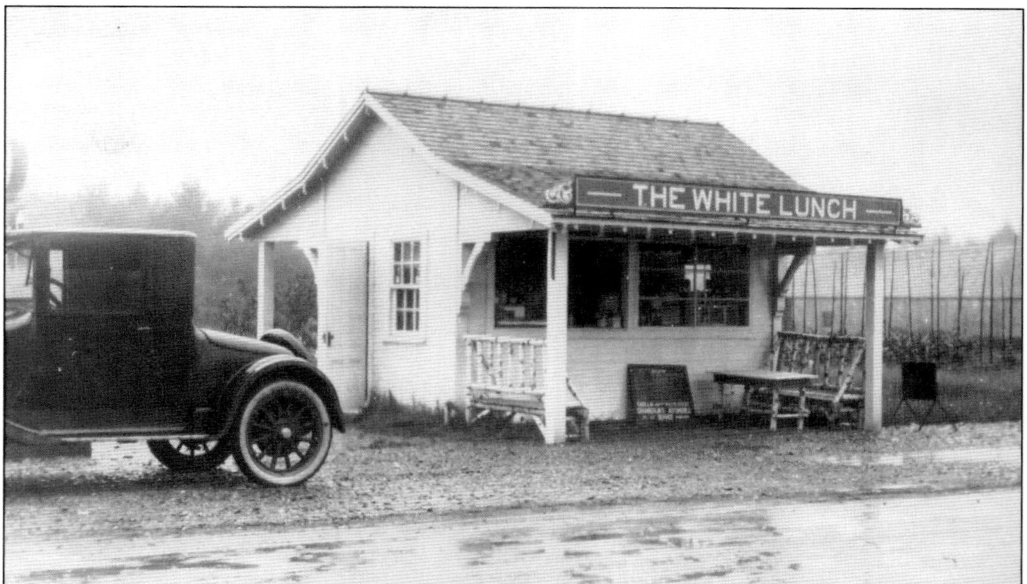

This luncheonette was located on Route 9, across from the present-day site of the Hackmatack Theater. It was owned by the Litchfield family in the early 1920s. Many locals frequented this popular luncheonette for many years to enjoy a quick midday meal.

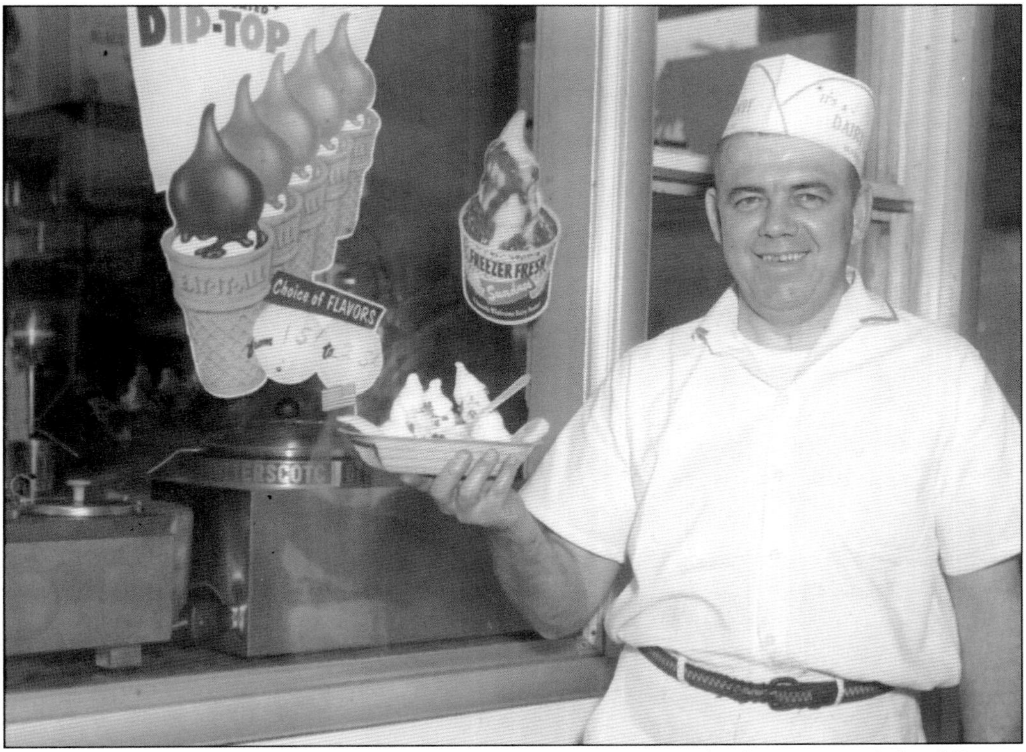

Charles Vigue, owner of Dairy Dandy, displays a tempting treat at his business on School Street. The establishment opened in 1952 as Dairy Dandy and then expanded to include lunch under the name Vigue's Luncheonette. The popular venue was family owned and operated at the former site of Thibeault's Garage.

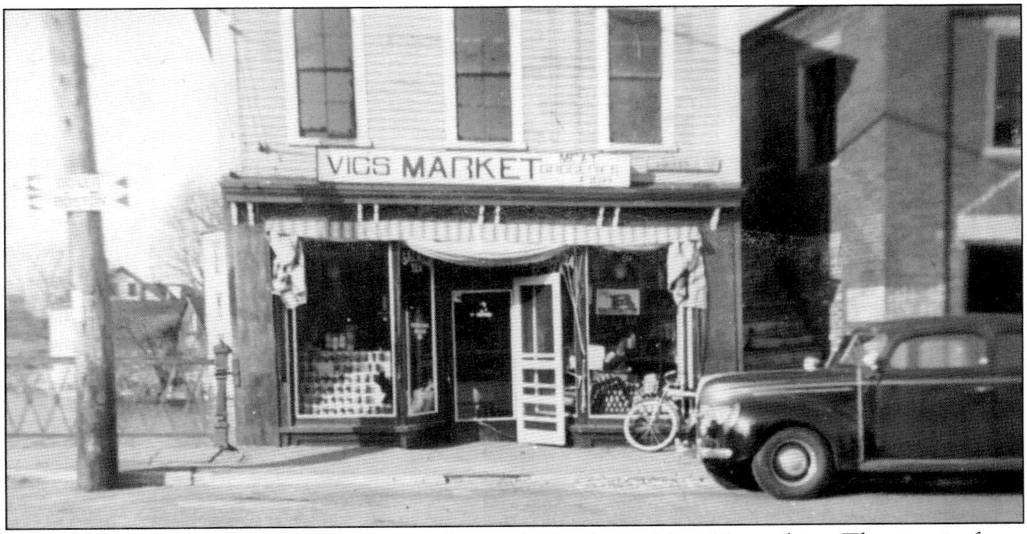

Vic's Market and an unknown store stand near the bridge to New Hampshire. The sign in front of the bridge indicates the path to Dover and Boston as motorists prepared to cross the state line. Canned goods can been seen stacked in a tall display inside the storefront window. A Ford Mercury, manufactured in the late 1930s, is parked in front of the store.

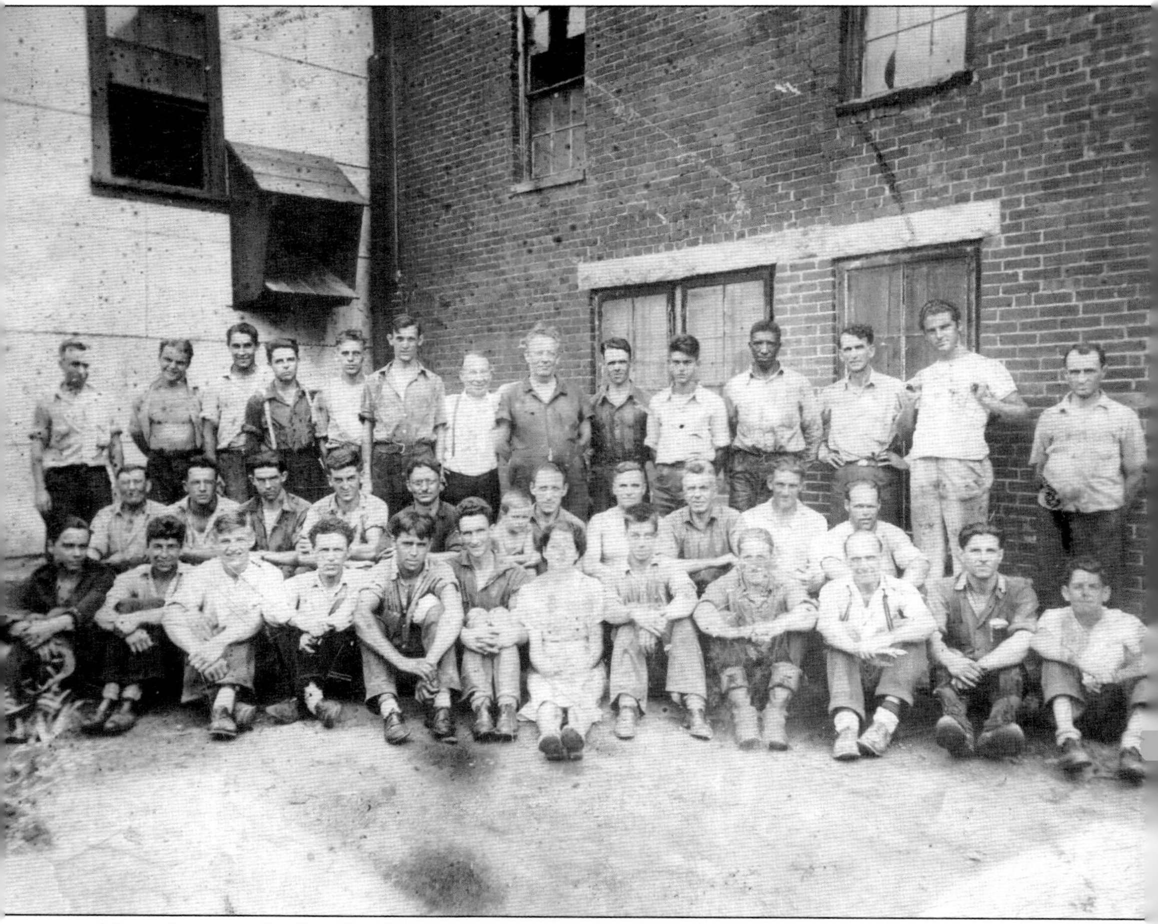

This photograph, dated 1936, was taken outside of Prime Tanning. In the first row at far left is Babe Plante. The man standing second from right is Lenard Kaplan. He was the son of Morris Kaplan, who founded the company in 1914. Lenard went on to become the chairman of the board for 40 years before passing the business on to his two sons, Steve and Mike Kaplan. Prime Tanning Company operated the largest vertically integrated wet blue and side-leather finishing tanneries in the United States. The location was previously occupied by Lennox & Nagle Sheepskin Tanners.

Five

Icehouses

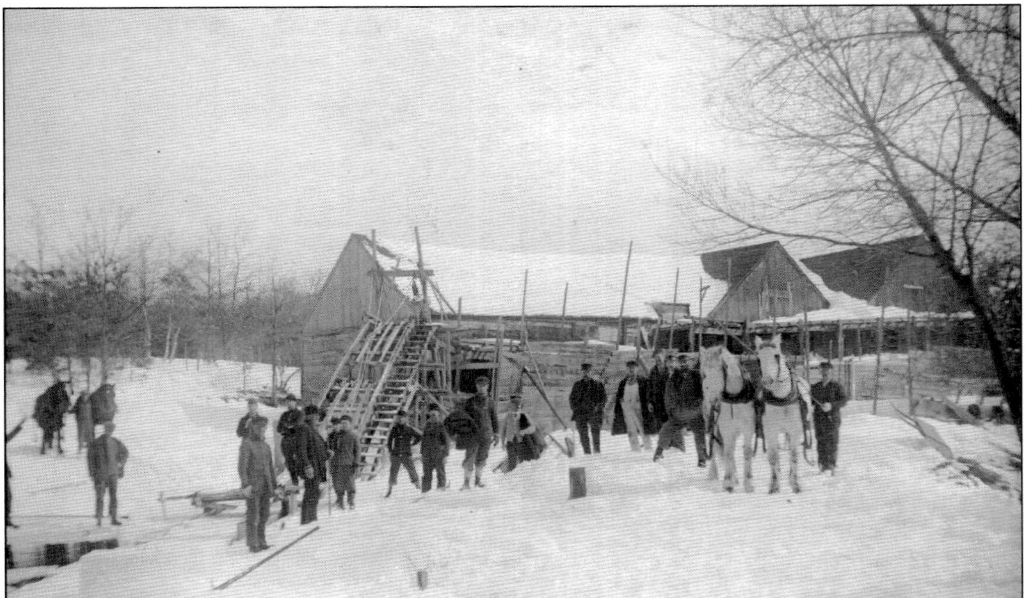

Workmen cut and store ice on Hall's Pond. In 1892, three ponds were created by digging up and damming marshy, spring-fed fields. The origins of the ice trade, also known as the frozen water trade, began in New England. The transport and sale of natural ice for domestic and commercial use became widely successful and quickly spread to other areas of the country.

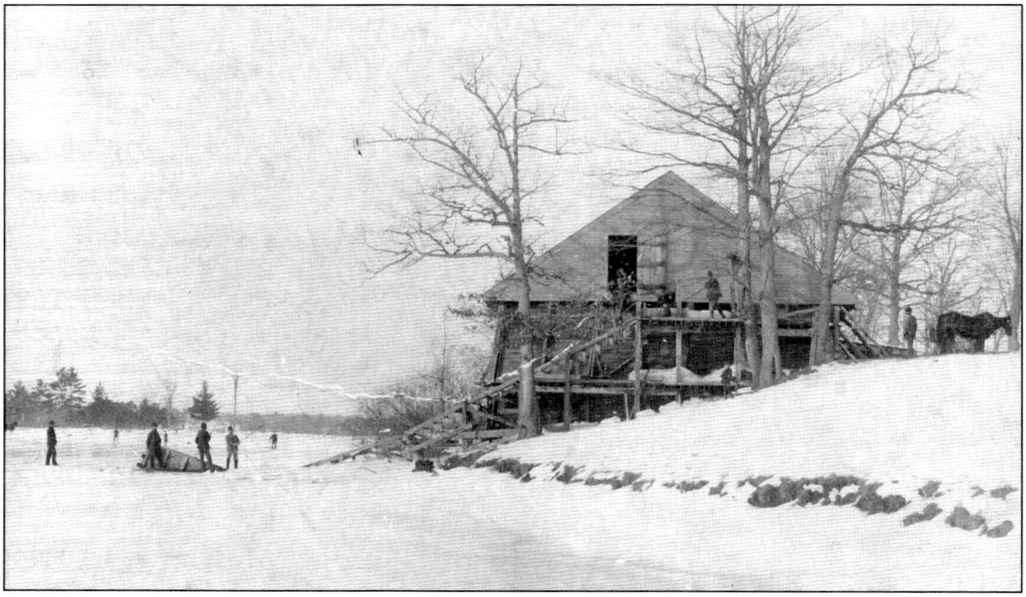

In the late 19th and early 20th centuries, the demand for ice was great. Berwick's main source of ice was a couple of ponds covering several acres, situated on the Hall property on what is now Route 9. Once cut, the ice was brought by horse to the icehouses, where it was stored in an insulated covering of sawdust. The sawdust was provided as a by-product from the local sawmills and was another source of "off-season" employment for local laborers. In addition to the storage for local use, a portion of the ice harvest was forwarded to the rail station in Somersworth, New Hampshire, for shipment to larger cities.

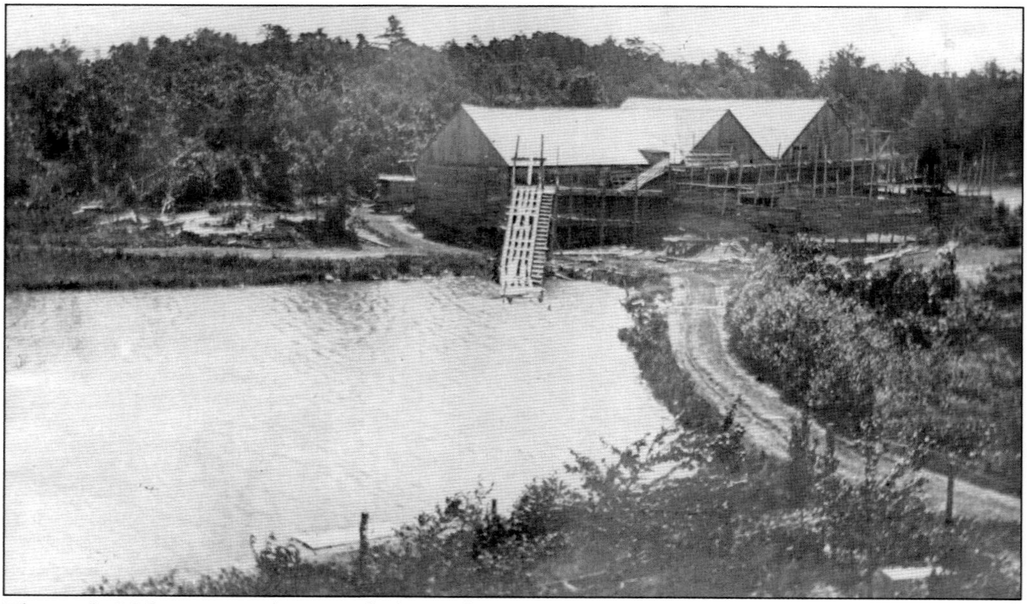

This early-20th-century photograph shows the George H. Hall Ice Company, established in 1892. During winter months, ice was stored here. Each block was moved up a chute with hooks to various levels of the icehouse. The facility was filled with blocks of ice, separated and surrounded by layers of sawdust supplied by lumber mills as an insulator.

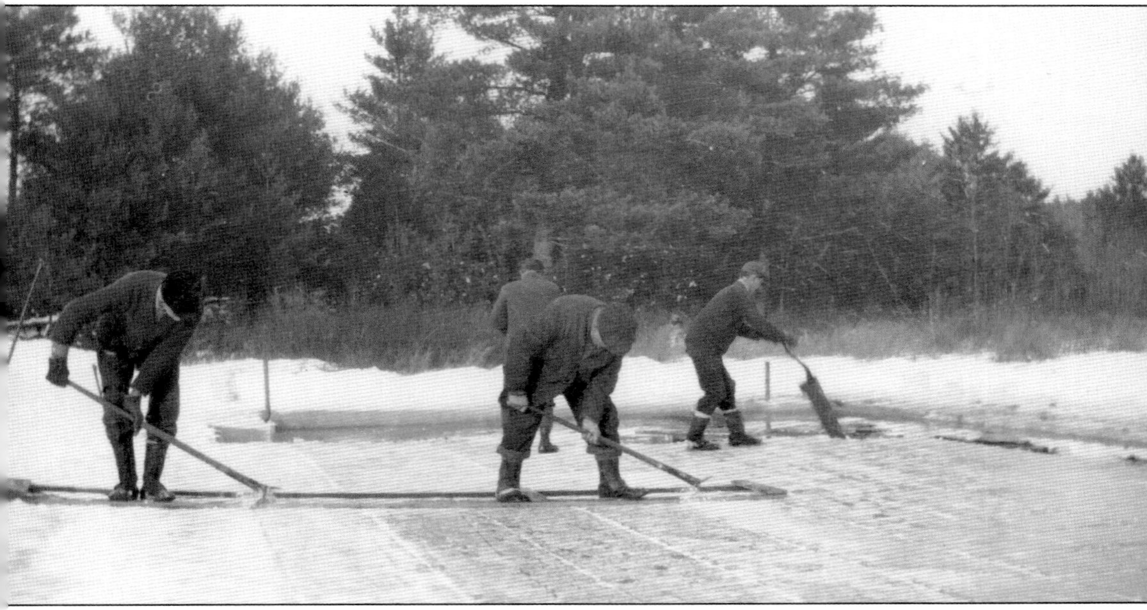

Men work to clear the ice on the pond behind the Hussey farm, located on Blackberry Hill Road, before cutting it. Long wooden planks were used to measure the grid lines. This was a primitive method for the time, as most areas were using horse-drawn ice cutters, fashioned after ploughs to draw the lines in the ice. Later, the Wyeth Company would manufacture a horse-drawn ice cutter that could cut the ice as well, replacing the handsaws that were initially used in the process. (Courtesy of Paul Boisvert.)

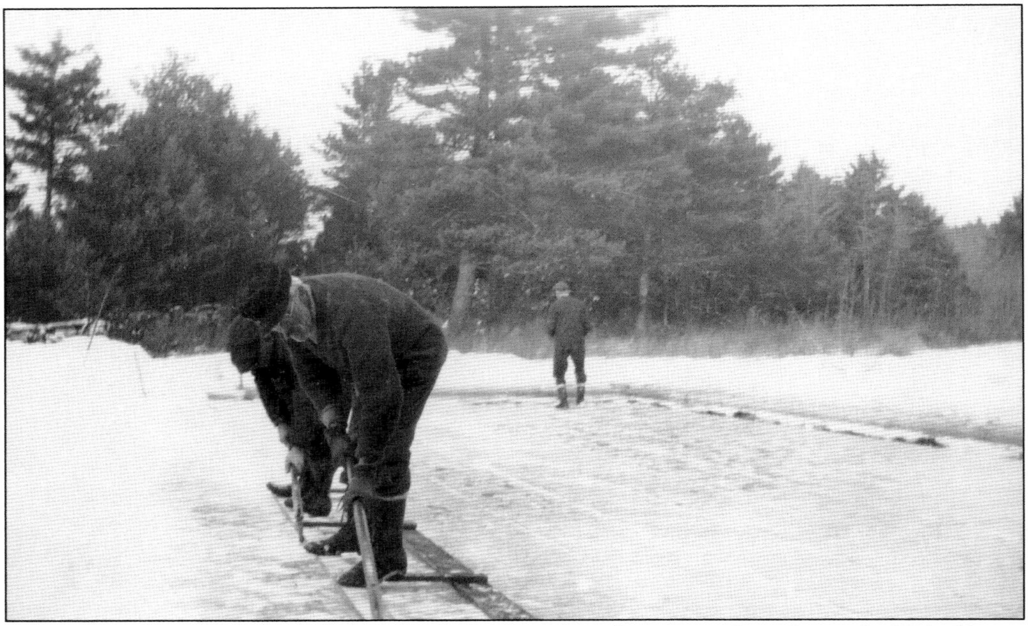

This photograph was taken in the early 20th century on the Hussey farm, located off Blackberry Hill Road. Here, two men (Clyde Farwell's father in front) draw grid lines in the ice, preparing it to be cut into blocks. The ice on the pond typically needed to be 18 inches thick before it could be cut, as it needed to be able to support the weight of the men and horses and be ideal for cutting into large blocks. (Courtesy of Paul Boisvert.)

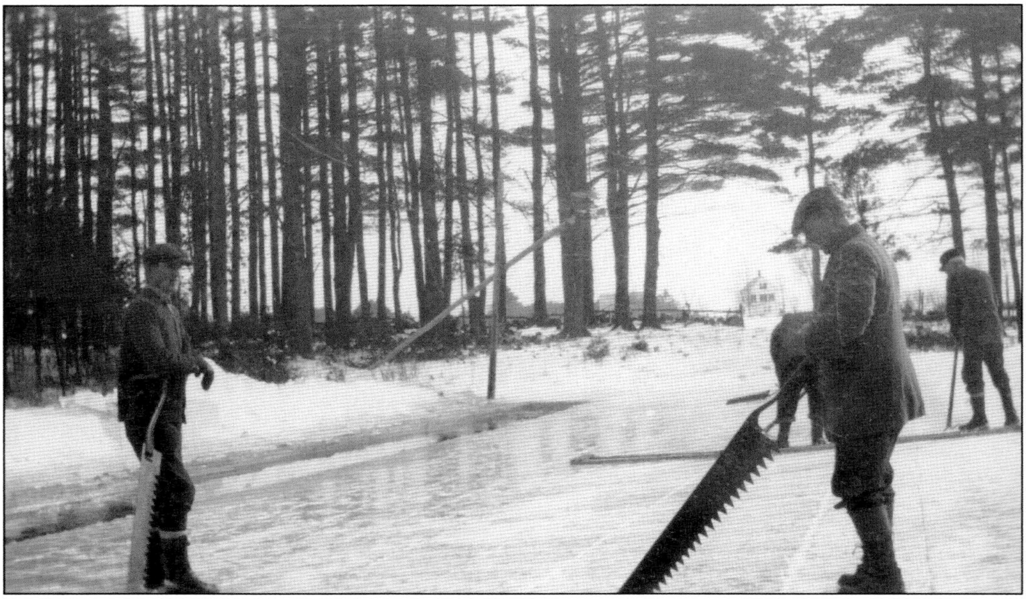

Clyde Farwell (left) uses an ice saw to cut ice on the pond behind the Hussey farm. With a desirable thickness, approximately 1,000 tons of ice could be harvested from a surface area of one acre. It was common in New England for an ice harvester to drill holes in the ice, allowing the cold air to reach farther below the surface to enhance the thickness. The Doran household on Blackberry Hill Road is in the background. (Courtesy of Paul Boisvert.)

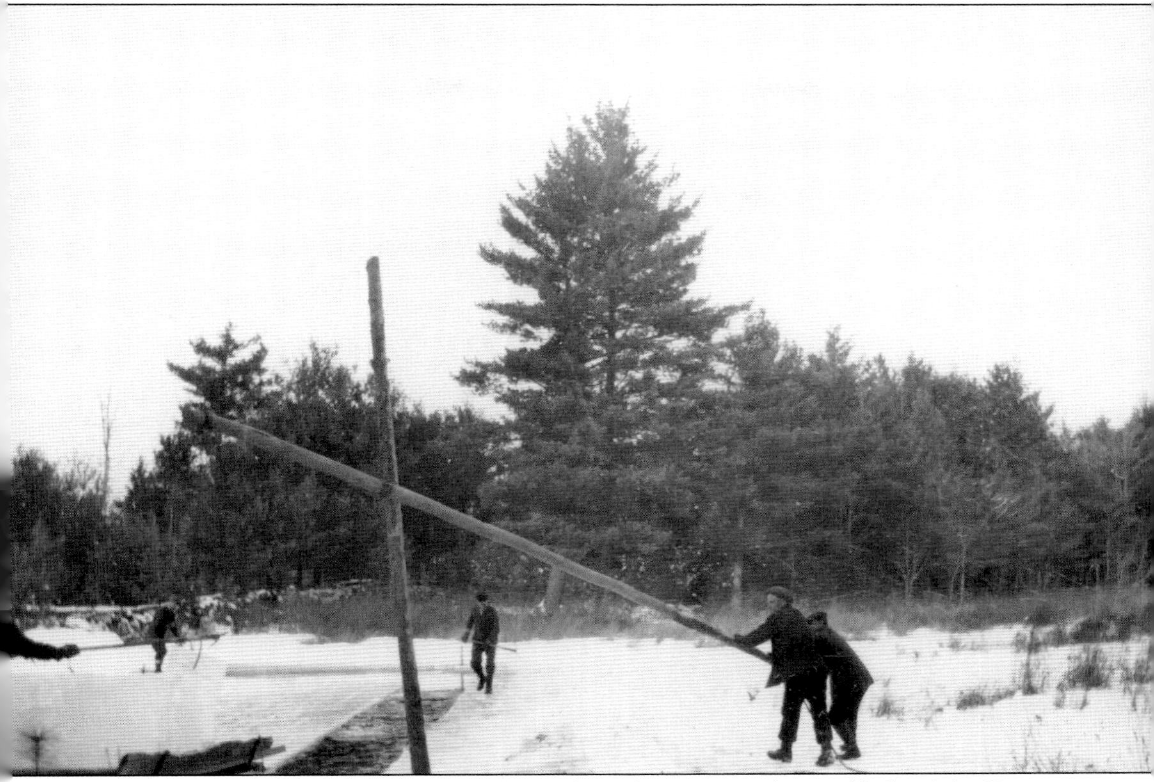

Men use long wooden poles as levers to lift the ice from the water on the pond behind the Hussey farm. Ice tongs were tied to the ends of the poles to secure the heavy ice blocks. A variety of other tools were used in the ice-harvesting process, including spiked horseshoes to prevent the horses from slipping on the ice. (Courtesy of Paul Boisvert.)

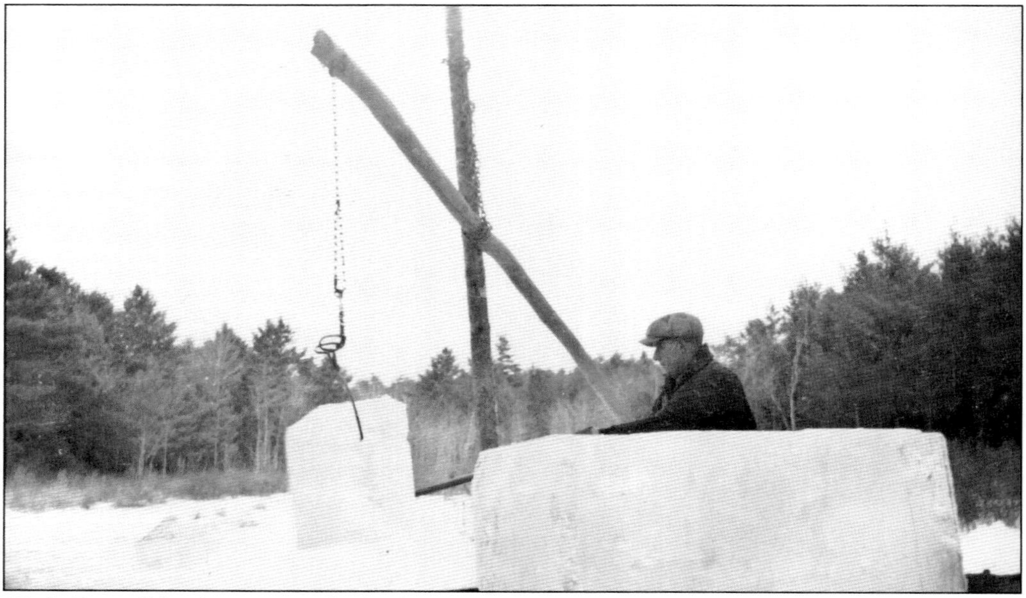

Clyde Farwell loads ice onto the back of a wagon behind the Hussey farm on Blackberry Hill Road. The ice was then transported to a nearby icehouse. During its peak at the end of the 19th century, the ice trade employed approximately 90,000 men in an industry capitalized at nearly $28 million. (Courtesy of Paul Boisvert.)

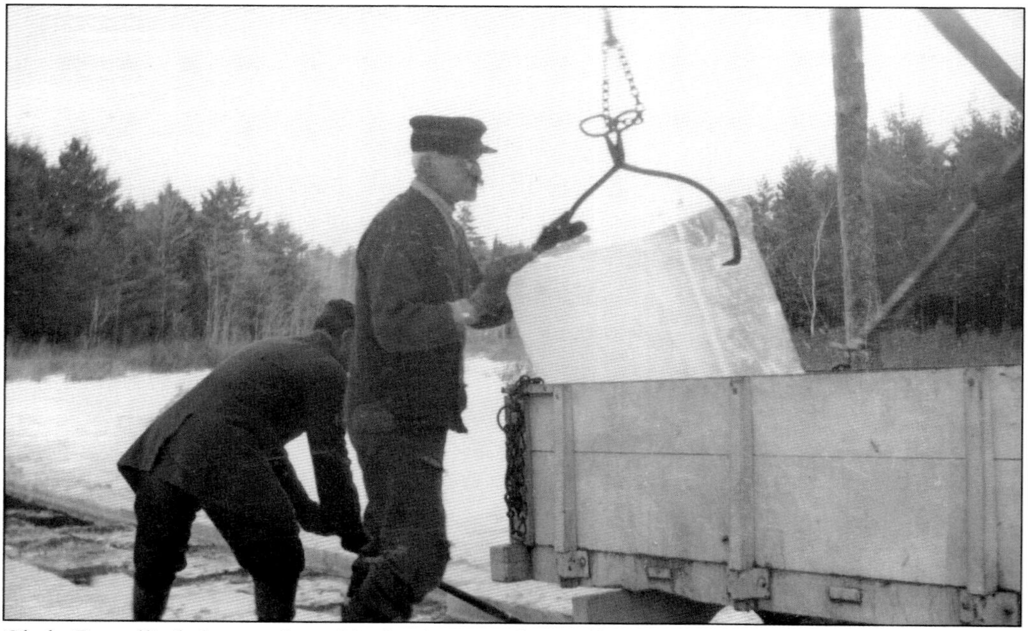

Clyde Farwell's father guides a block of ice, traditionally cut in dimensions of 22 inches by 32 inches, into the back of a wagon for transportation. Behind him, another man continues to prepare the Hussey farm ice for cutting. These blocks of ice would likely be loaded into refrigerated cars used by the railroad company to transport meat. (Courtesy of Paul Boisvert.)

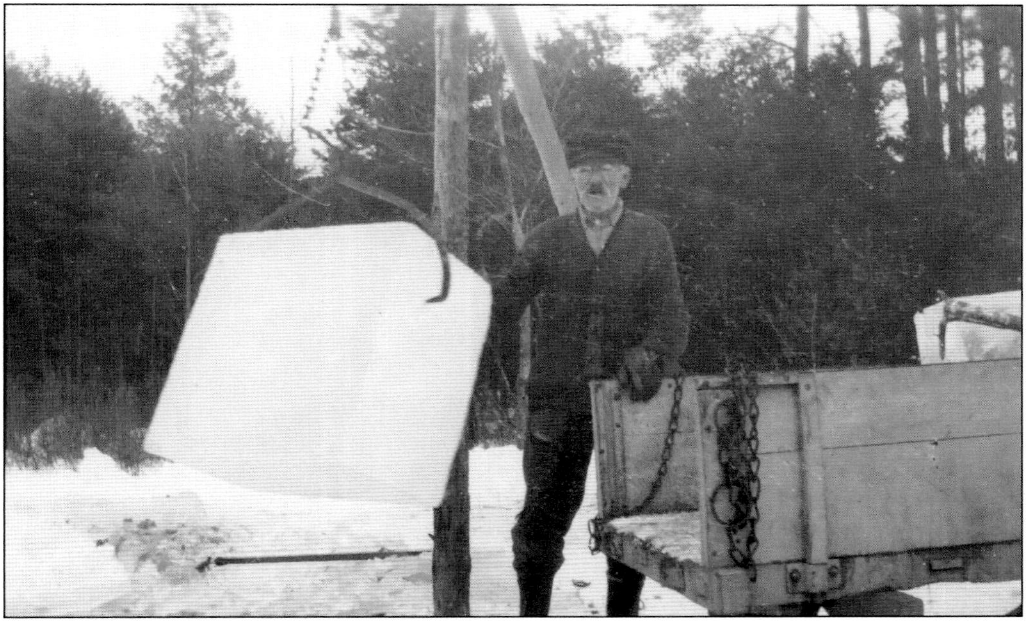

Clyde Farwell's father guides a block of ice into the back of a wagon. An ice pick used for drawing grid lines lies in the snow in the background. This photograph was taken on the pond behind the Hussey farm on Blackberry Hill Road in the early 1900s. (Courtesy of Paul Boisvert.)

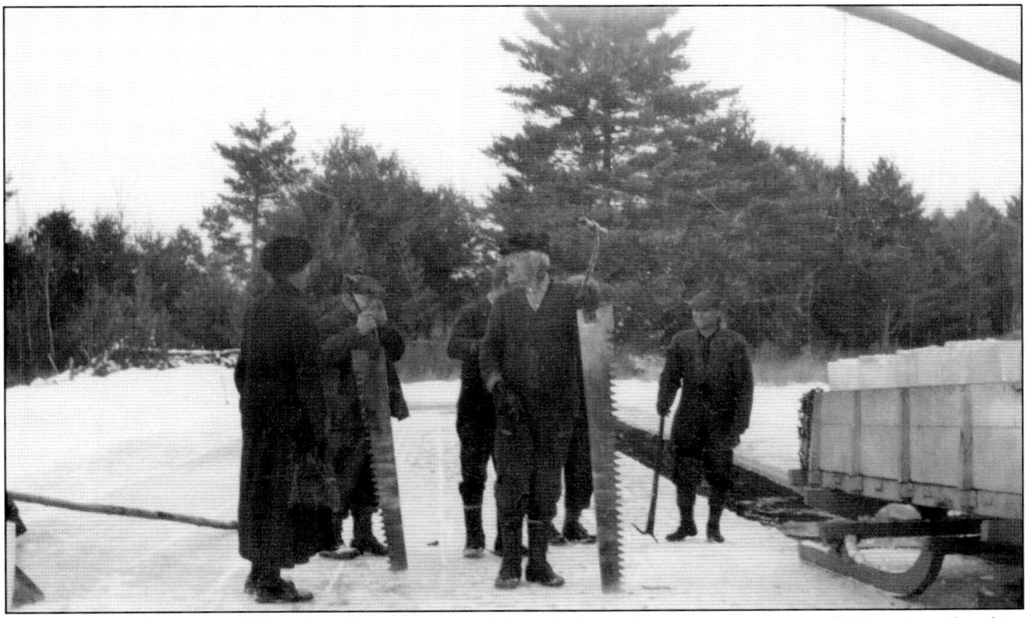

Members of the Farwell family take a moment's break from the extreme manual labor involved in ice harvesting. On display are long ice saws used for cutting ice. The ice at this location, behind the Hussey farm on Blackberry Hill Road, was typically two feet deep. A sleigh wagon full of ice waits to be transported to a nearby icehouse. (Courtesy of Paul Boisvert.)

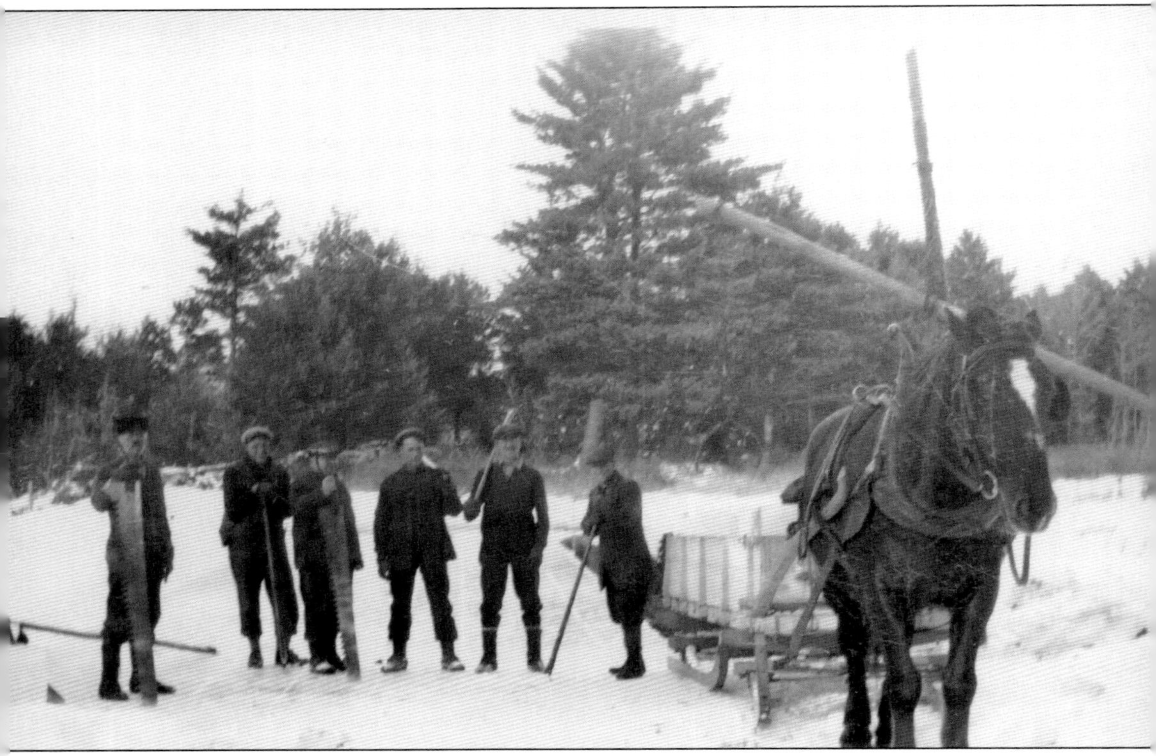

In this photograph, several men look on as the horse drags away a sleigh full of ice freshly cut from the pond behind the Hussey farm on Blackberry Hill Road. The ice-harvesting process was labor intensive, requiring 20 to 100 men over a period of four to eight weeks. (Courtesy of Paul Boisvert.)

Six

SCHOOLS

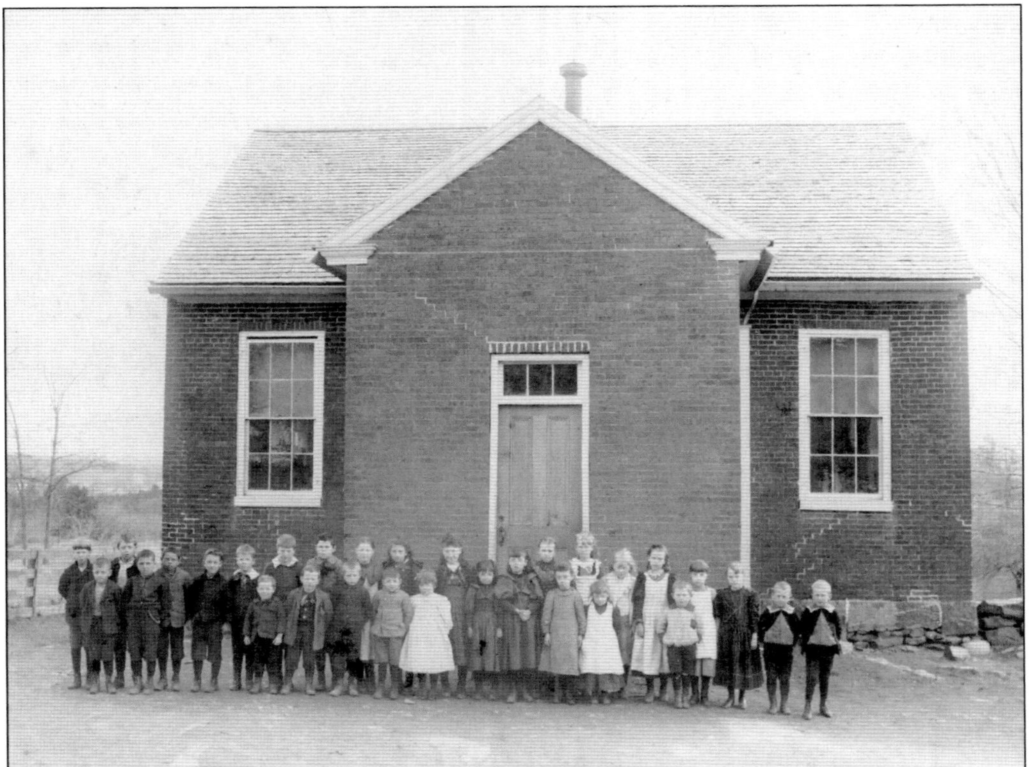

The class of 1895 poses in front of the Little Brick Schoolhouse located on Cranberry Meadow Road. This is one of the first classes to ever be taught in this one-room schoolhouse. The little girl in the white dress in the center is Marion Shaw.

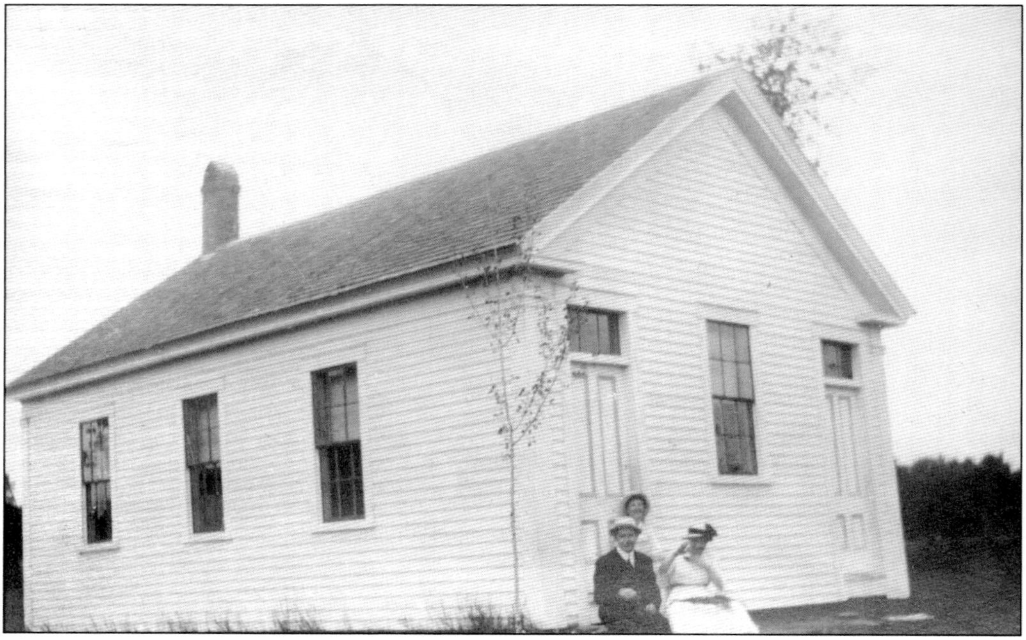

The Hubbard School was at one time located on the corner of Hubbard and Walnut Grove Roads. The building was eventually purchased as a private residence and moved to an unknown location.

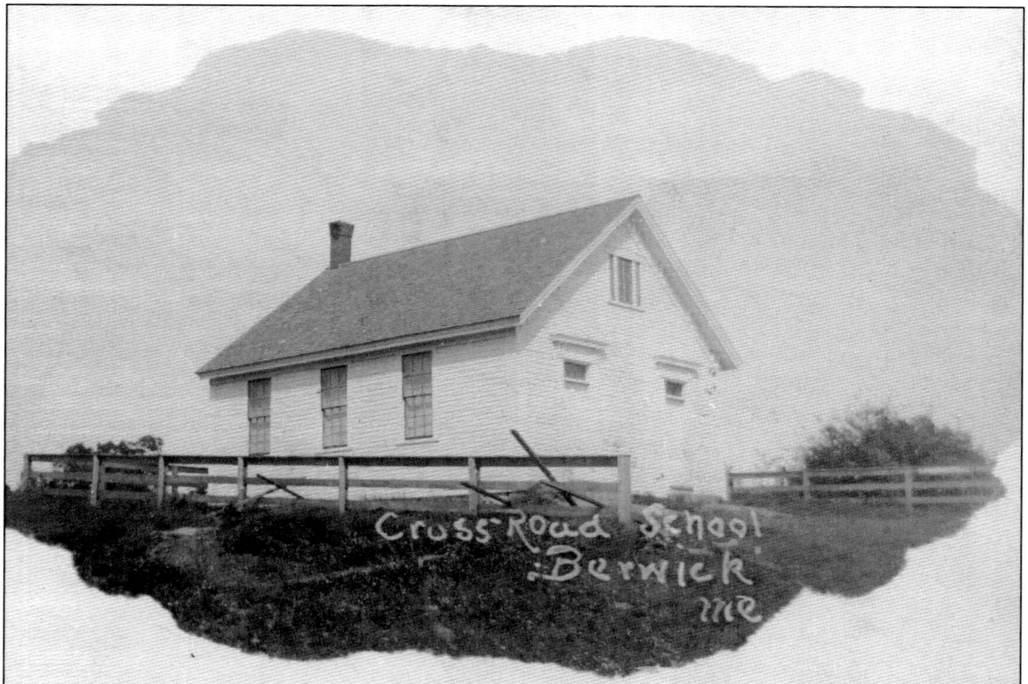

This is a photograph of the one-room Cross Road Schoolhouse. It was originally located on Route 9. Visible at the front of the building are two separate doors, indicating a time when girls and boys were segregated. This building was later moved to Pine Hill Road, where it would eventually serve as a private residence.

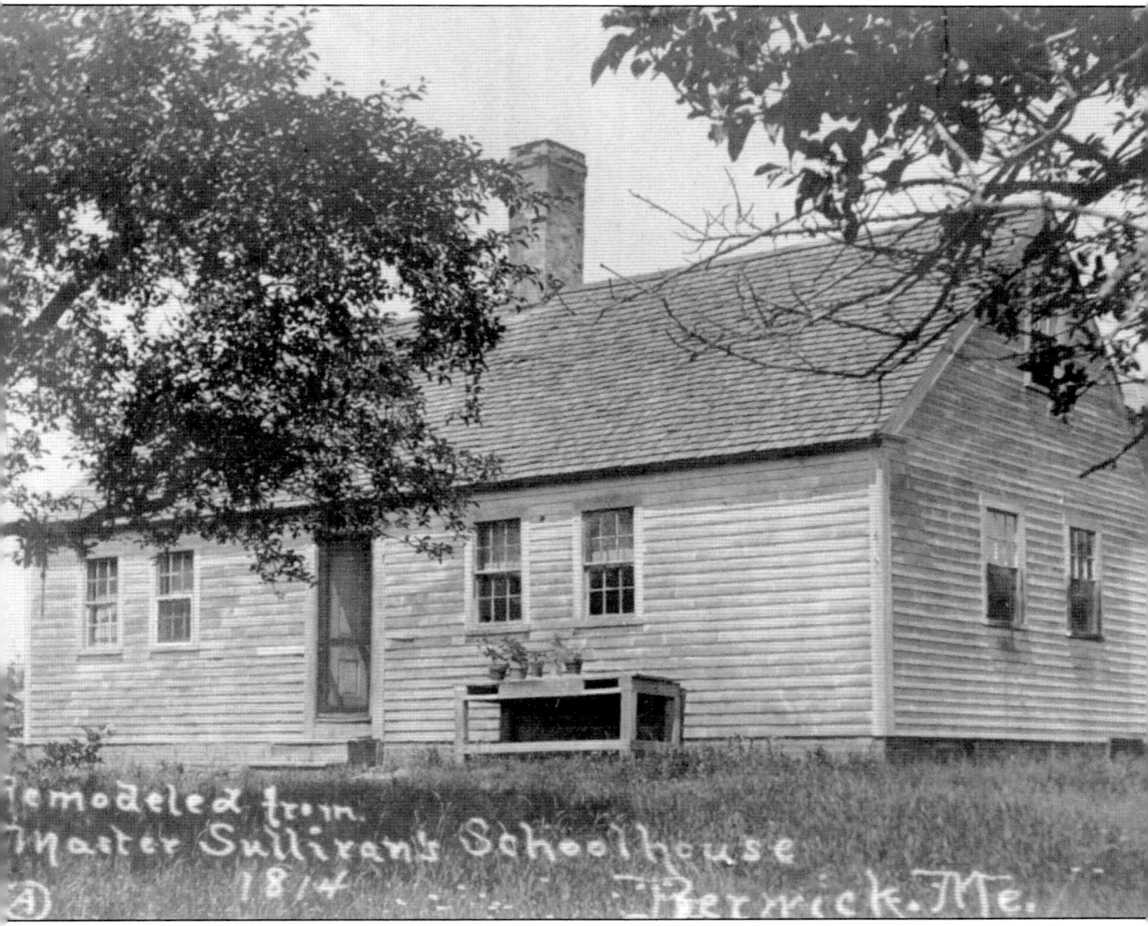

This house was built in 1743 by William Hooper, a shoemaker. In 1761, John Sullivan, father of Maj. Gen. John Sullivan of the Revolutionary War, purchased this house to use as Berwick's first schoolhouse. The house was moved by oxen in 1814 from a site near Worster Brook to its present location on the corner of School Street and Old Pine Hill Road. Eventually, the house became the property of the town and was sold at an auction in 1945 to Walter Hall, who remodeled it.

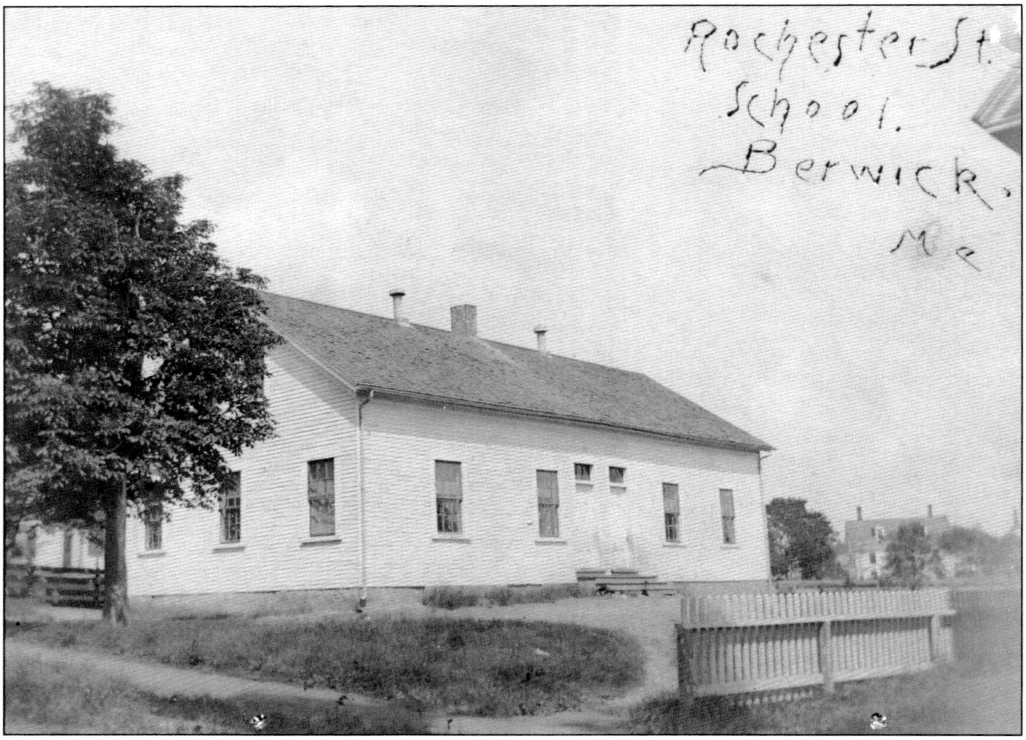

The Rochester Schoolhouse, located on Rochester Street, was one of the first schools to be built in the village area. The front of the building showcases two doors, one for the boys and the other for the girls. This building would later become known as Austin's woodworking shop.

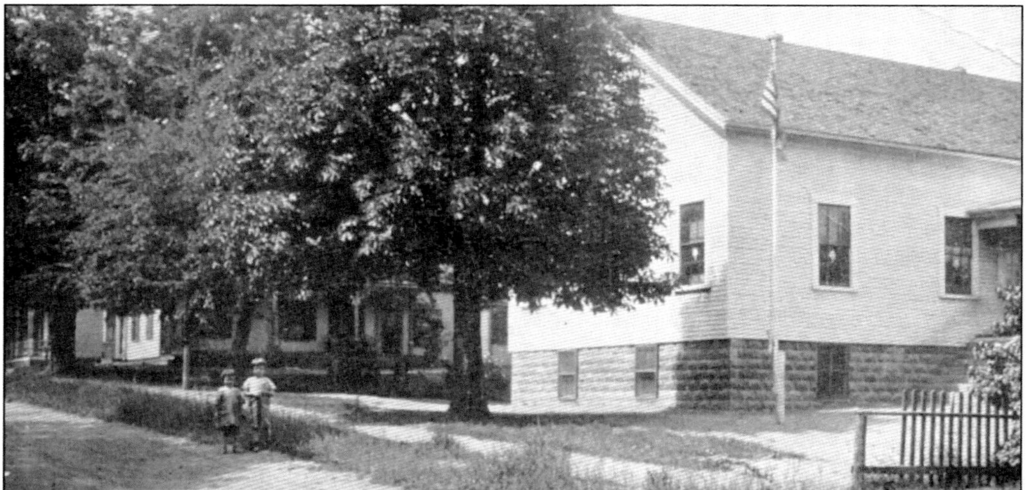

This postcard shows two youngsters standing outside the Rochester Street Schoolhouse. This photograph was taken in the early part of the 20th century. The private residences of Rochester Street can be seen in the background.

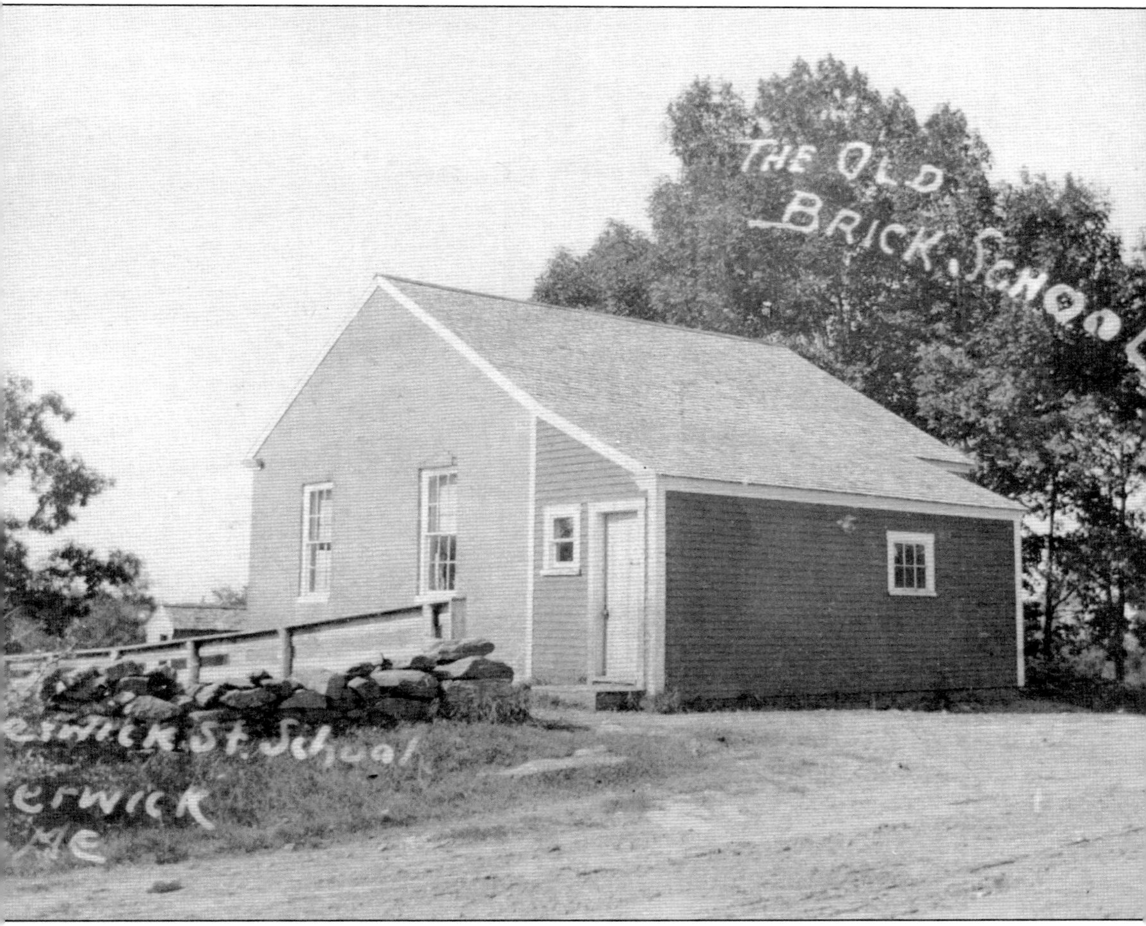

This building was first known as the Old Brick Schoolhouse. This one-room schoolhouse, on Berwick Street, housed grades one through eight, taught by one teacher. During that time, most teachers were unmarried women who lived with a family member. Often, these teachers were also former students of the same schoolhouse. In the 19th century, schools often had two, sometimes three semesters: summer, fall, and winter, each lasting 10 to 14 weeks. This building later served as the residence of Leola Pepler. Ultimately, it was destroyed by fire and no longer stands today.

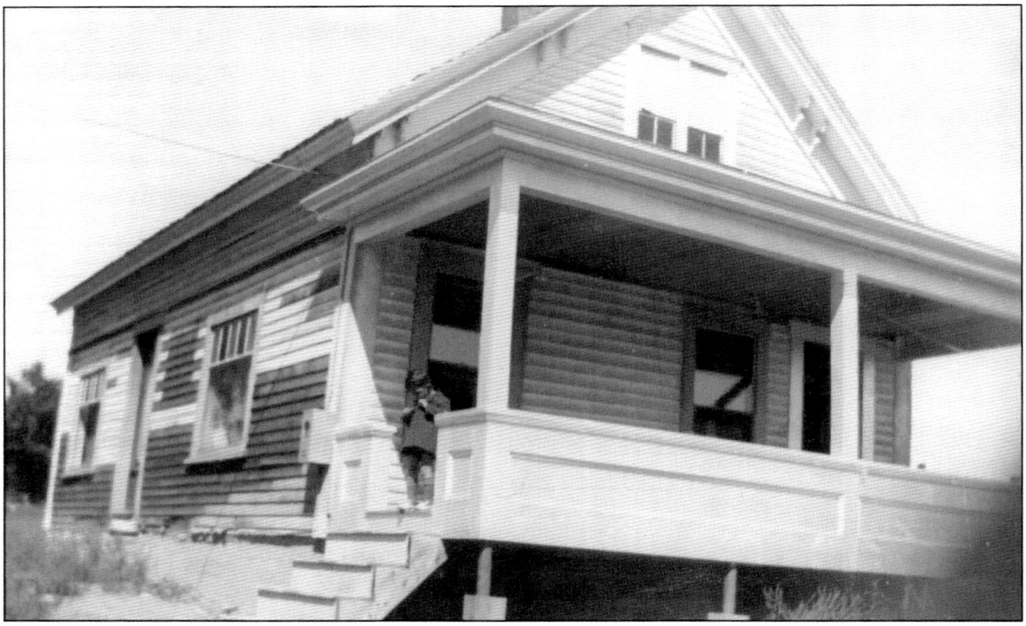

A student of the Messenger's Bridge Schoolhouse inspects the buttons of his coat on the porch of the one-room schoolhouse. This building is now part of a private residence located on Pine Hill Road.

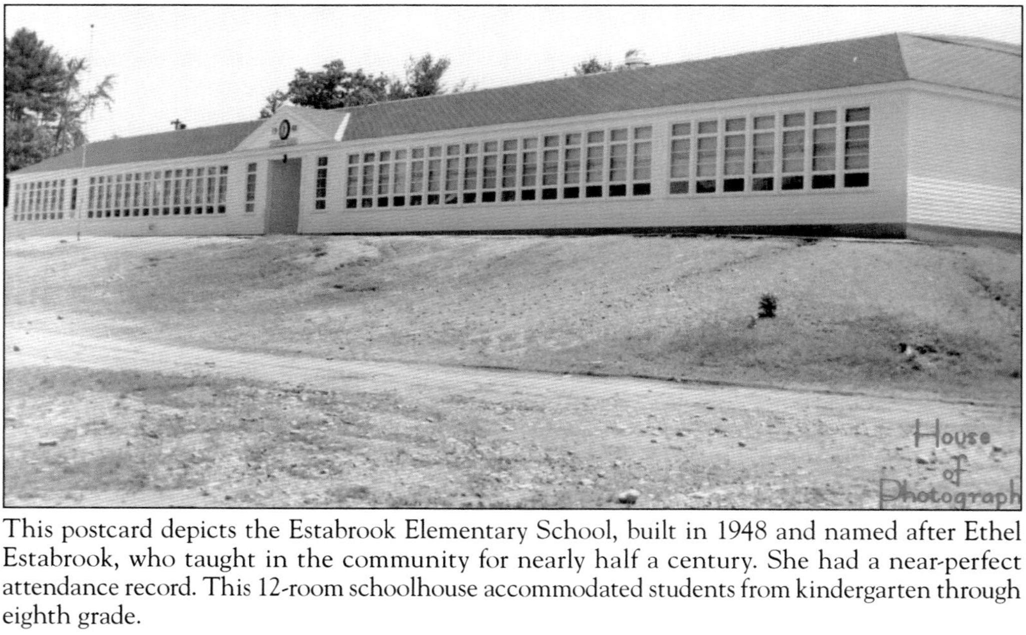

This postcard depicts the Estabrook Elementary School, built in 1948 and named after Ethel Estabrook, who taught in the community for nearly half a century. She had a near-perfect attendance record. This 12-room schoolhouse accommodated students from kindergarten through eighth grade.

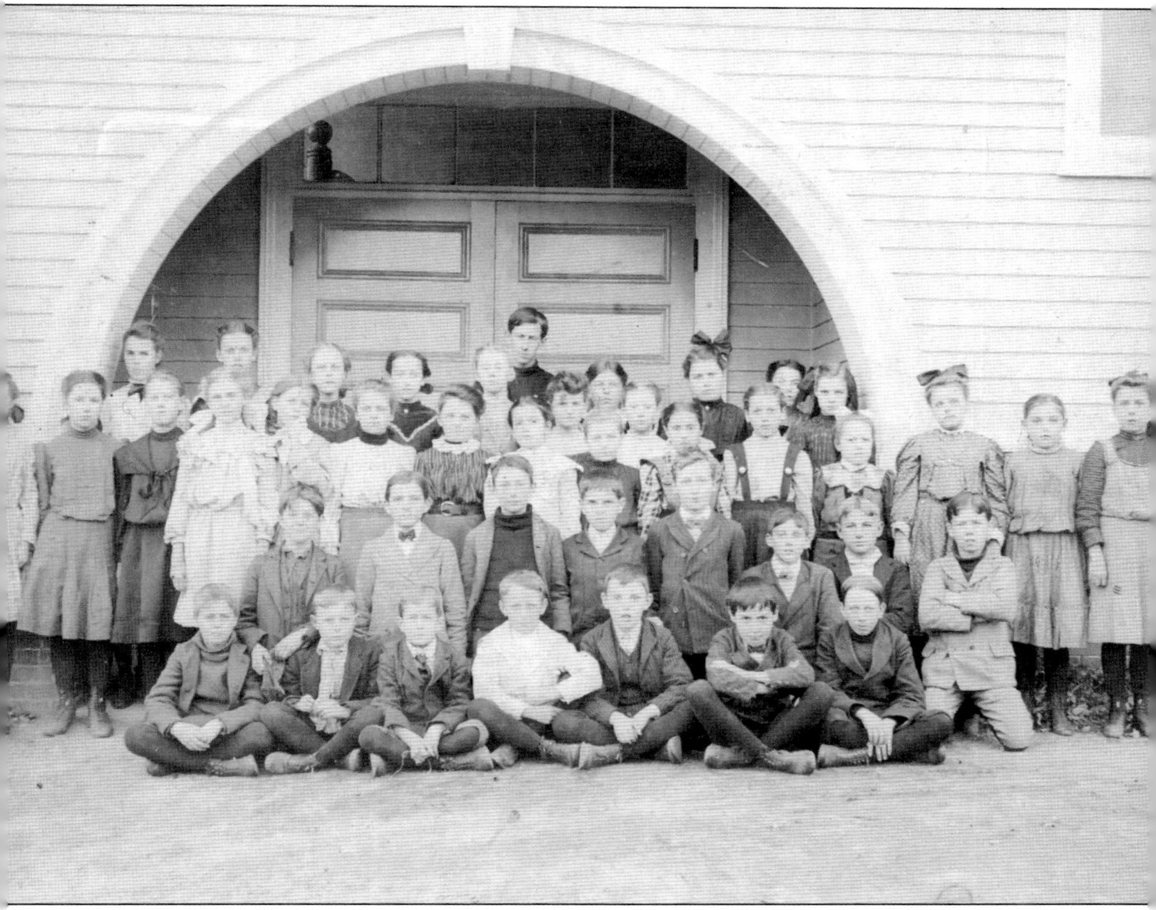

Students pose for their class picture outside the Sullivan High School located on School Street. This is the second of three schools to be built at this location. Both the first and second school at this location was sometimes referred to as the Sullivan High Grammar School because it encompassed all grades. After losing the first two to fires, the third was built from brick. The third school was called Berwick High School.

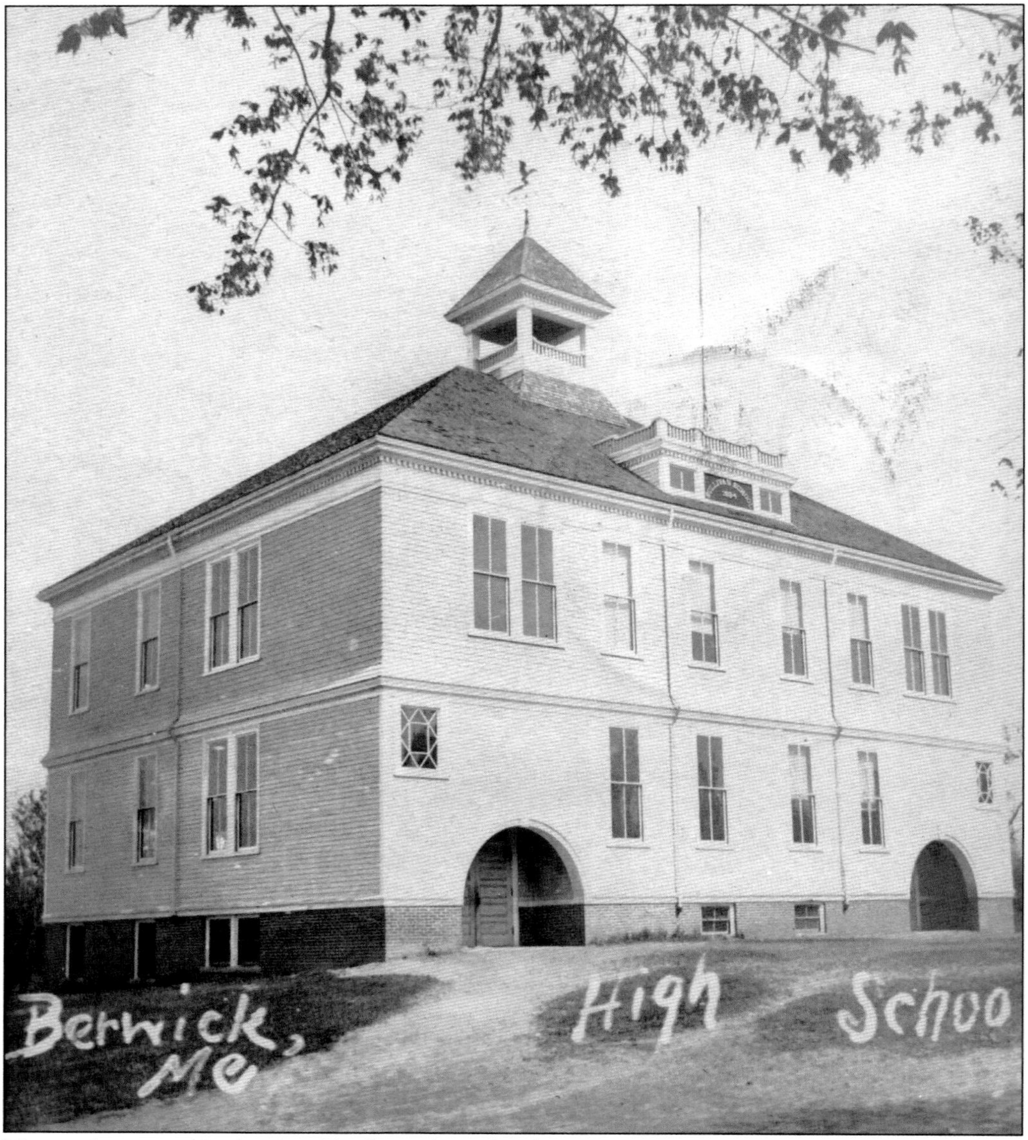

This is the second high school built on the School Street site. It was named after its predecessor, the Sullivan High School. Erected at the end of the 19th century, it was destroyed by fire on June 6, 1927.

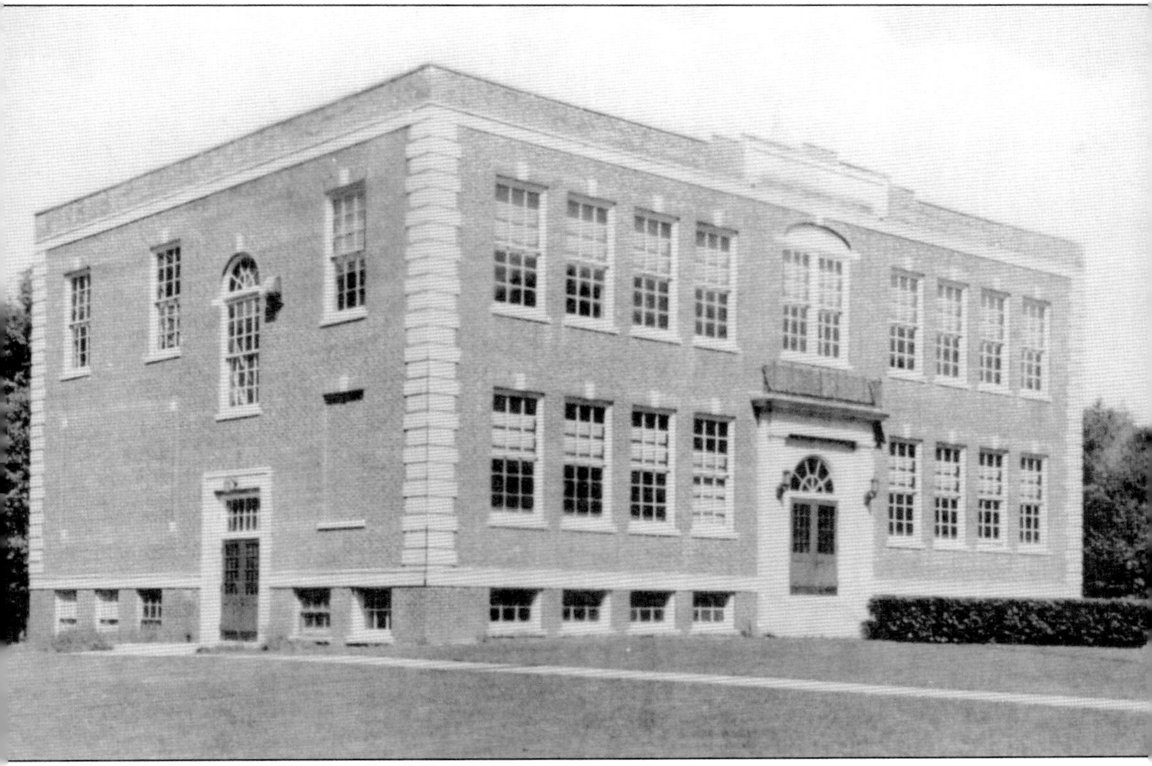

The Berwick High School was built in 1928. This is the third school to be built at this location. A wing was added to this building in 1953, and another wing was added in 1961. It is now used an apartment complex on School Street.

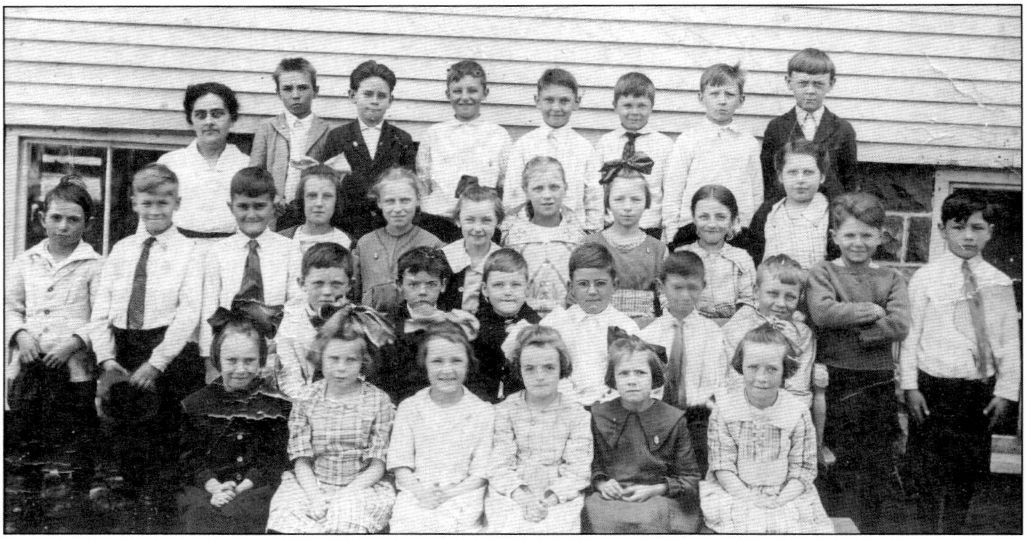

Schoolteacher Ruth Stone and her students pose in front of the Rochester Street School. This school was located in the one of the districts that formed Sullivan School District in 1872. The photograph is thought to date to the 1930s.

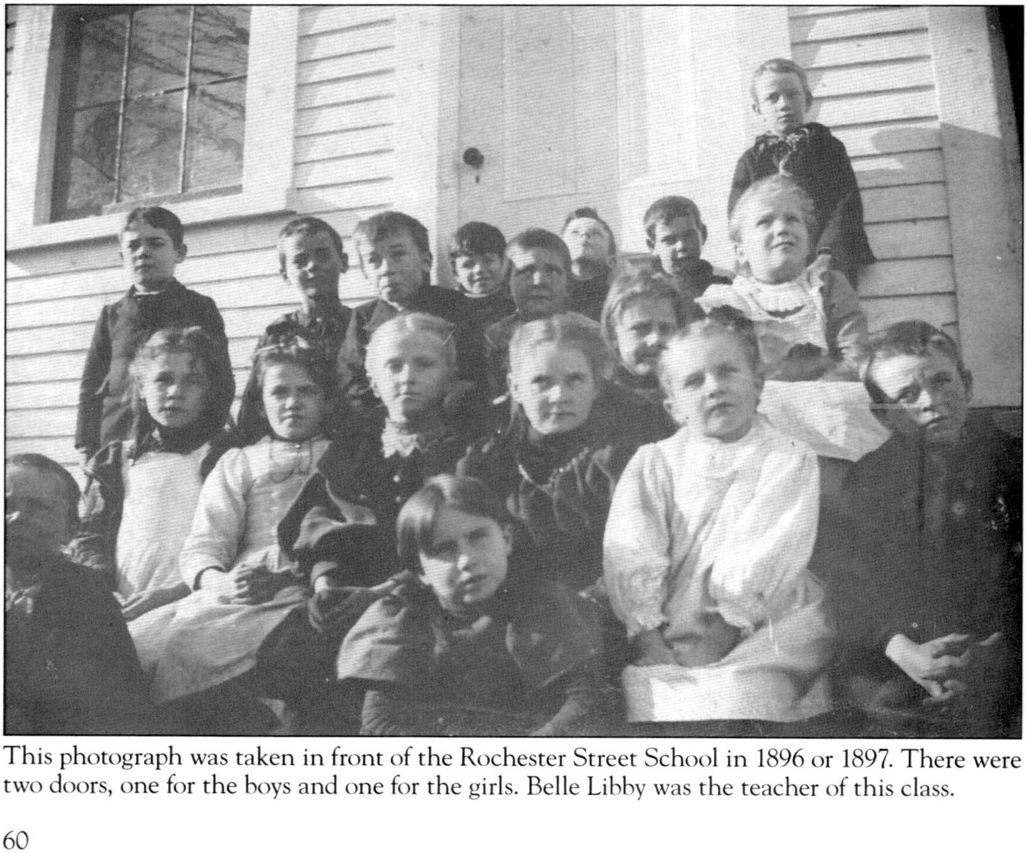

This photograph was taken in front of the Rochester Street School in 1896 or 1897. There were two doors, one for the boys and one for the girls. Belle Libby was the teacher of this class.

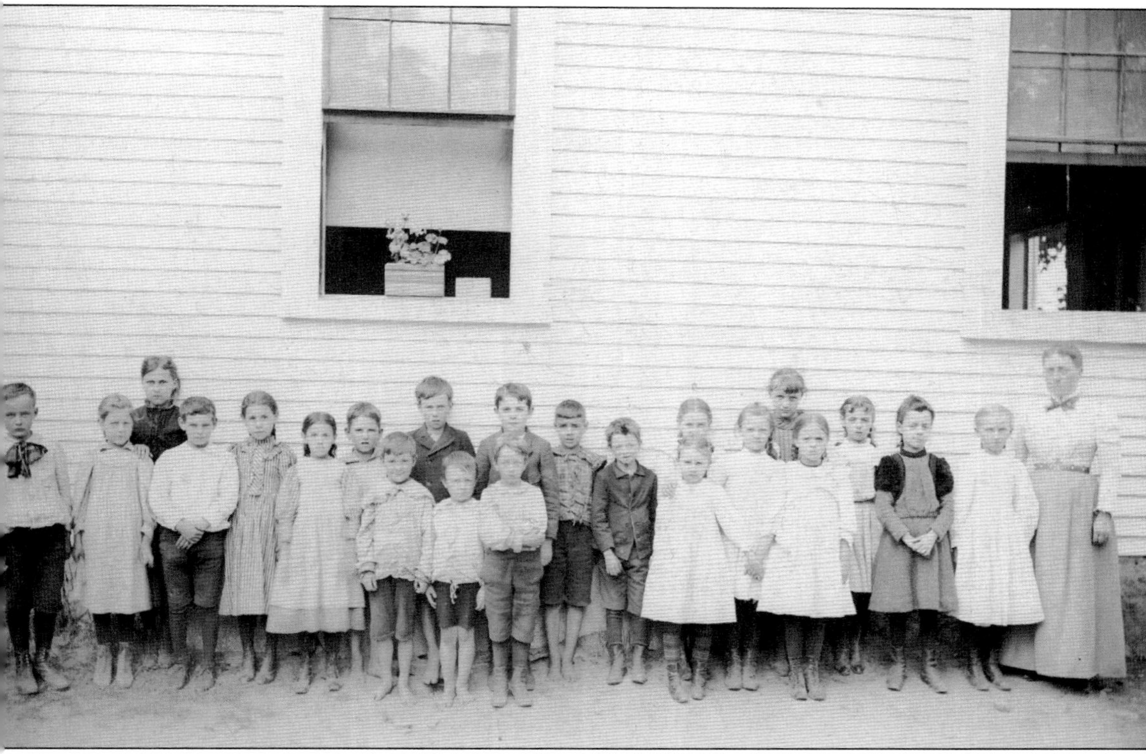

Students line up for their class photograph with their teacher, Belle Libby, on the side of the Rochester Street School in 1898. Some of these students are posing in bare feet. It was not uncommon for some children not to have shoes to wear during the warmer months of the year.

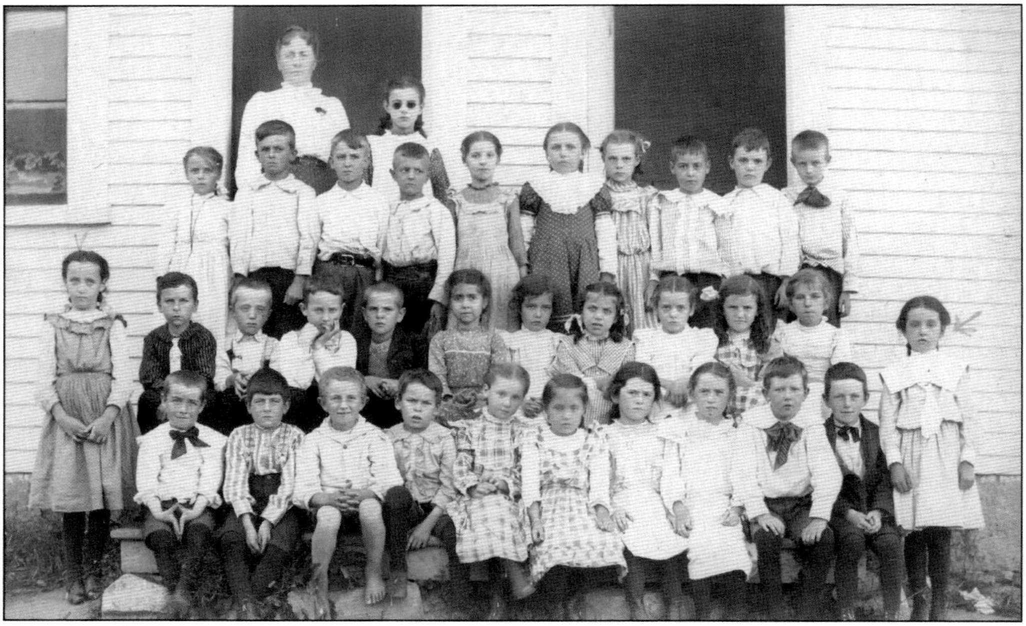

Schoolteacher Belle Libby stands in front of the Rochester Street School with her students on September 12, 1902. Lura Brown is in the first row, fifth from the left. Marion Tibbetts is standing in the first row at far right. Lena Hatch is standing in the second row at far left.

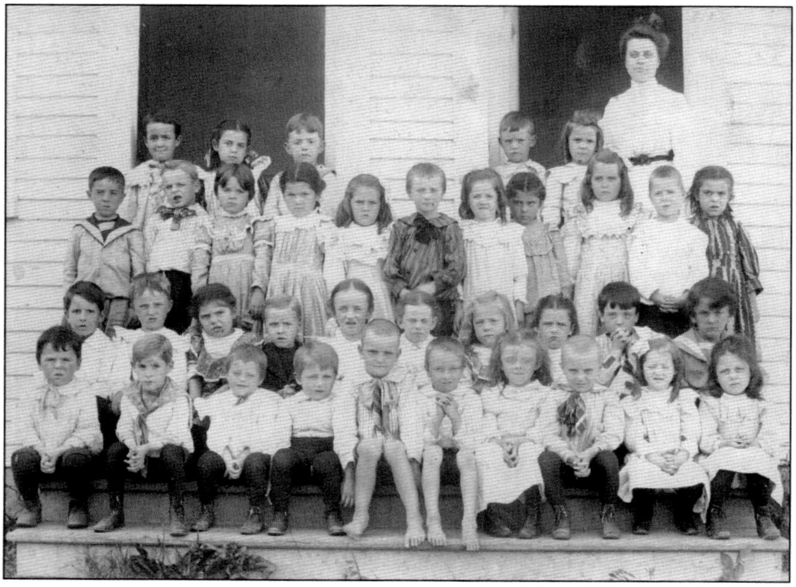

Belle Libby stands behind her students sitting on the front steps of the two-room schoolhouse on Rochester Street. The two barefoot children sitting on the front step are a good indication that this photograph was taken in the late spring or early summer.

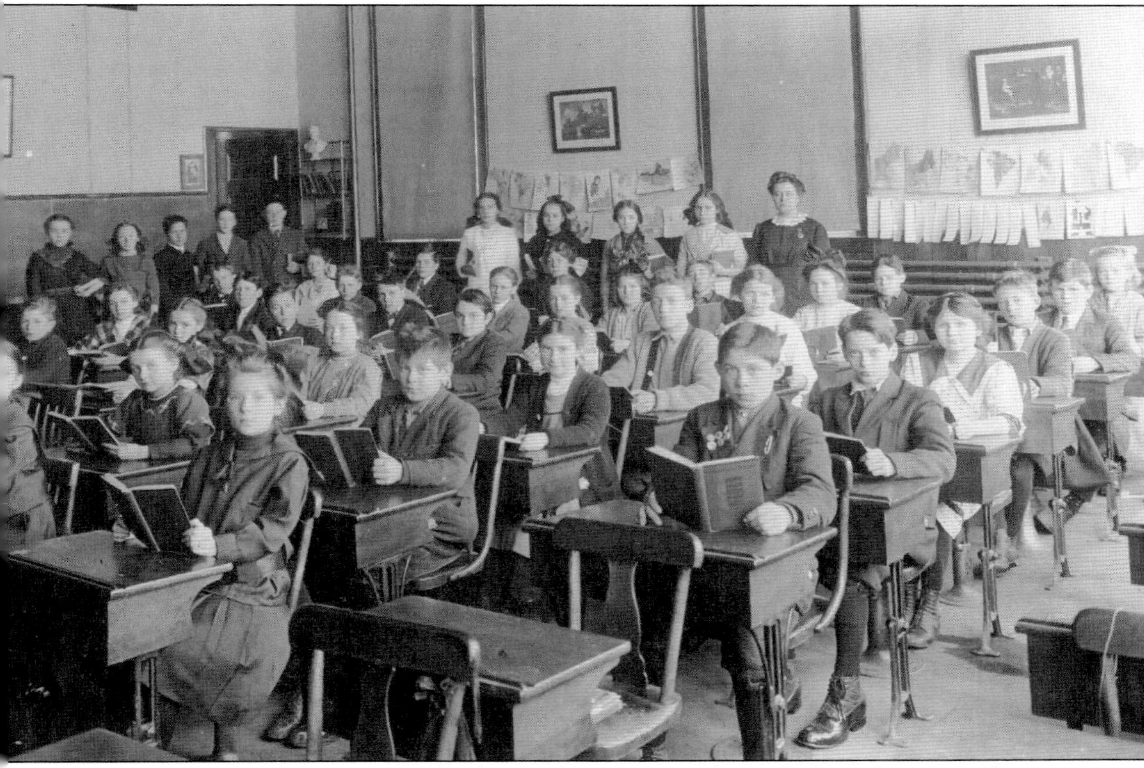

A class at Sullivan High Grammar School poses for a photograph inside their classroom. Shown here, starting with the right row, are, from front to back, (first row) Eric Sevigny, Charles Downes, May Gerrish, Harold Jones, Elinore Hanscom, and Ethel Moulton; (second row) Marjorie Ames, Geo Guptill, Ethel Mason, Elisha Leach, Helen Whitehouse, unidentified student, and Arthur Worster; (third row) Grace Brackett, Helen Kimball, Evelyn Rice, Lester Bragdon, Mable Richer, Beulah McIntyre, and Harry McIntyre; (fourth row) Hazel Austin, Marton Burell, Leland Mullen, Benard Downes, and Olive Bryant; (fifth row) Lester Mathews, Ester Baker, Ralph Cheney, and Chester Mathews. Those standing are, from right to left, Beautrice Coffin, Bernice Coffin, two unidentified students, Wayne D., Beautrice Dame, Hazel Mathews, Gladys Goodwin, Harriet Hurd, and the teacher, Gertrude Downes.

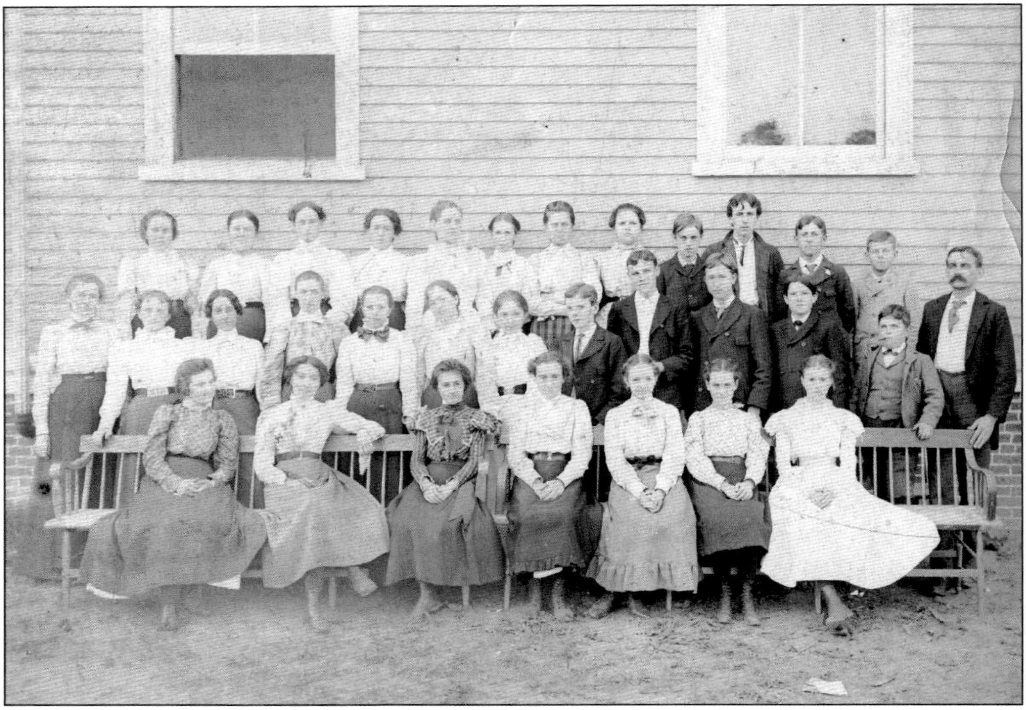

Students of the Sullivan High Grammar School, and some of their parents, sit outside for their class photograph. It was not uncommon during that time for parents to sit in on the classroom studies.

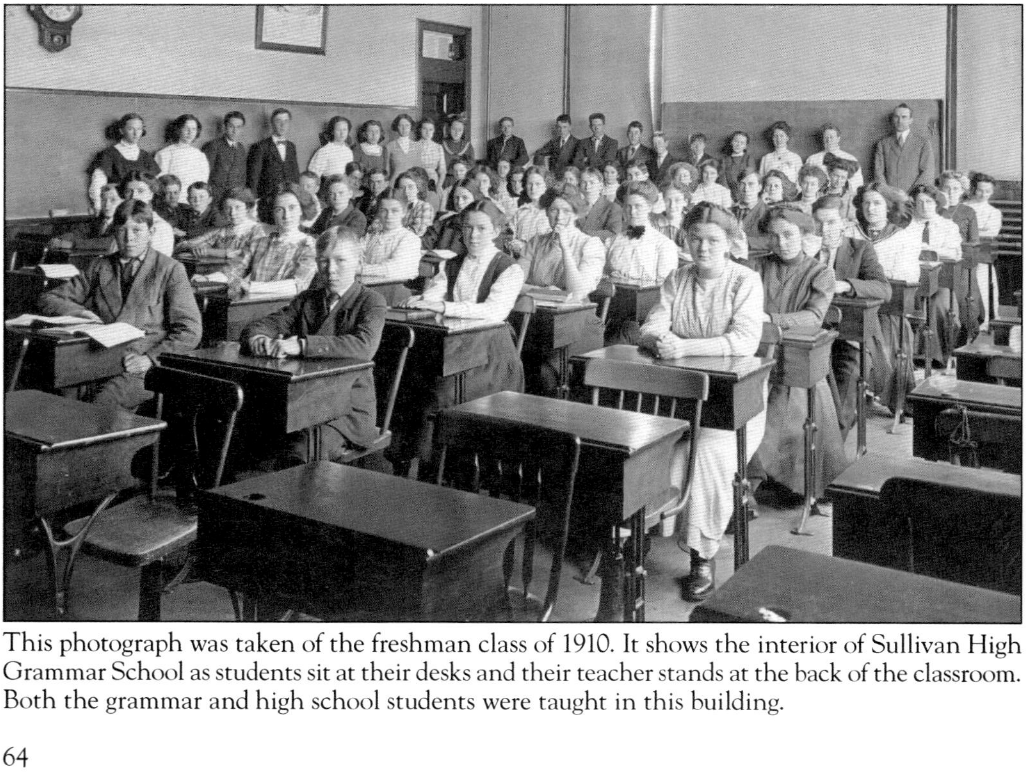

This photograph was taken of the freshman class of 1910. It shows the interior of Sullivan High Grammar School as students sit at their desks and their teacher stands at the back of the classroom. Both the grammar and high school students were taught in this building.

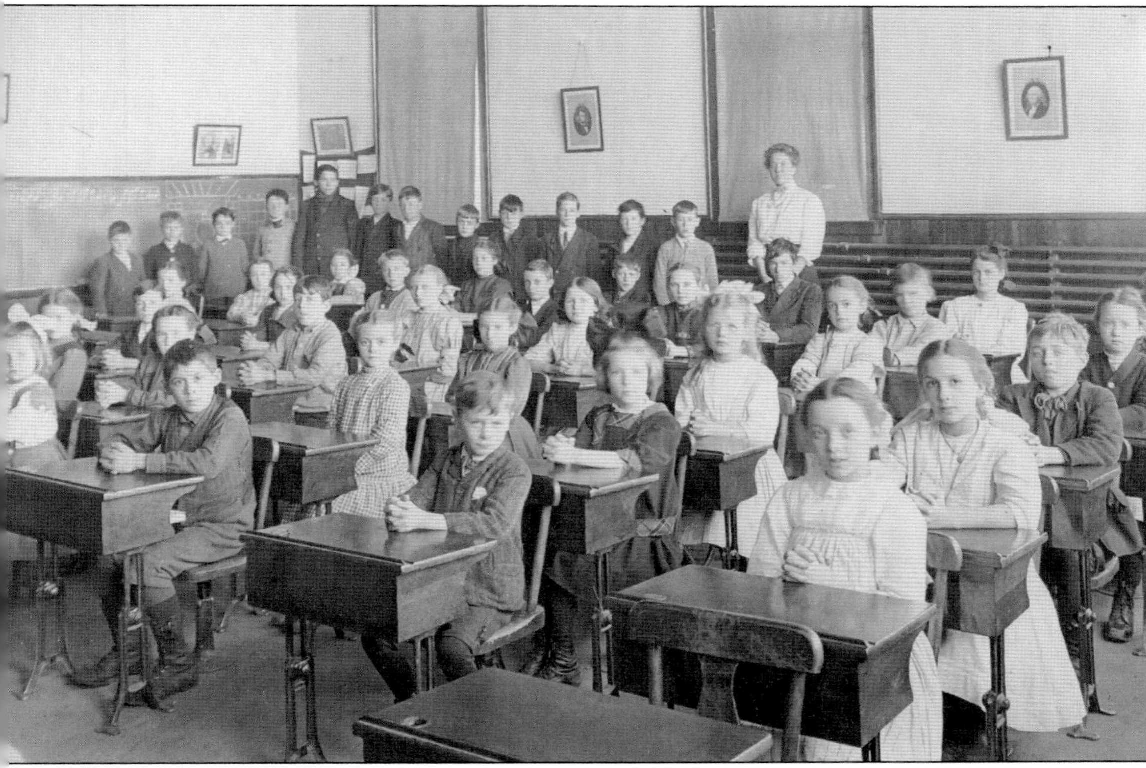

Students and their teacher pose for a class photograph in Sullivan High Grammar School. Shown here are, starting from the right row and from front to back, (first row): Mildred Cooper, Beautrice H., Harry McIntyre, Evelyn Rice, and unidentified; (second row) unidentified, Marjorie Ames, Helen Whitehouse, Grace Brackett, Elenore Hanscom, and unidentified; (third row) Eric S., Ethel Moulton, Ethel Mason, May Ester Gerrish, Marjorie Guy, and unidentified; (fourth row) Helen Kimball, unidentified, Ralph Cheney, two unidentified students, and Buster Mathews; (fifth row) unidentified, Olive Downes, Hazel Mathews, and Elisha Leach; (sixth row) all unidentified. The students standing are unidentified.

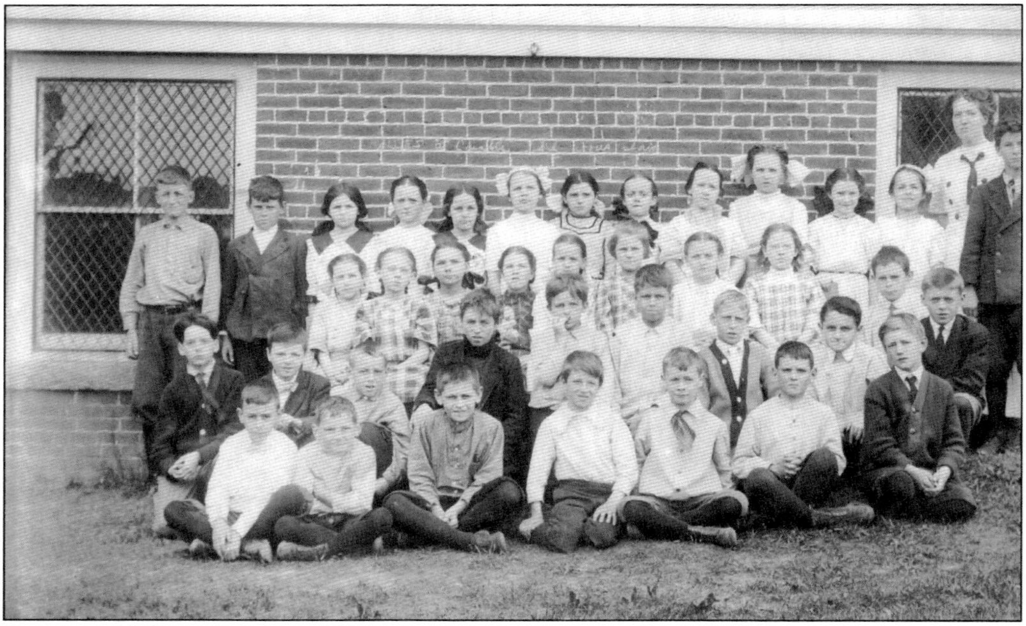

Fourth and fifth graders from Sullivan High Grammar School pose for their 1910 class photograph. Shown here are, in the best known order, from left to right, (first row) unidentified, Eric Sevigny, Geo Guptill, Arthur Cooper, unidentified, Verne Hanscom, and Harry Jones; (second row) Charles Downes, Hugo Young, Harry McIntyre, Lindsey Leach, Cecil Horne, Lester Bragdon and two unidentified; (third row) Irene Worcester, Yula Bridges, unidentified, Clarina Schulmauer, Kathren Reynolds, Helen Kimball, Marjorie Ames, unidentified, Auther Worcester, and Wellard Downes; (fourth row) two unidentified, Elisha Leach, Elenore Hanscom, May Ester Gerrish, Helen Whitehouse, Beulah McIntyre, Ethel Moulton, Evelyn Rice, Marjorie Guy, Ethel Mason, Grace Brackett, Mary Hall (the teacher), and Henry Staples.

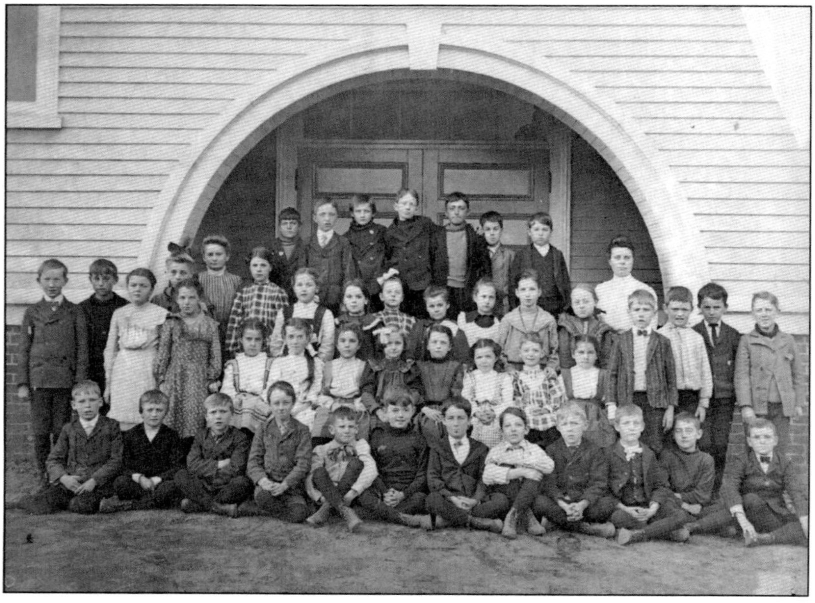

Students and their teacher pose outside Sullivan High Grammar School for their class portrait. Note how the girls are kept at the center of the gathering. At that time, it was common to keep boys and girls separated inside the class.

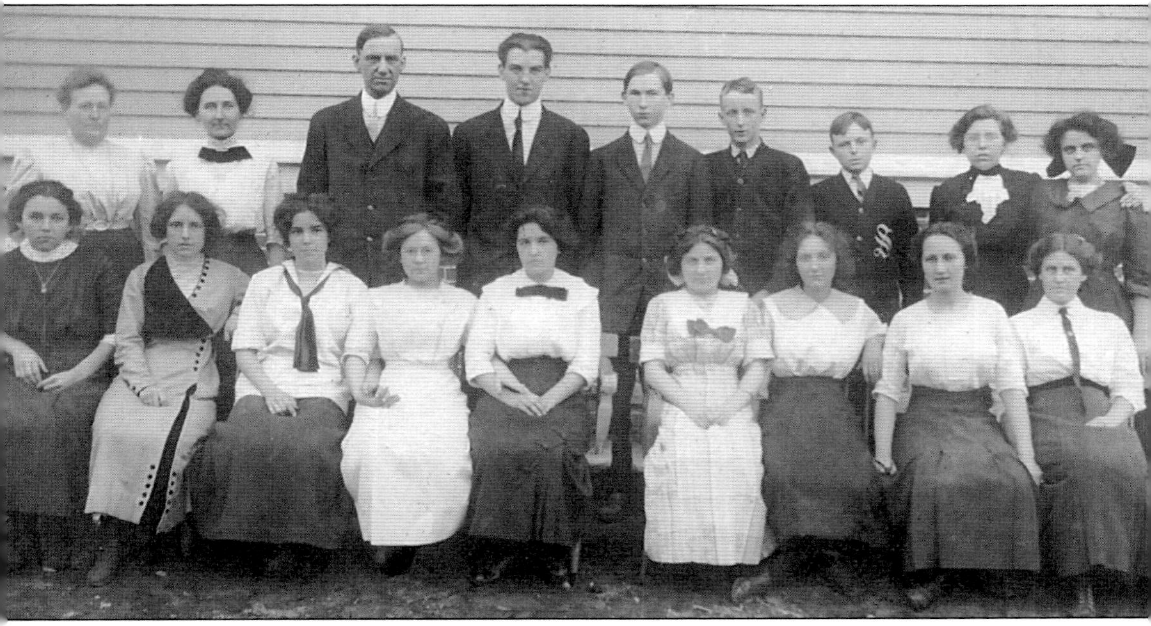

This photograph depicts the 15 students of the graduating class of 1913 at Sullivan High Grammar School. The graduates are, in no particular order, as follows: Fannie May Guptill, Hazel Emily Johnston, Mabel Estelle Hanscom, Olive Armine Spencer, Burton Roscoe Day, Edwin Harold Gerrish, Moses Winthrop Morrill, Luceile Marion Stevens, Wallace Kendall Tibbetts, Viola Ethel Ricker, Vera Ruth Stone, Ruth Calista Brackett, Lura Martha Brown, Muriel Gladys Hanscom, and Marion Ruth Tibbetts. Also appearing in the photograph in the upper left corner are two teachers and the schoolmaster; all are unidentified.

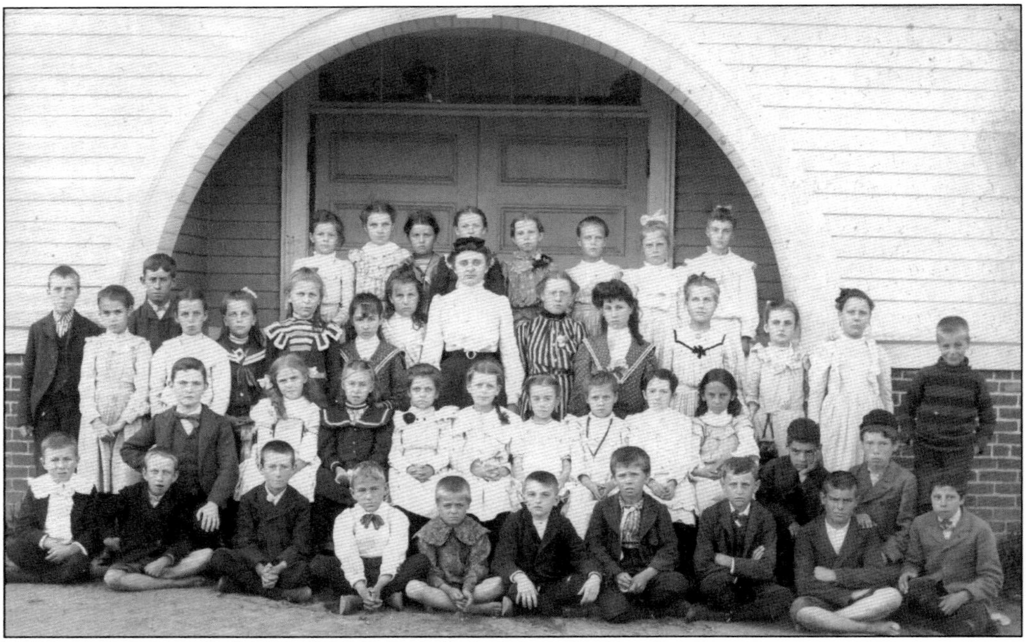

Students and their teacher pose outside Sullivan High Grammar School. This photograph was taken in September 1902.

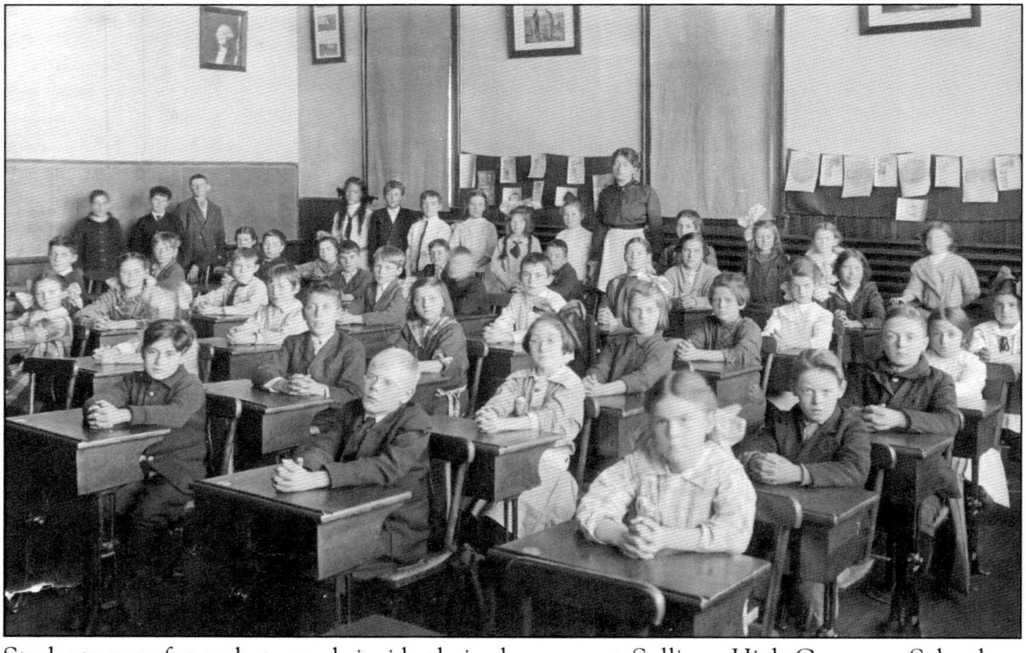

Students pose for a photograph inside their classroom at Sullivan High Grammar School on School Street in the early 1900s. Their teacher is standing in the back of classroom.

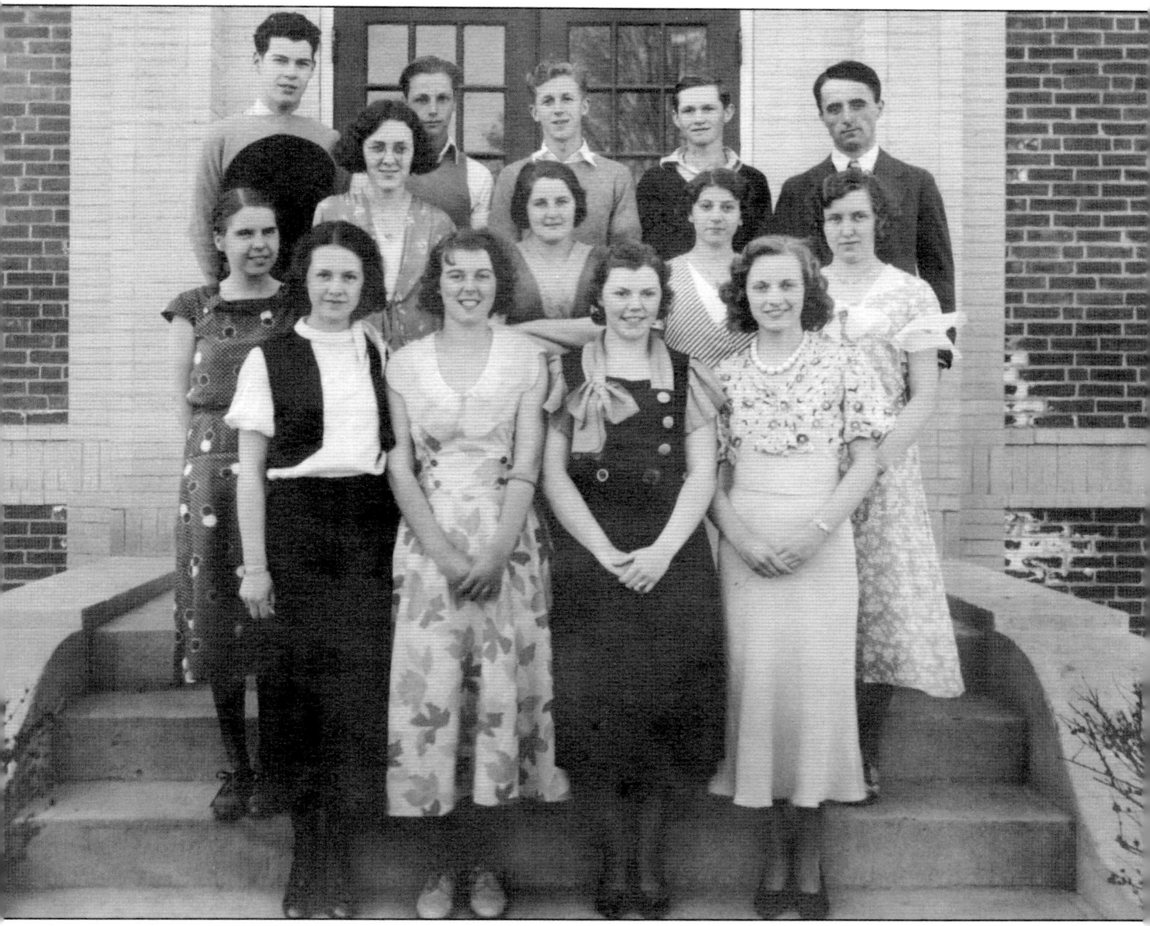

The 13 graduating students of the class of 1933 stand on the front steps of the Berwick High School located on School Street. From left to right are (first row) Carolyn Cheney, Beverly Mathews, Florence Garnett, and Bernice Neilson Libby; (second row) Gertrude Frost Yemma, Ruth Randall, Arlene Tanguay, Catlin ?, Martha Ross, and Annie Matthews Goodwin; (third row) Paul Gallup, Harold MacKenzie, Harold Coffin, Nelson Varney, and Arthur Coffin.

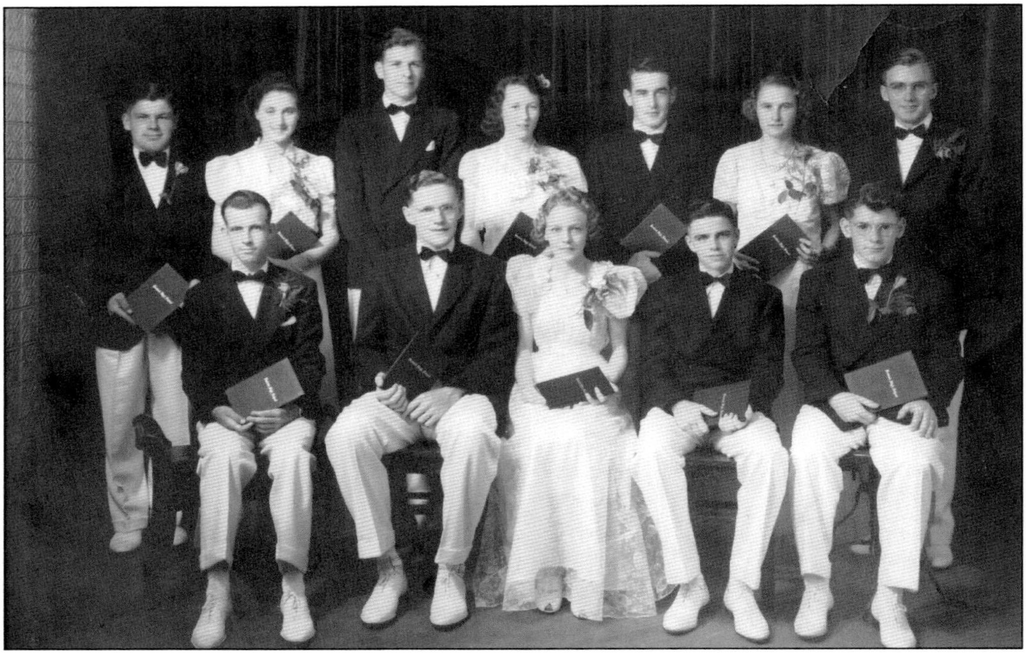

Sullivan High Grammar School students pose for their class photograph. Shown here are, from right to left, (first row) Carlton Spencer, Phil Matthews, Alice Garland, Ernest Ricker, and Clyde Randall; (second row) Paul Scruten, Ellen Ham, Frank Chapman, Pearl Hoyl, Jack Moran, Eleanor Martin, and Burton Kimball.

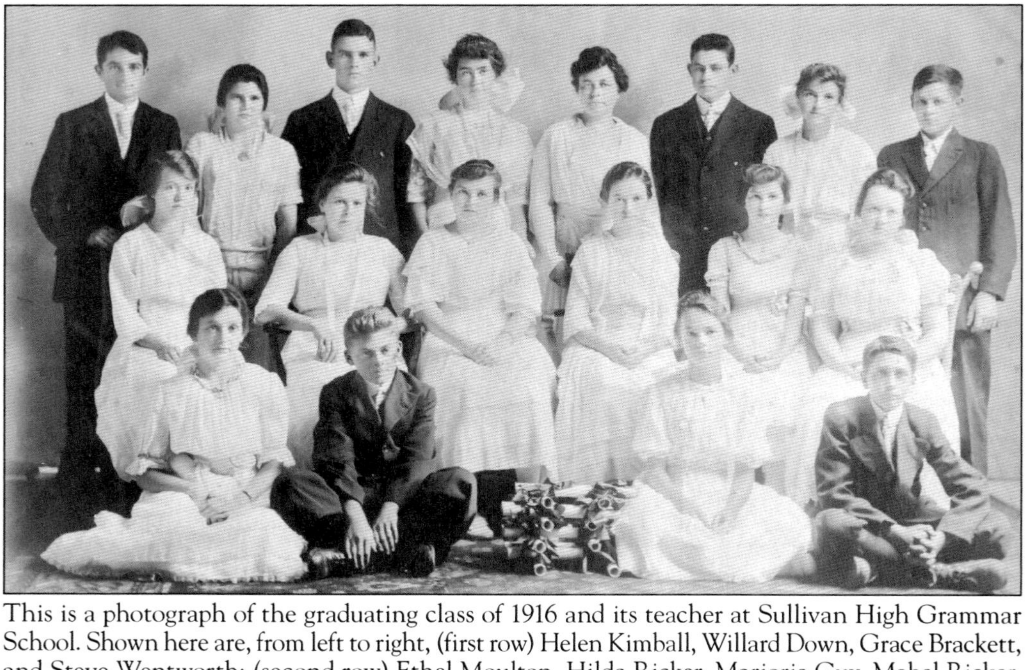

This is a photograph of the graduating class of 1916 and its teacher at Sullivan High Grammar School. Shown here are, from left to right, (first row) Helen Kimball, Willard Down, Grace Brackett, and Steve Wentworth; (second row) Ethel Moulton, Hilda Ricker, Marjorie Guy, Mabel Ricker, Ether Mason, and Evelyn Rice; (third row) Lester Bragdon, Beulah McIntyre, Eleanor Hanscom, Etta Wilson, Gertrude Downs (teacher), Arthur Worster, Suzy Ricker, and George Guptill.

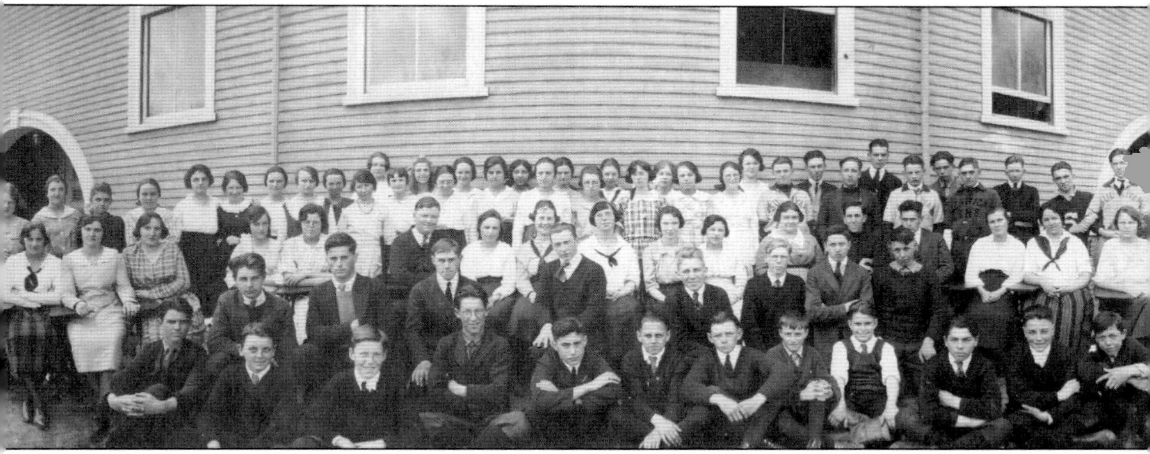

Sullivan High Grammar School students pose outside the building for their class portrait in the 1920s. This photograph was taken shortly before the fire that destroyed the building in 1927. (Courtesy of Dawn Milbury.)

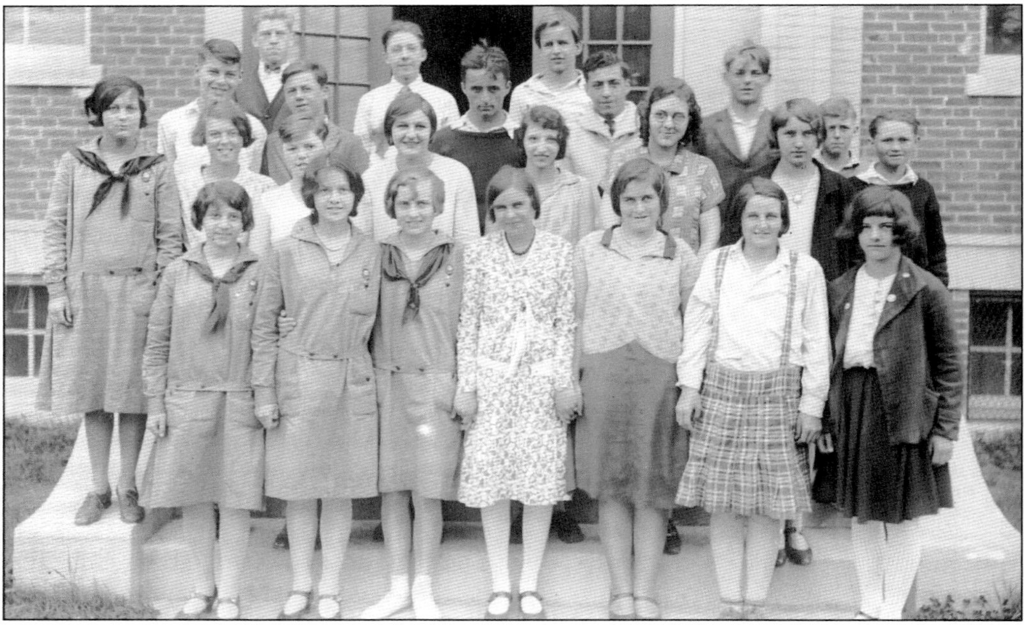

The class of 1933 poses for their class photograph on the steps of the Berwick High School. This photograph was taken during their freshman year, in May 1930.

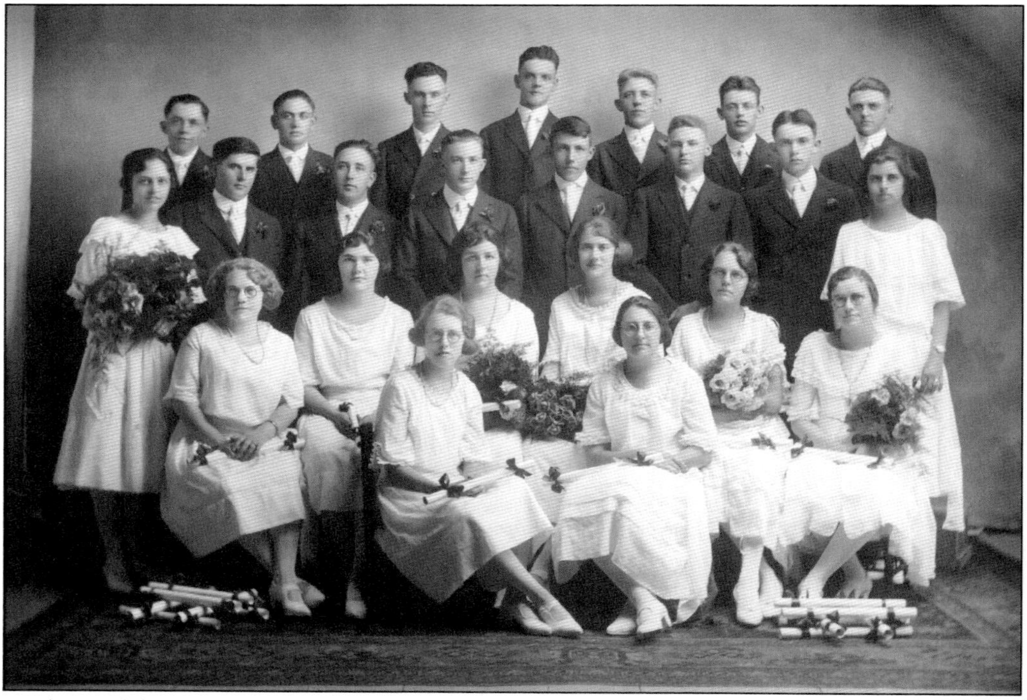

Students of the class of 1922 pose for their portrait. Frances Mathews is in the second row, fifth from left. Their teacher stands in the back row at far right.

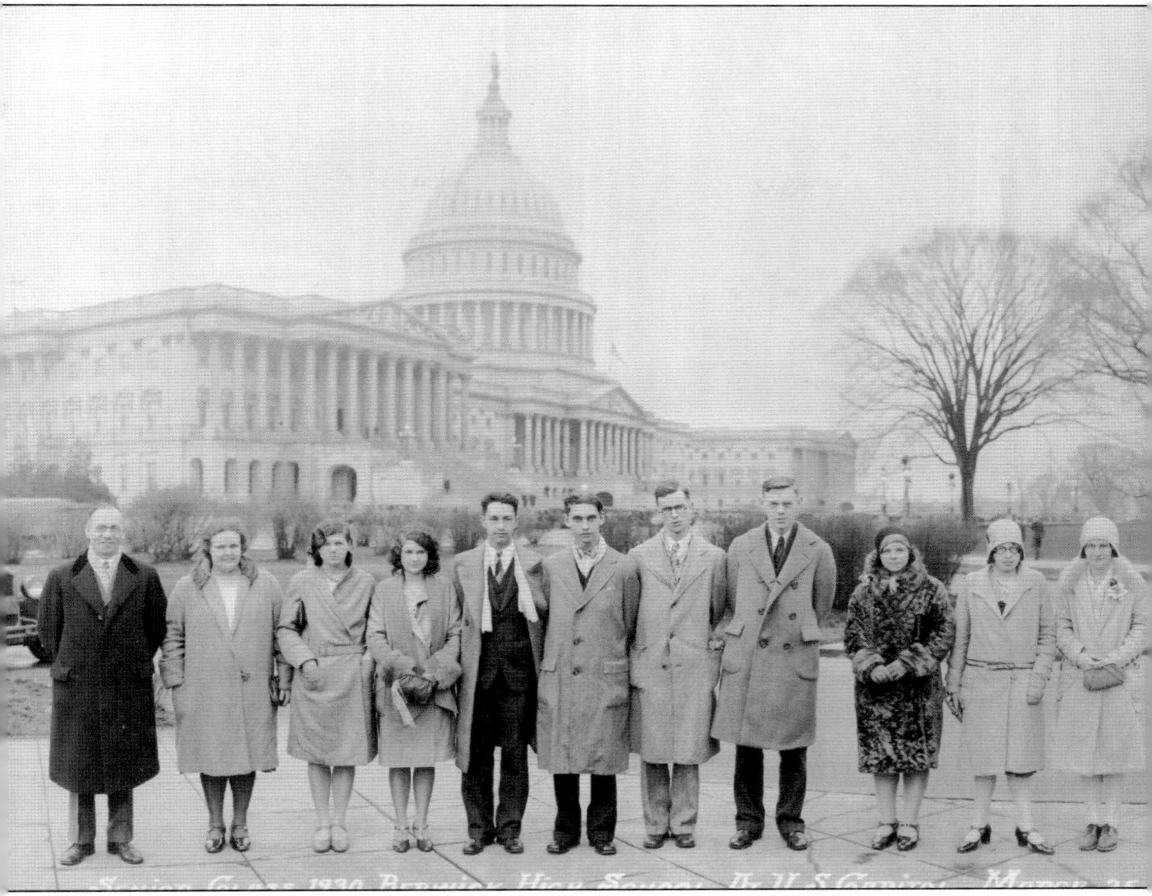

Berwick High School's senior class poses in front of the state capital building while on a class field trip. This photograph was taken in 1930.

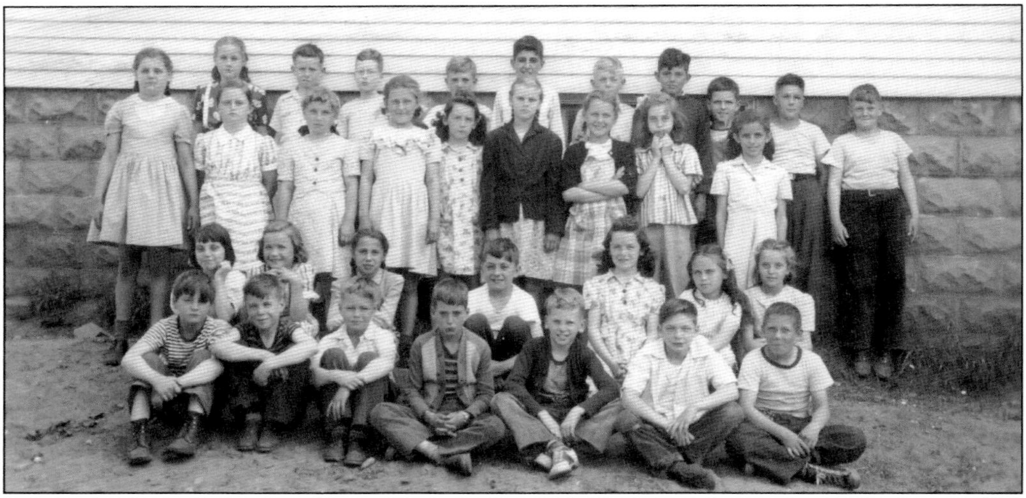

Third and fourth grade elementary school students pose in front of the Estabrook Elementary School located on Wilson Street. The school was named after a long-standing local teacher, Ethel Estabrook, who was reported to have never missed a day of school in 20 years. Today, this building sits empty, although an addition that was later added to the structure is now currently the location of the Berwick Police Department. This photograph was taken in 1945. The boy in middle with white T-shirt is Brian Cincotta, who is now one of the town historians.

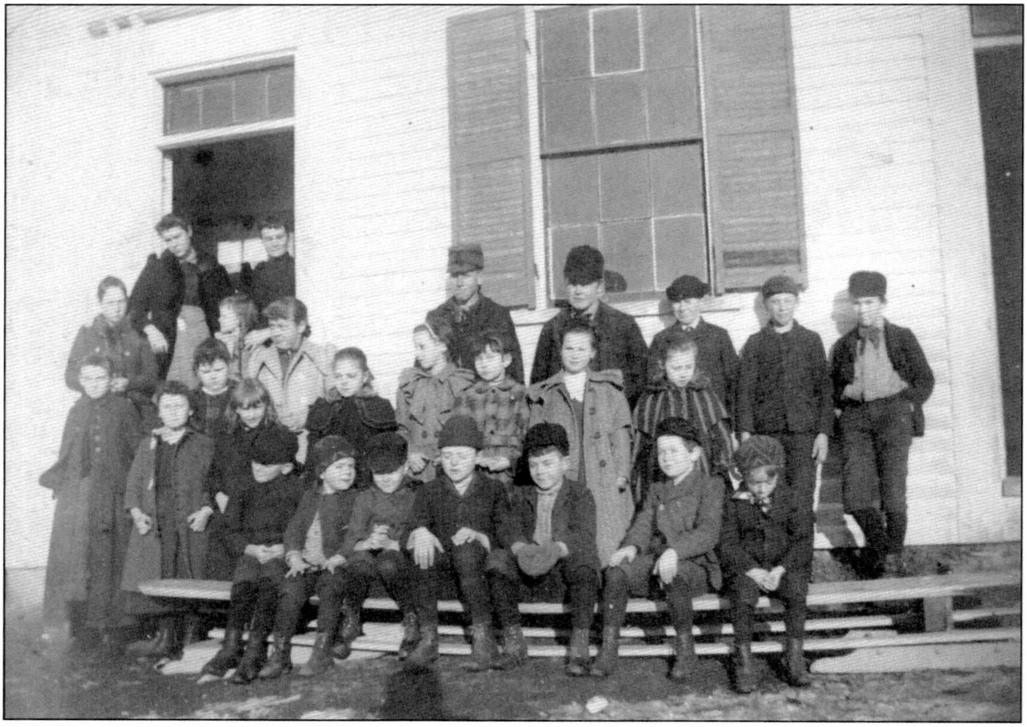

This photograph from the early 20th century was taken in front of the Pine Hill School. During this time, it was common to see two separate doors on the front of a schoolhouse. The door on the left was for girls, and a separate door on the right was used for boys. The teacher can be seen standing in front of the left door.

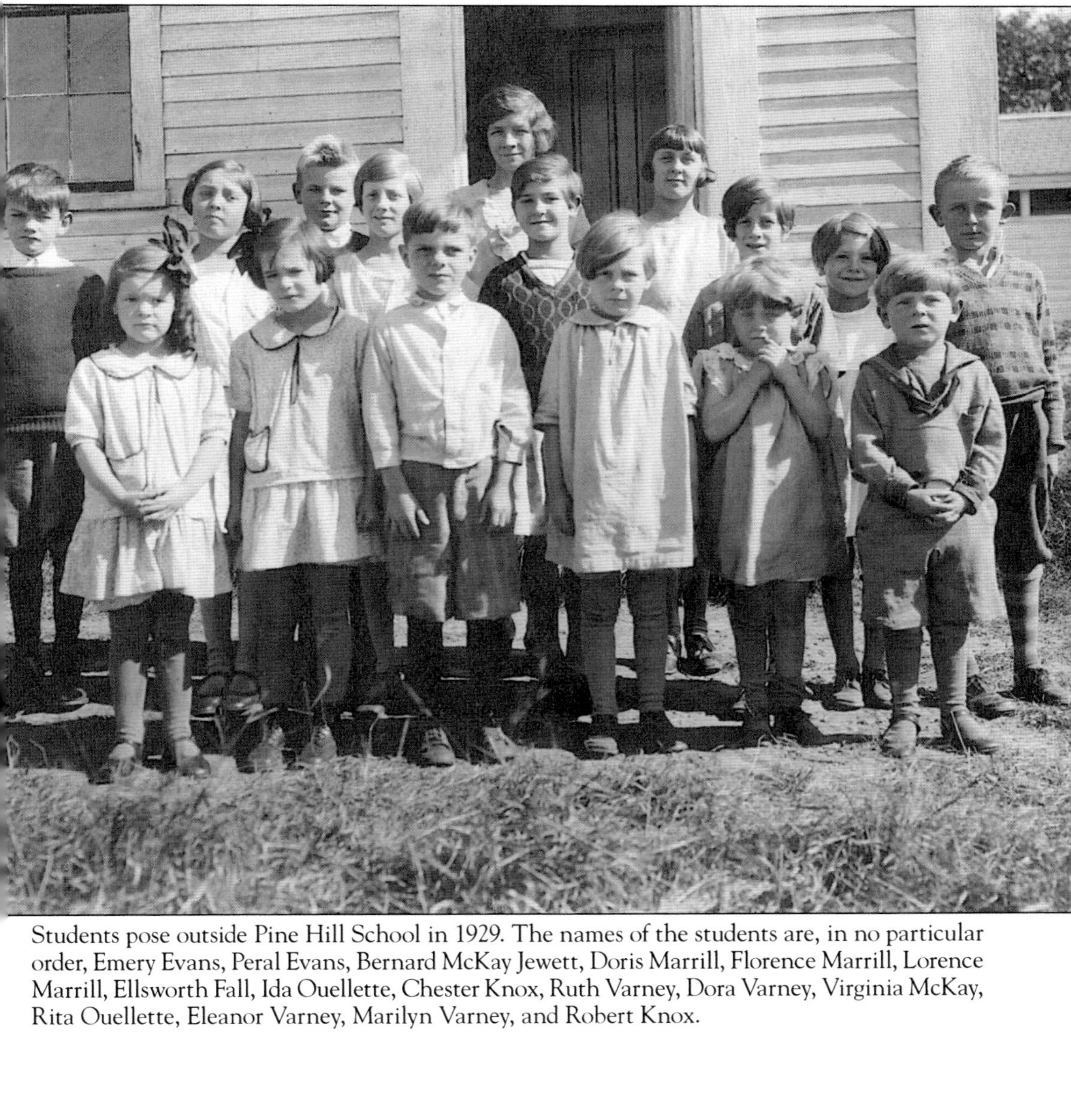

Students pose outside Pine Hill School in 1929. The names of the students are, in no particular order, Emery Evans, Peral Evans, Bernard McKay Jewett, Doris Marrill, Florence Marrill, Lorence Marrill, Ellsworth Fall, Ida Ouellette, Chester Knox, Ruth Varney, Dora Varney, Virginia McKay, Rita Ouellette, Eleanor Varney, Marilyn Varney, and Robert Knox.

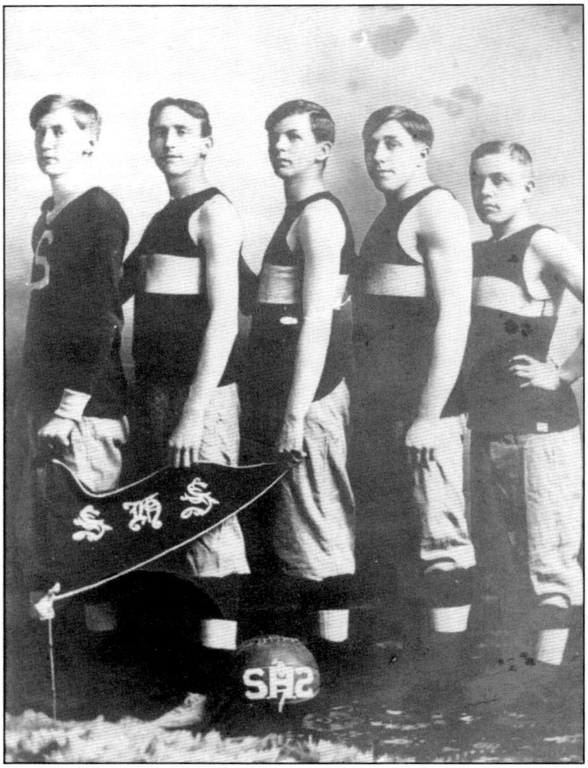

Here, five members of the Sullivan High School basketball team pose for a photograph, thought to be taken in 1906. The initials of the school can be seen on both the flag and the basketball.

On this postcard, dated March 24, 1906, three students of Sullivan High School pose for the camera. The back of the card reads simply, "We won." The young man on the right appears to be wearing an early umpire's uniform.

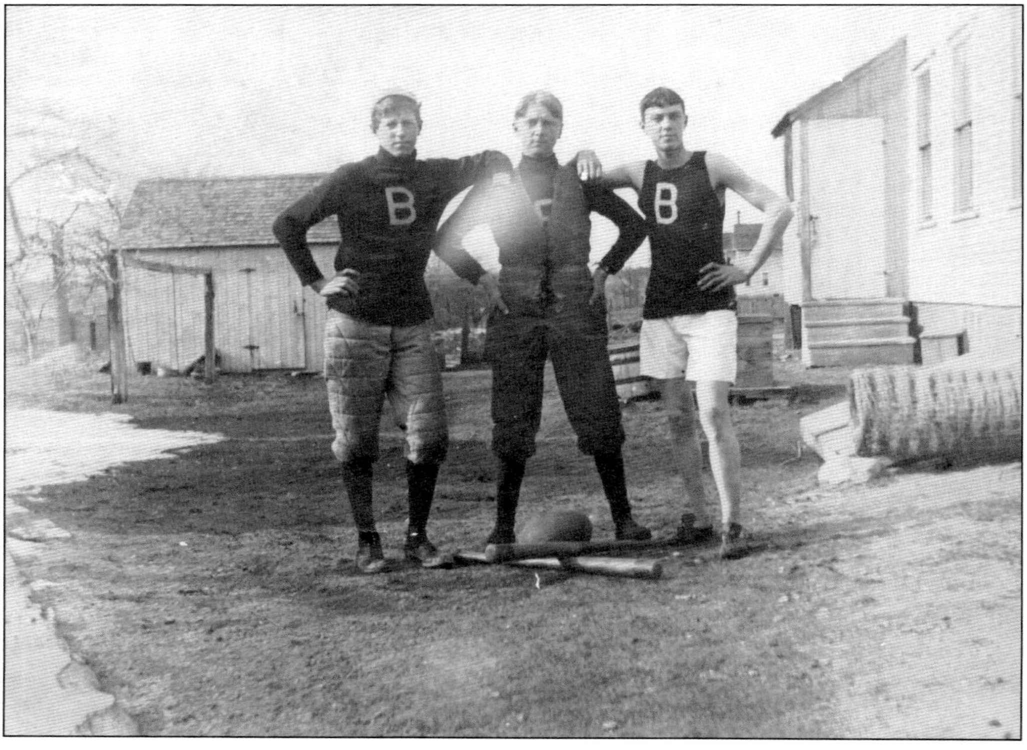

Seven

FARMS AND HOMESTEADS

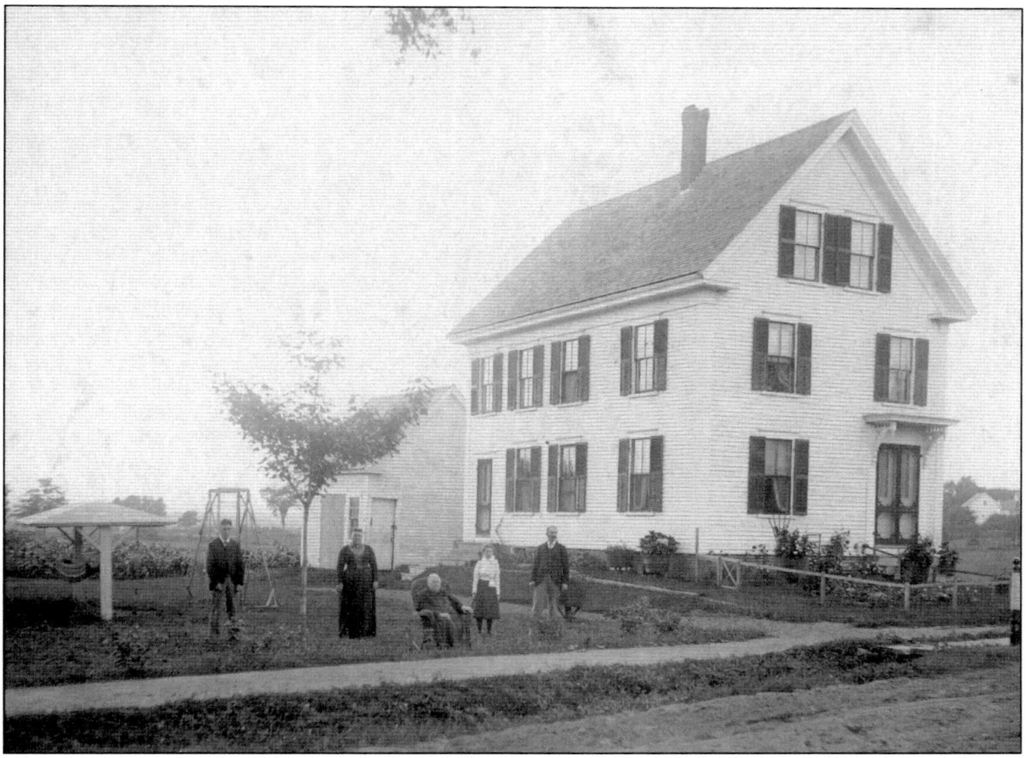

This is a 20th-century photograph of the Chisholm home, located on Pine Hill Road. The start of a cornfield can be seen in the background. By the mid-19th century, Maine, especially the southern portion, was scattered with family farms that produced a variety of crops, most of which were for use of the family and its animals.

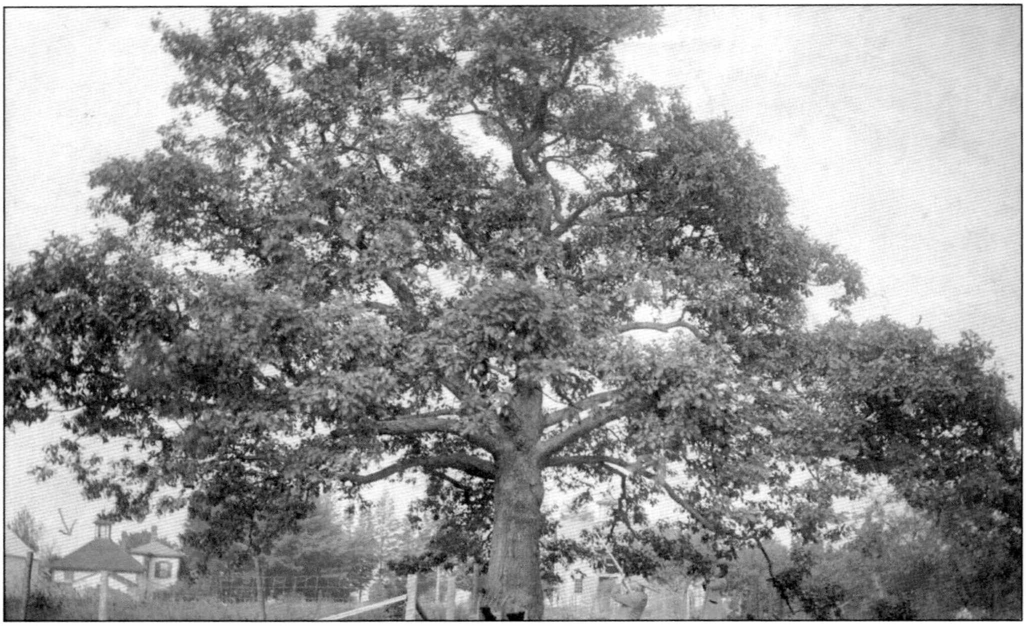

Dr. James Chase, a dentist, prepares to shoot a critter out of the old oak tree on the Grant property while his wife, Belle Grant Chase, watches anxiously. The house at lower left is located at 85 Sullivan Street and was built by George Wilber Stillings in 1876 or 1877.

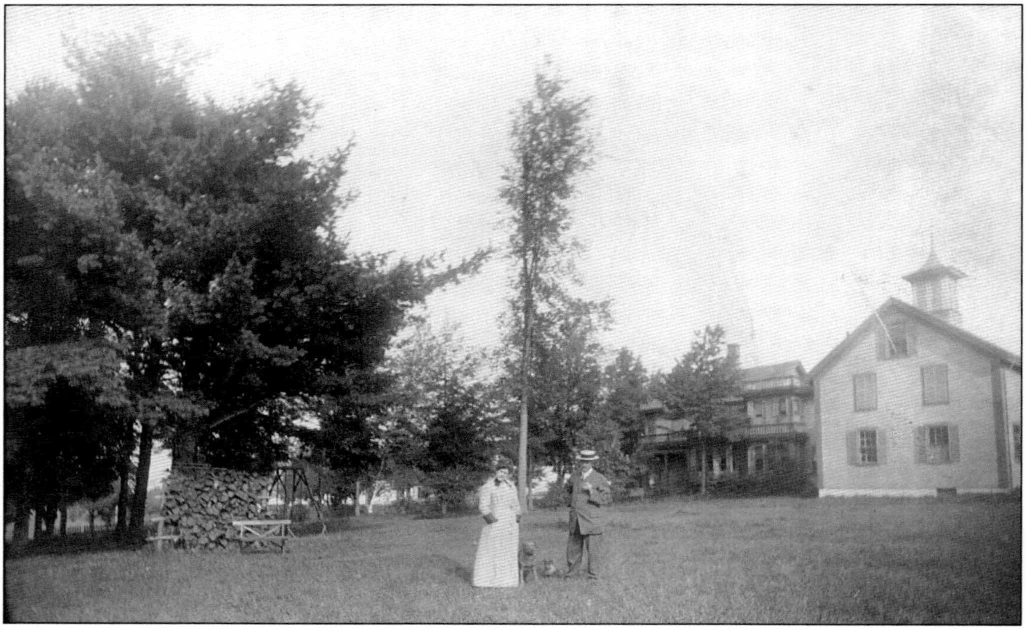

Dr. James Chase and his wife, Belle Grant Chase, stand on the Grant property located on Sullivan Street in Berwick. Visible at right is the back of the Advent Christian Church, also located on Sullivan Street.

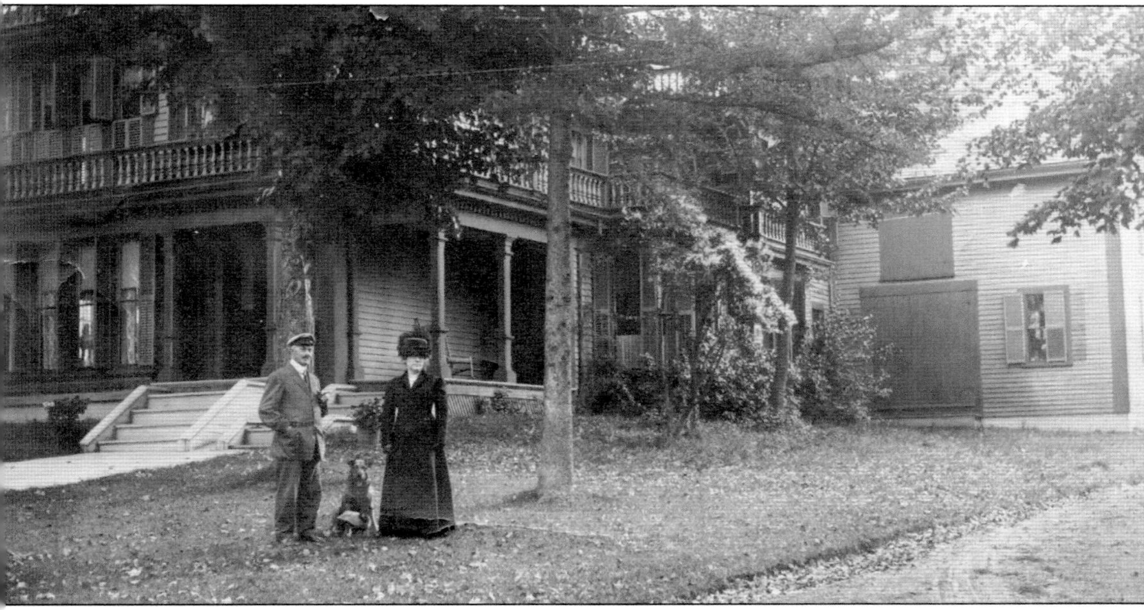

Belle and James Chase stand in front of the Grant home on Sullivan Street. Their two dogs join in for the family photograph. A close look reveals that the smaller dog is wearing a jacket. This photograph was taken in the early 1900s.

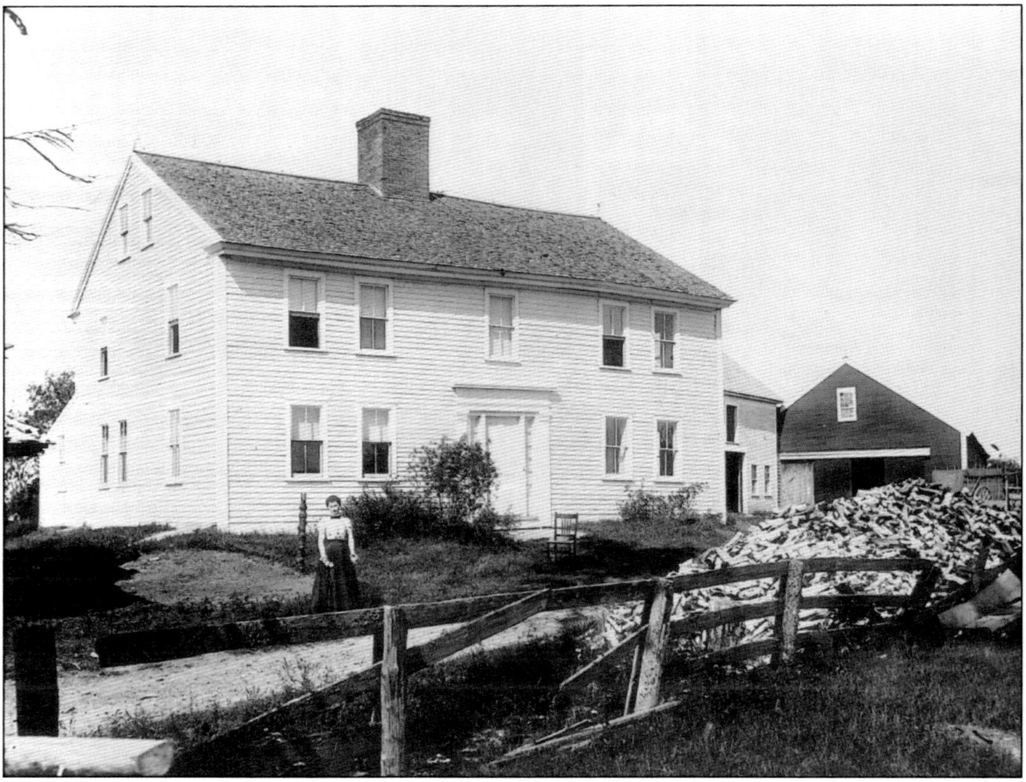

Carolyn Fall stands in front of the Fall homestead in the late 19th century. This residence was once located off Pine Hill Road. Ancestors of the Fall family still reside in Berwick.

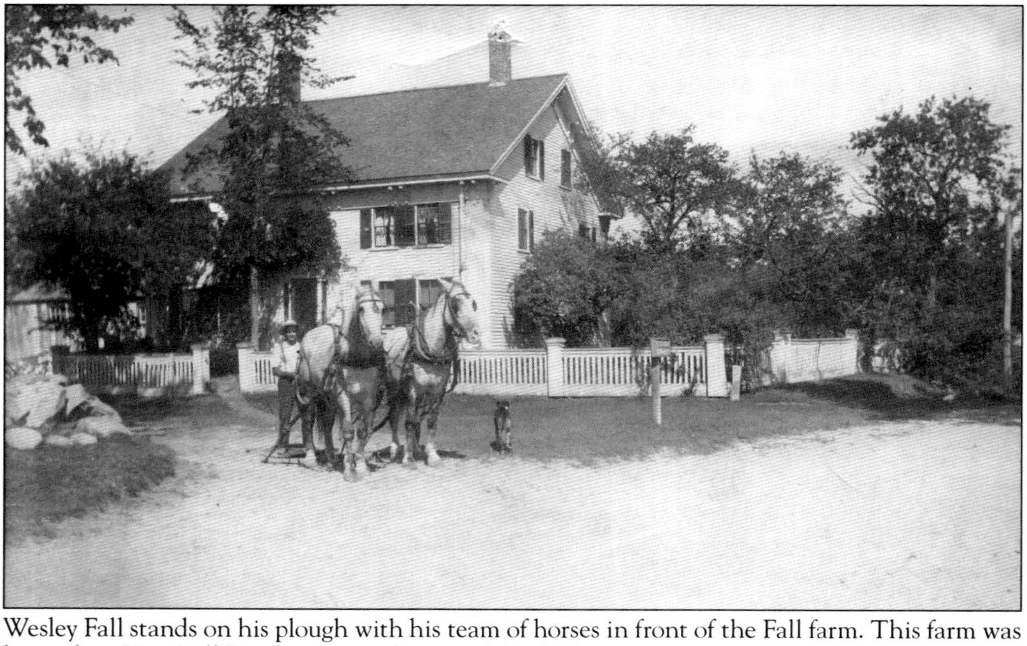

Wesley Fall stands on his plough with his team of horses in front of the Fall farm. This farm was located on Pine Hill Road in the early part of the 20th century.

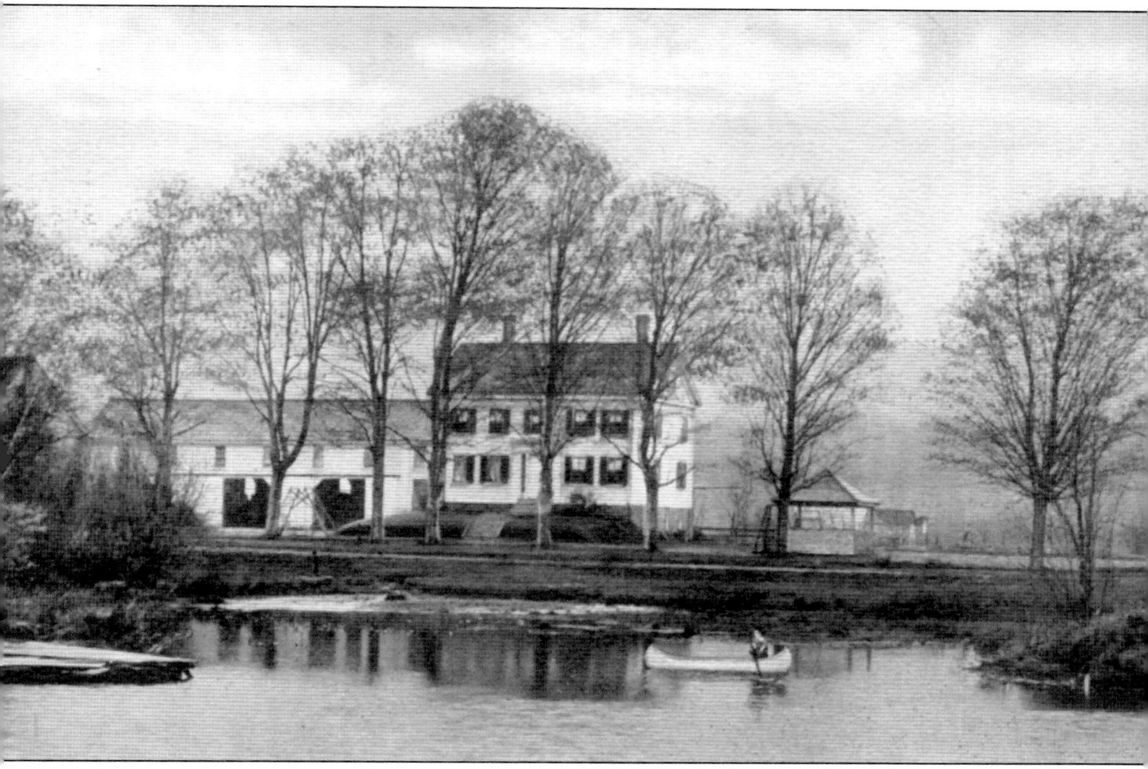

This illustrated postcard of the Chapman residence is dated August 4, 1924. The property has since been purchased by Dana Hall. The small shed to the right of the house recently burned down.

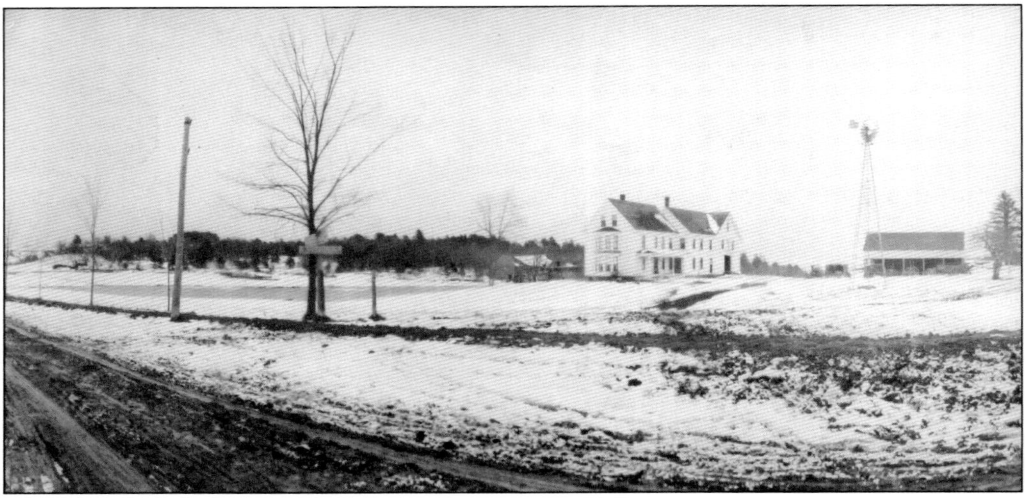

These early-20th-century photographs show the George Hall farm, located on the corner of Route 9 and Old Pine Hill South. Windmills served as an early source of power for many Maine farms. This location would later become the site for Berwick's first ambulance service. It is one of the most recognizable properties in Berwick today.

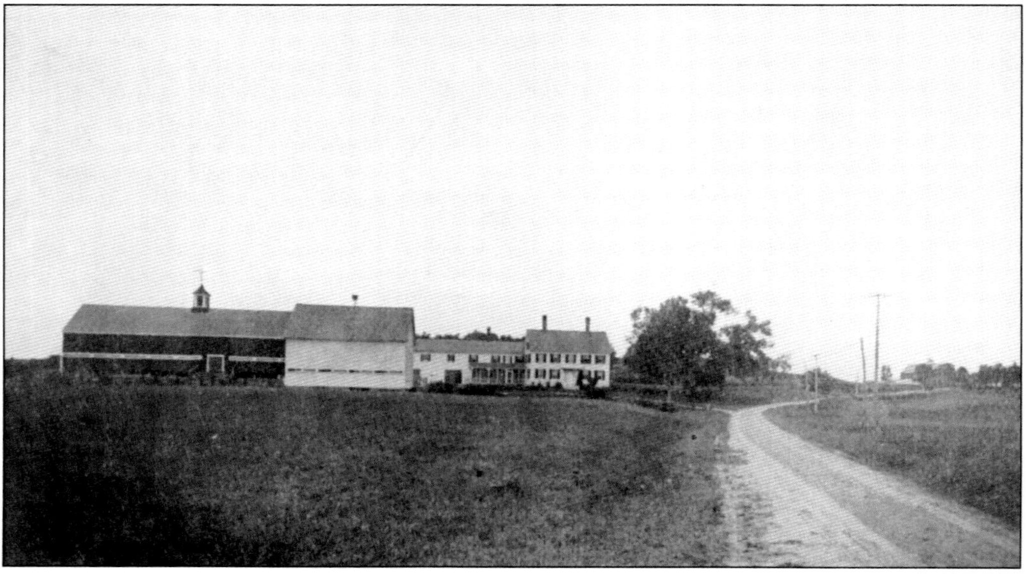

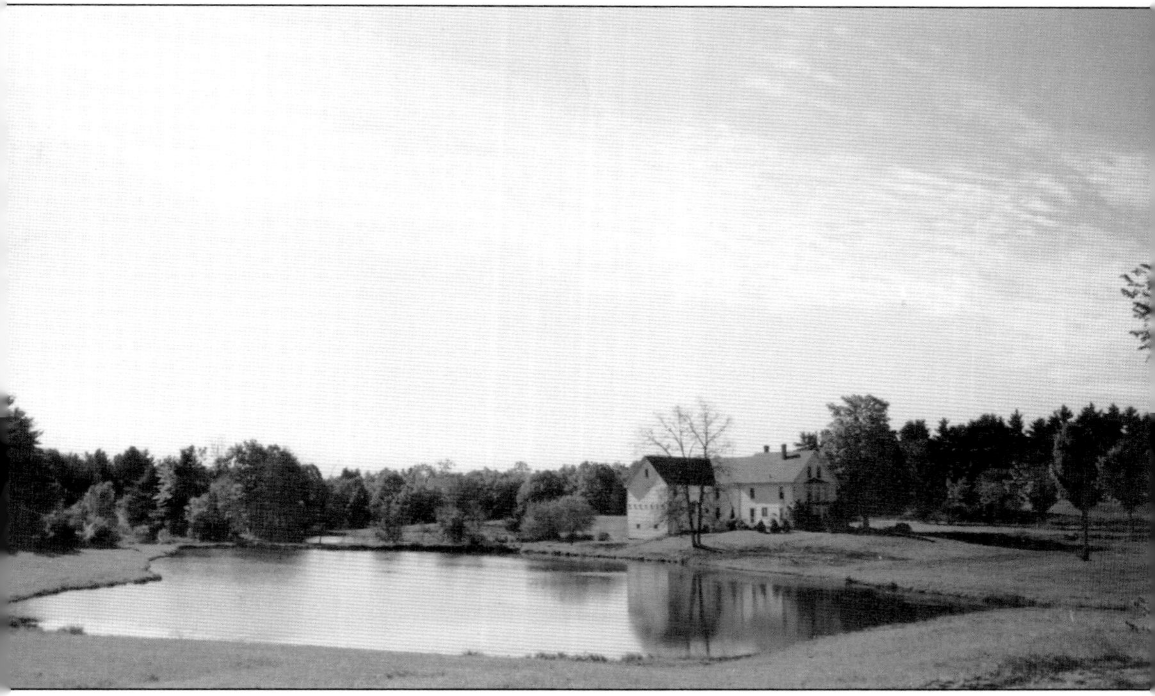

This postcard of Hall's Pond was sent on July 17, 1953. It shows the Hall property, located off Route 9, in the background. This pond was one of three in Berwick that was used for ice harvesting in the late 19th century and the early part of the 20th century.

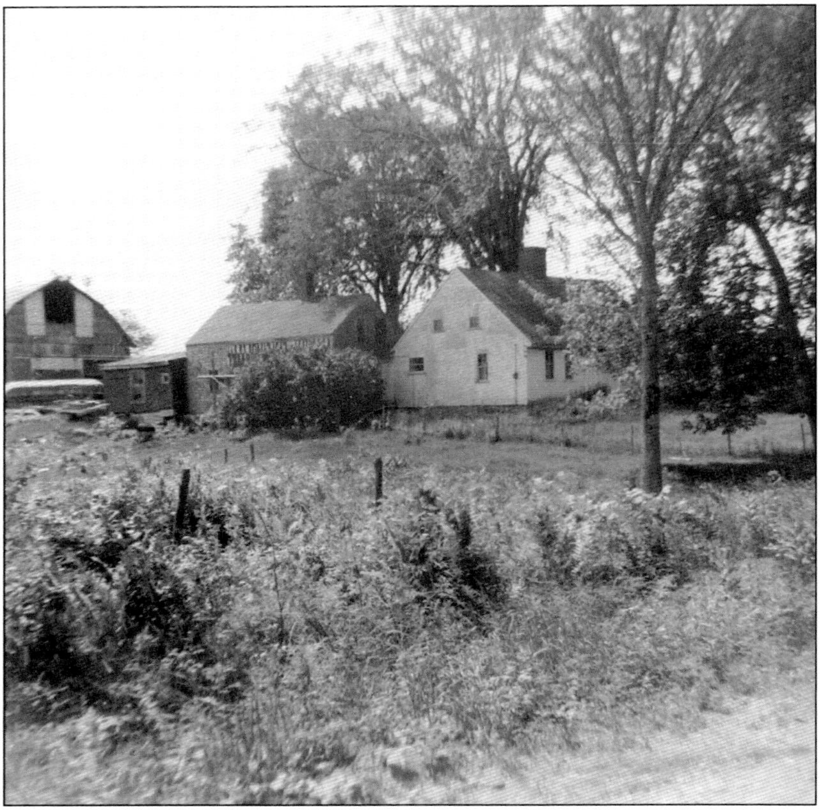

The Worster Dairy Farm, located at 74 Worster Road, was originally owned by Arthur Worster. In the 20th century, this was one of the dairy farms that produced a surplus of product and began offering butter or cream to neighbors and local stores. (Courtesy of Dawn Milbury.)

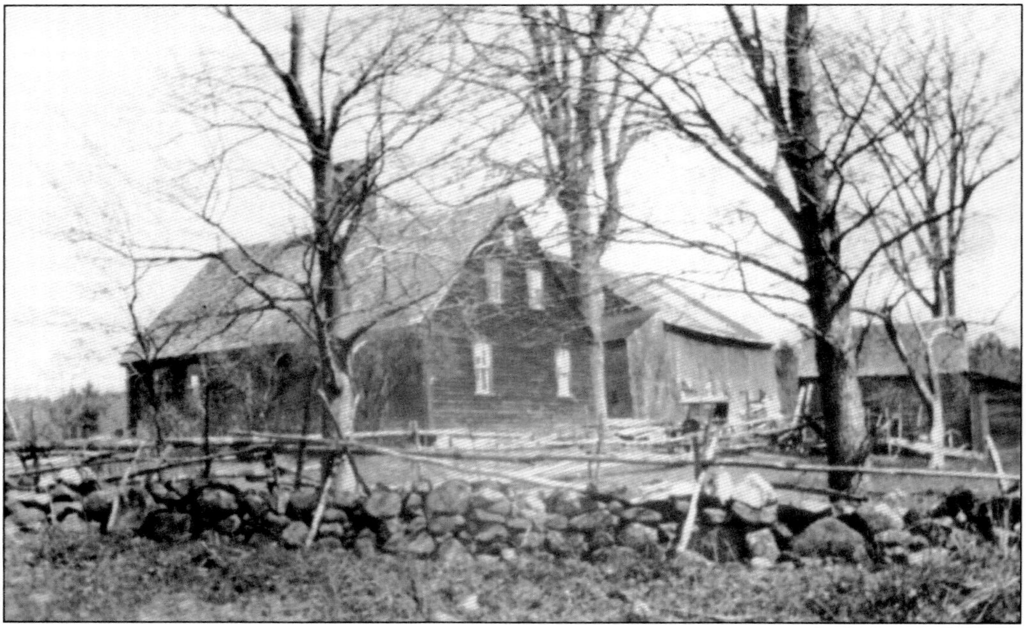

The Worster farm served as a dairy farm for many decades. Today, the barns no longer exist, and the property is a private residence. (Courtesy of Dawn Milbury.)

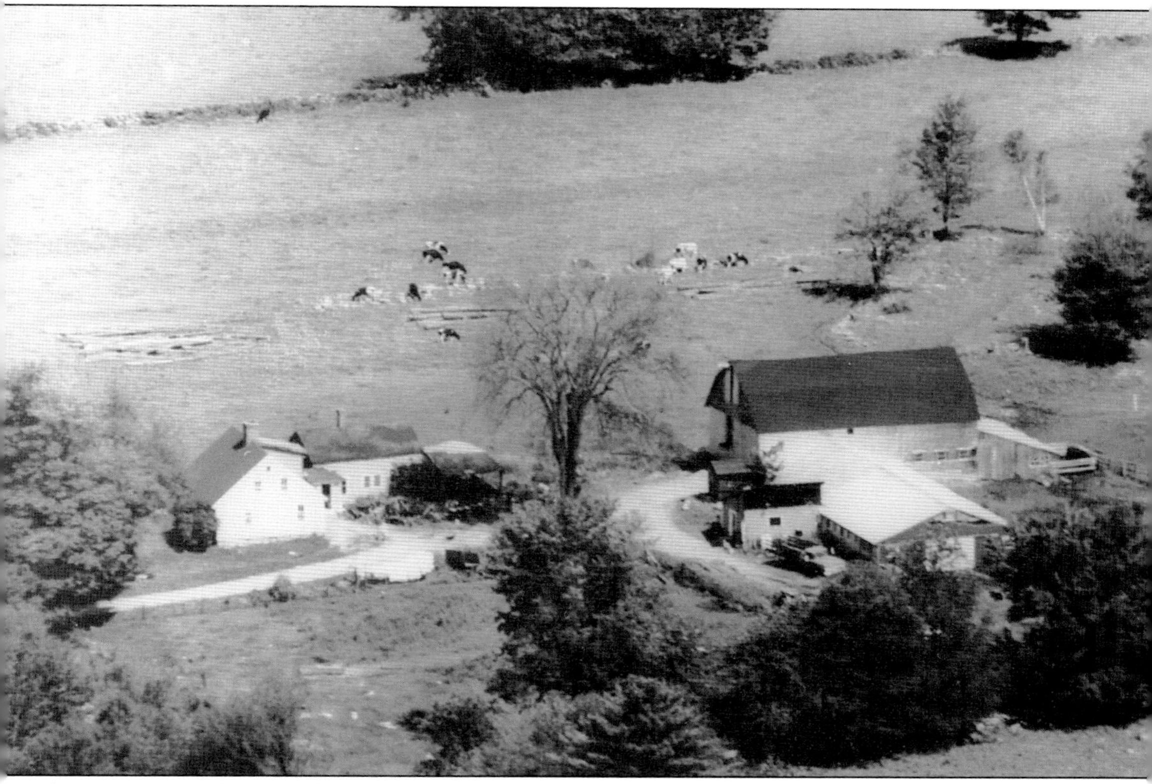

This is an aerial photograph of the Worster farm, taken in the late 1950s. The barns are no longer standing. The Worster farm was one of the best-known dairy farms in Berwick, during a time when dairying was one of Maine's most visible agricultural industries. (Courtesy of Dawn Milbury.)

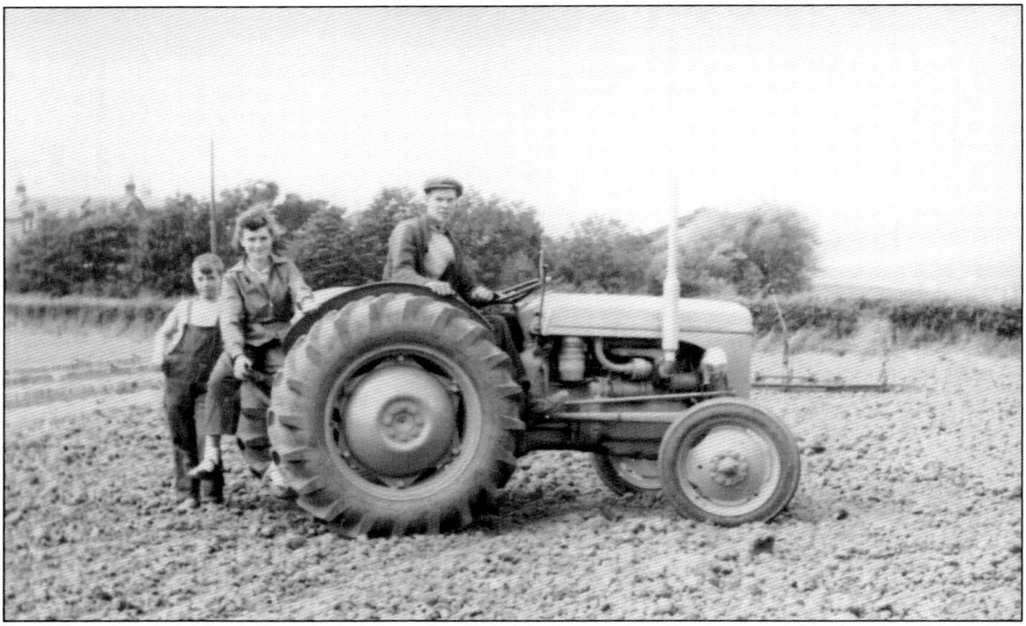

Here, some youngsters farm the fields at the Worster property in 1955. The back of the photograph reads, "Drew and John with a girl who works here during her summer holidays." (Courtesy of Dawn Milbury.)

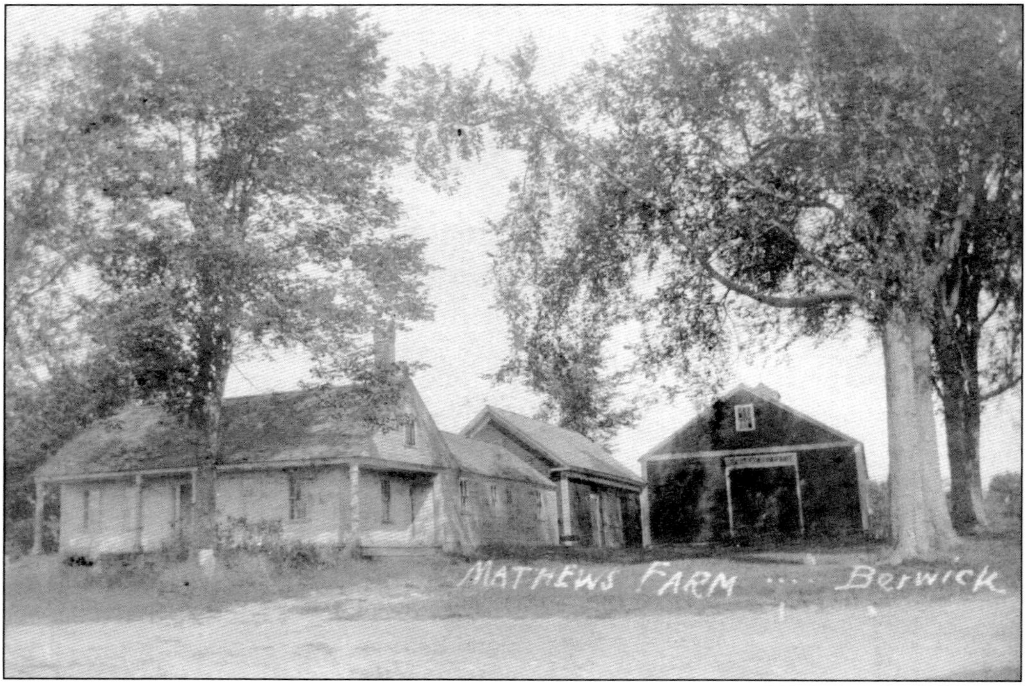

The Mathews farm, located on Cranberry Meadow Road, was built in 1916. The main house was torn down in 1938.

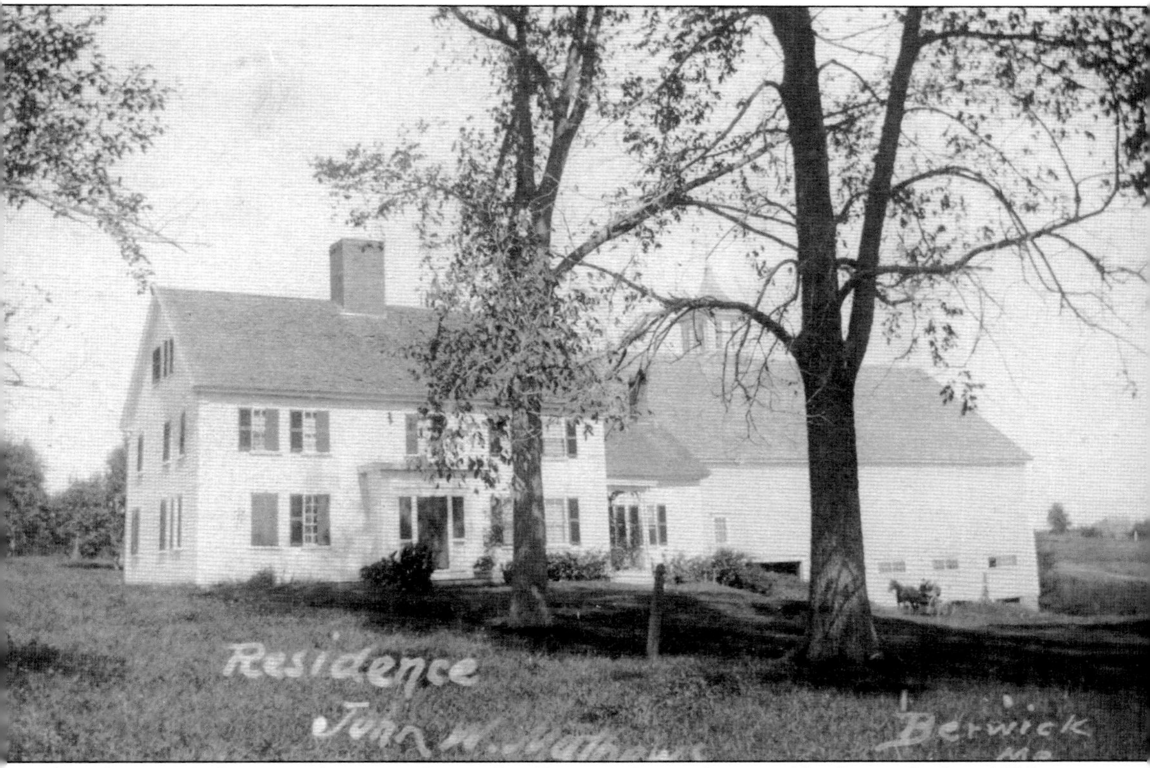

The John W. Mathews residence was located on Route 9. It was destroyed by fire in the late 1920s. A horse-drawn wagon in front of the barn can be seen in the lower right of the photograph.

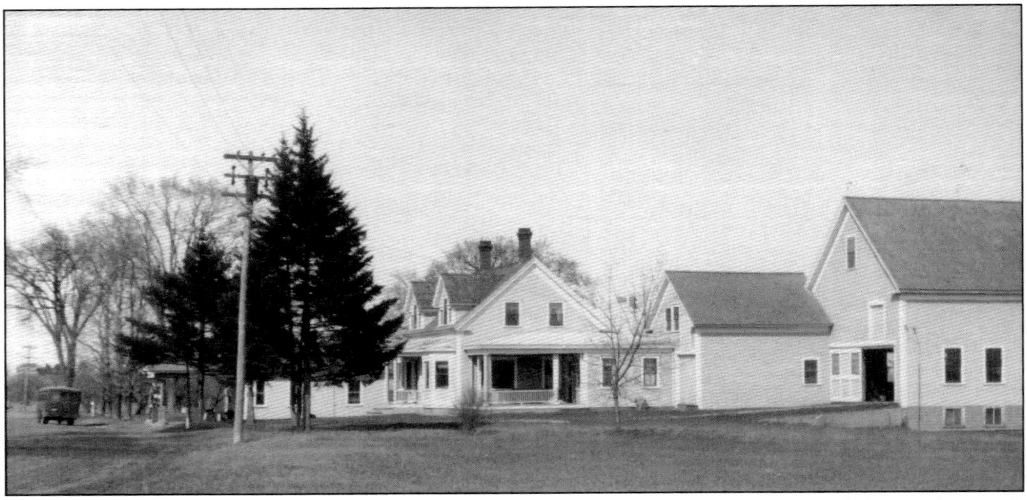

This is the Guptill farm as it appeared in 1925. Today, it is known as the location of the Hackmatack Playhouse on Route 9.

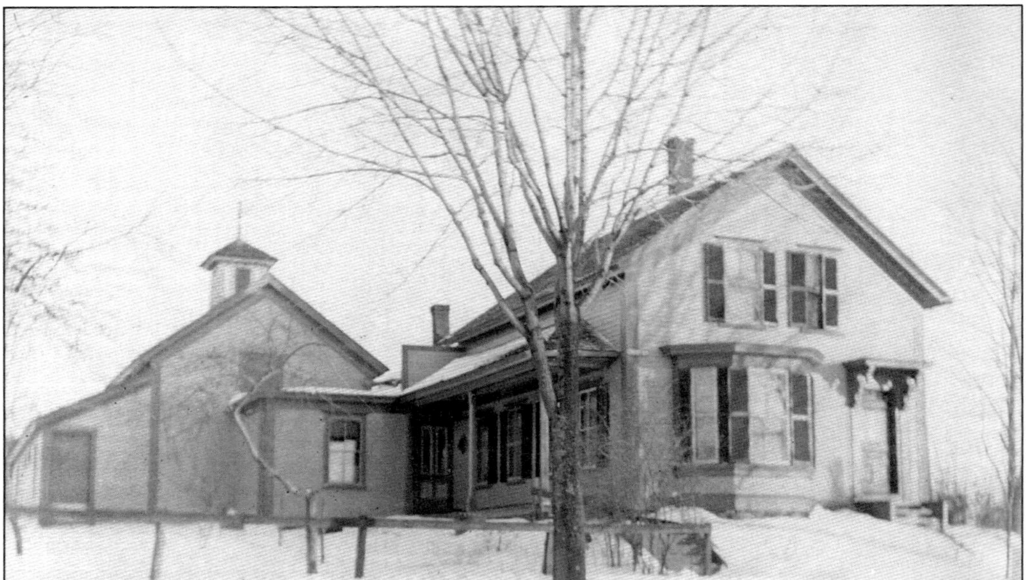

The Luther Nason house is located on the corner of Merriam and Berry Streets. The canted bay window rising from the ground was a popular Victorian feature in houses of this period.

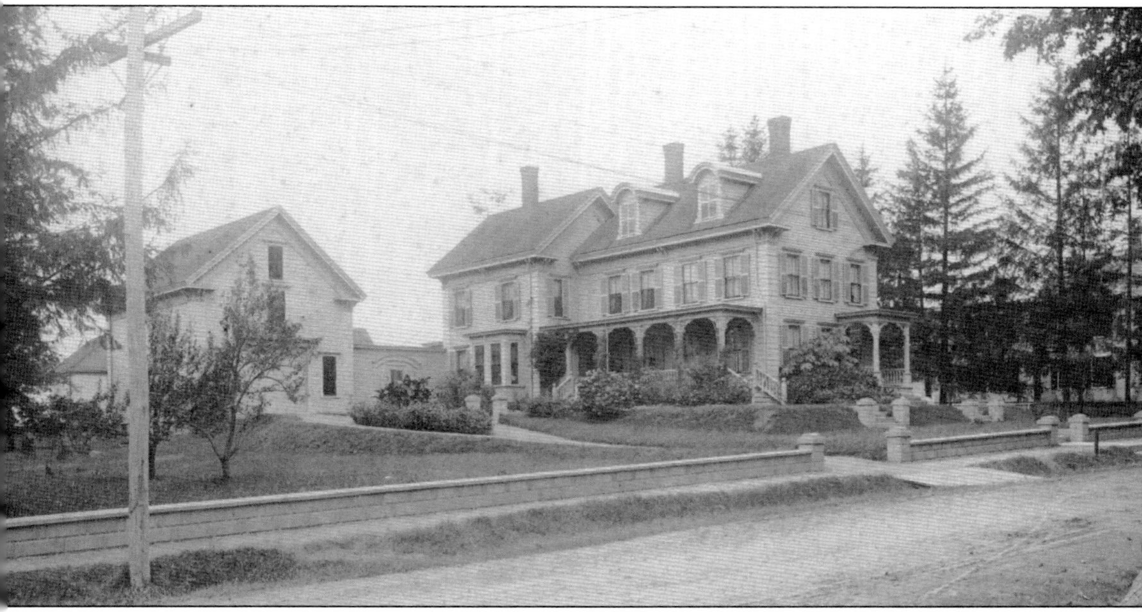

This is the home of Dr. Bonano, located on Rochester Street. It was also known as the home of George Moore. The bonneted dormers, named after their arched shape, can be seen on the side of the house. This feature was popular in Victorian-style homes.

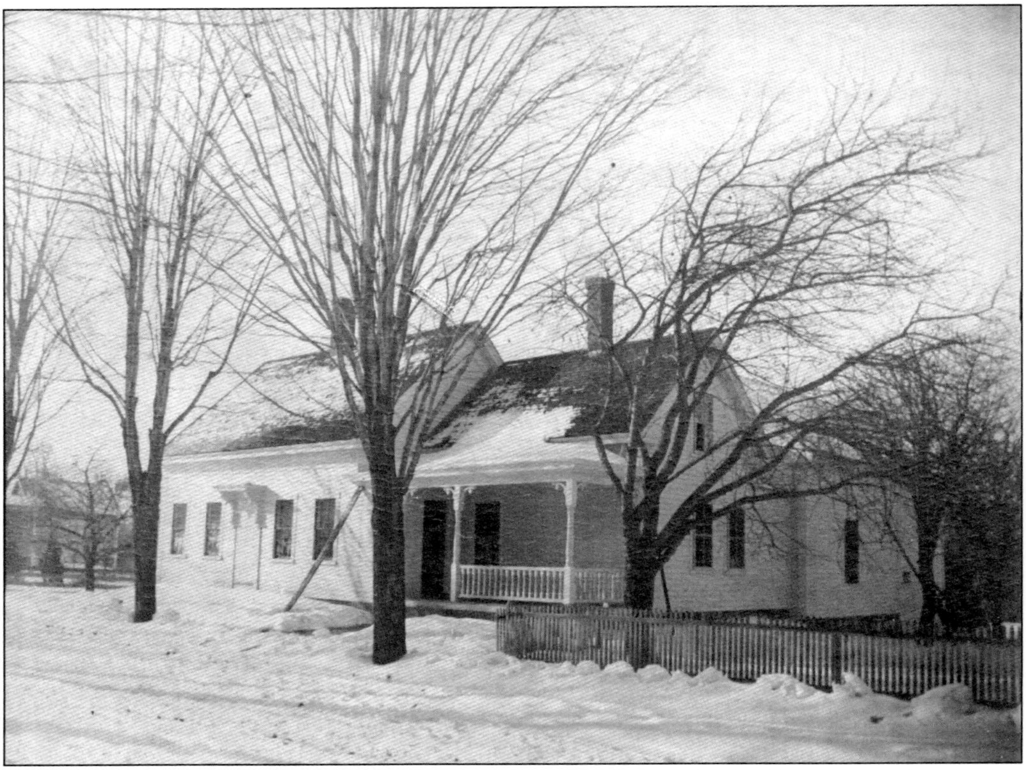

This house, located on First Street in Berwick, was once owned by the Hemingway family. It is typical of homes built in the late 19th century. It was occupied by upper-class town dwellers. The Hemingway descendants no longer live in Berwick.

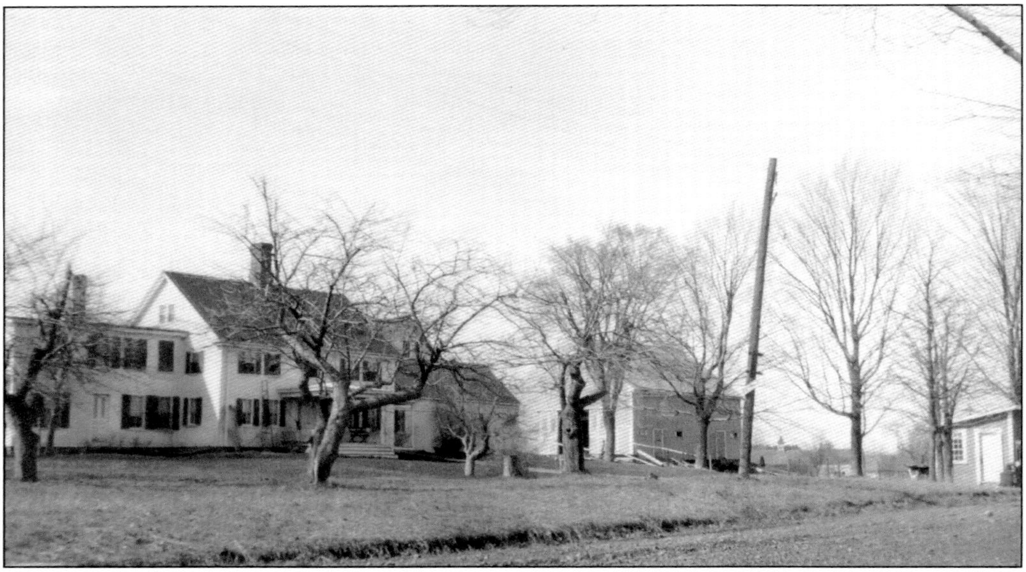

The Litchfield farm, located on Route 9, was once the home of a popular photographer. It stills stands in Berwick, located across from the Hackmatack Playhouse. The small building on the right was once occupied by The White Lunch, where locals went to purchase a midday meal.

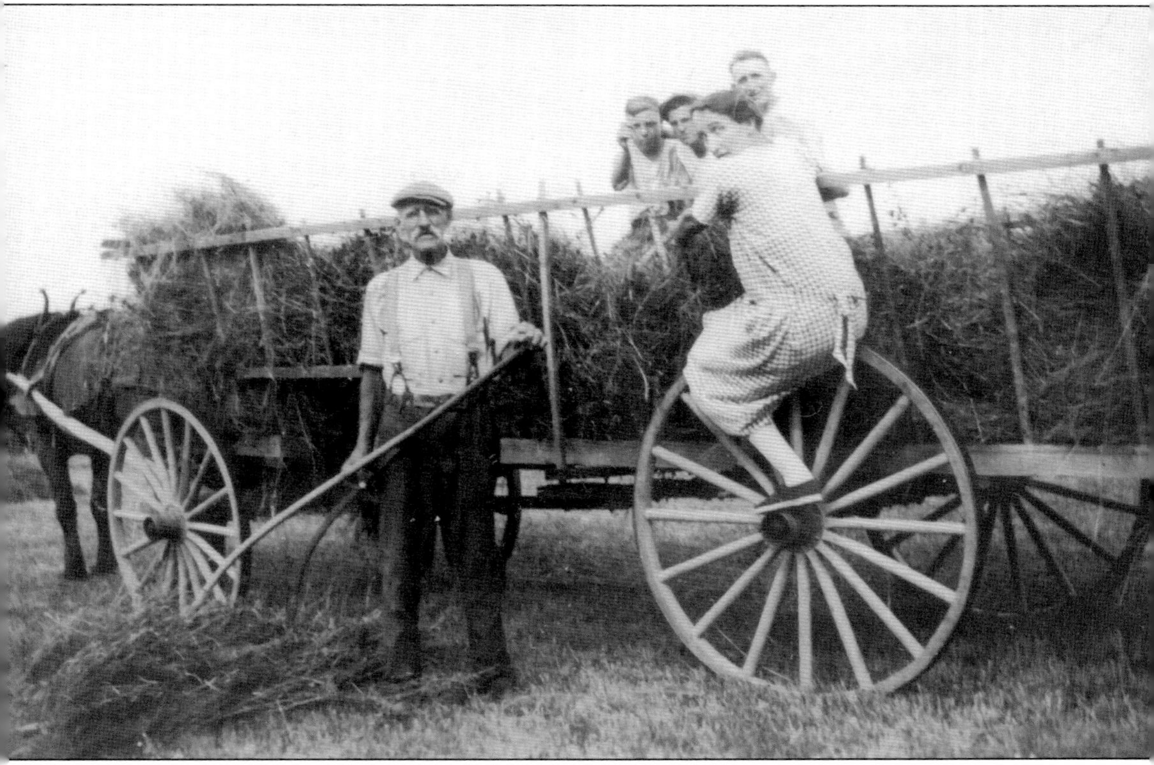

Teenagers are haying the fields on the Hussey farm, located on Blackberry Hill Road. Clyde Farwell is the tallest person on the far side of the wagon. His father holds a large wooden haying pitchfork. (Courtesy of Paul Boisvert.)

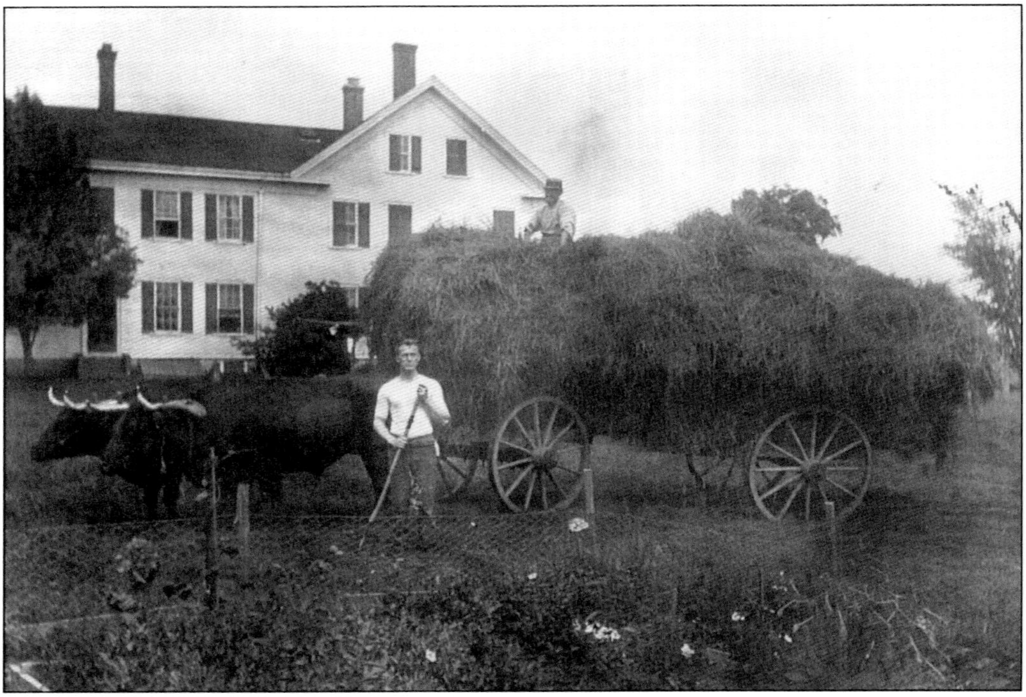

This is a photograph of Samuel and John Perkins haying on the Perkins farm in 1892. This property still stands on Blackberry Hill Road today. (Courtesy of Patricia J. Fulton and Nancy W. Fulton.)

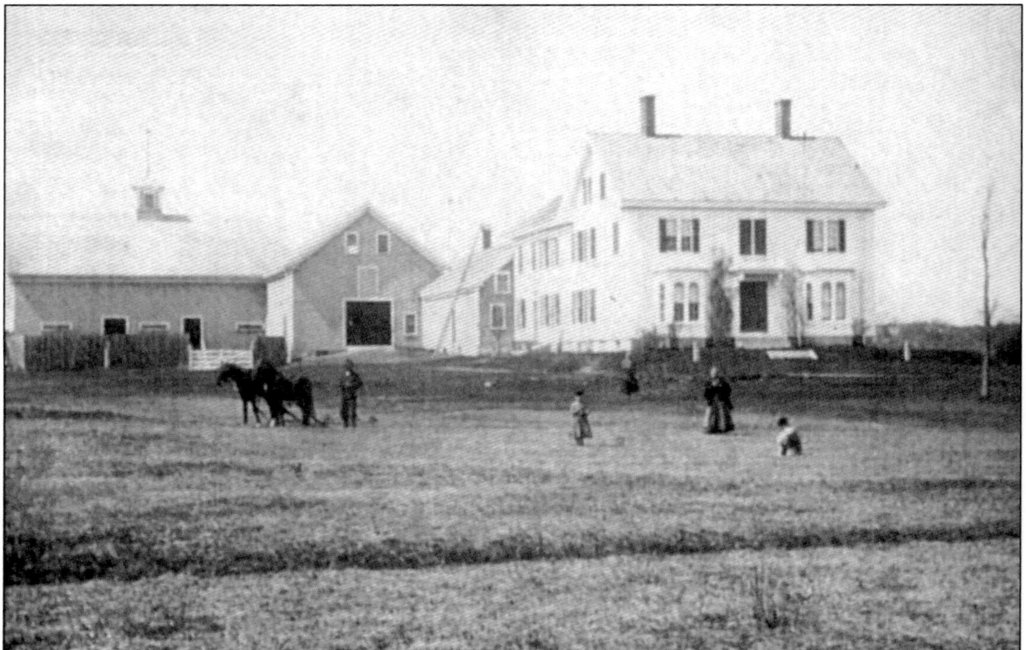

A man can be seen plowing the field in front of the Perkins farm in the later part of the 19th century, while his wife and children stand aside in the yard. This property is located on Blackberry Hill Road, but it no longer functions as a farm. (Courtesy of Patricia J. Fulton and Nancy W. Fulton.)

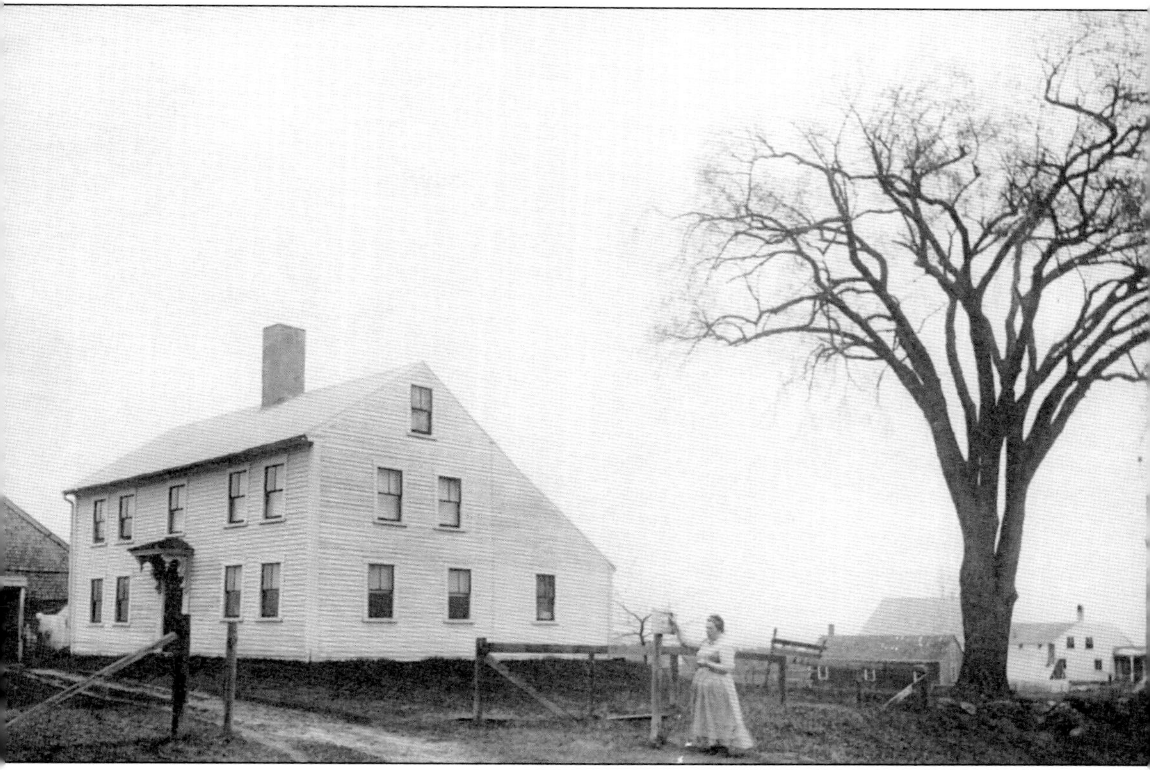

This photograph depicts the Fall residence, located on Pine Hill Road. It is a classic example of a saltbox house. The name comes from the structure's resemblance to a wood-lidded box in which salt was kept. This Colonial style of architecture originated in New England in 1650. These homes had one story in back and two stories in front.

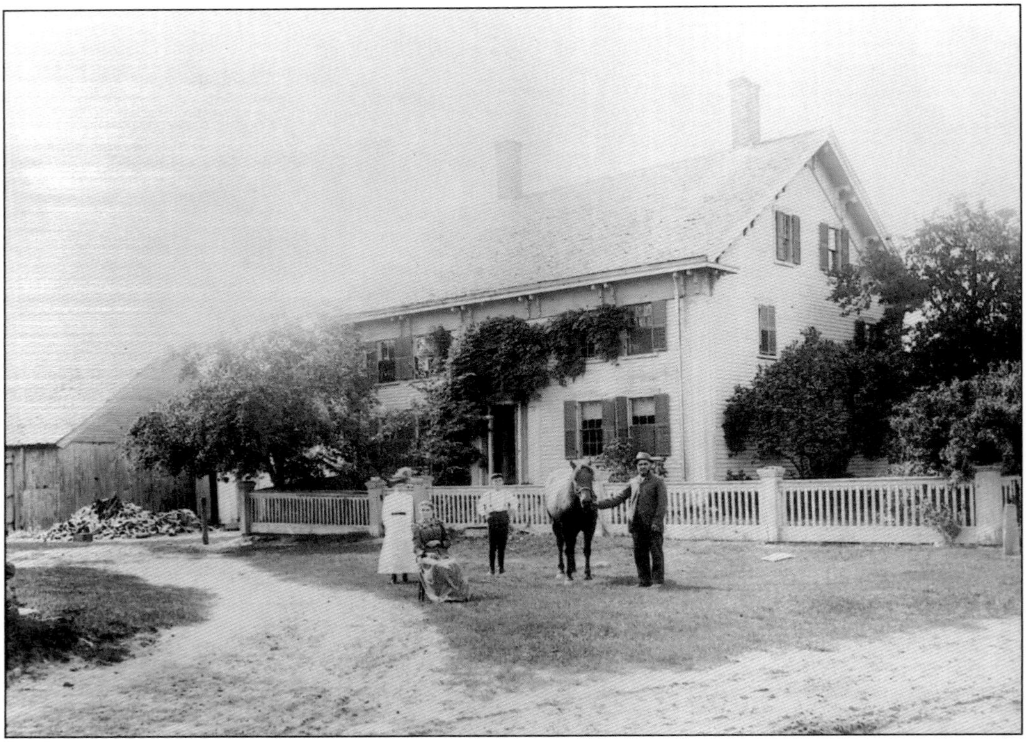

Elizabeth Fall and John Fall stand behind their seated mother in front of their Pine Hill home. Their father, Wesley Fall, holds the reins of one of the farm's horses. This photograph is thought to have been taken around 1880.

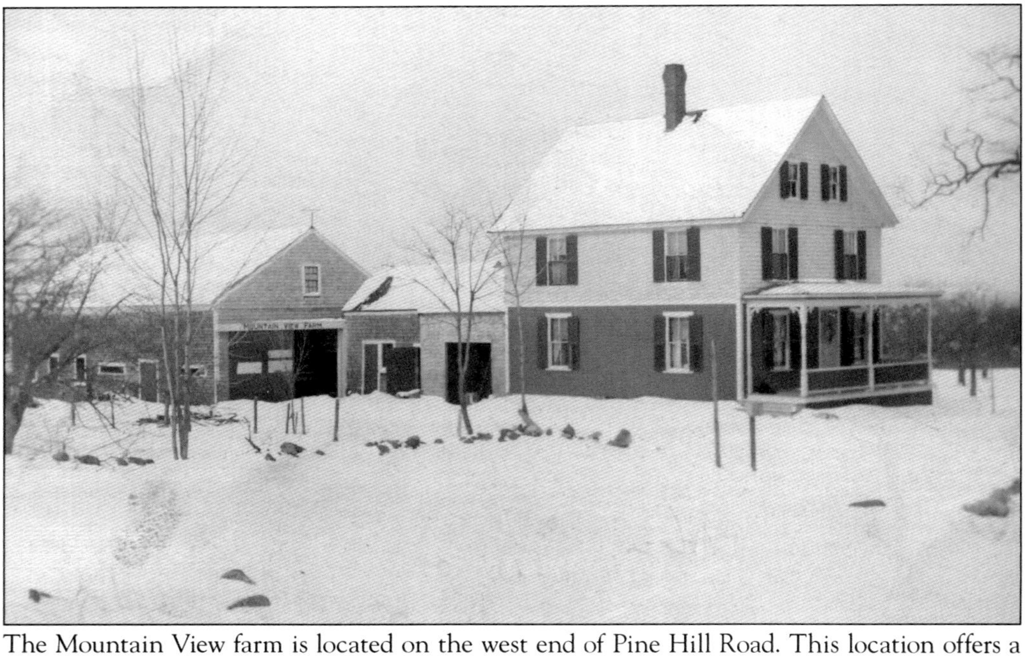

The Mountain View farm is located on the west end of Pine Hill Road. This location offers a unique view into Rochester, New Hampshire.

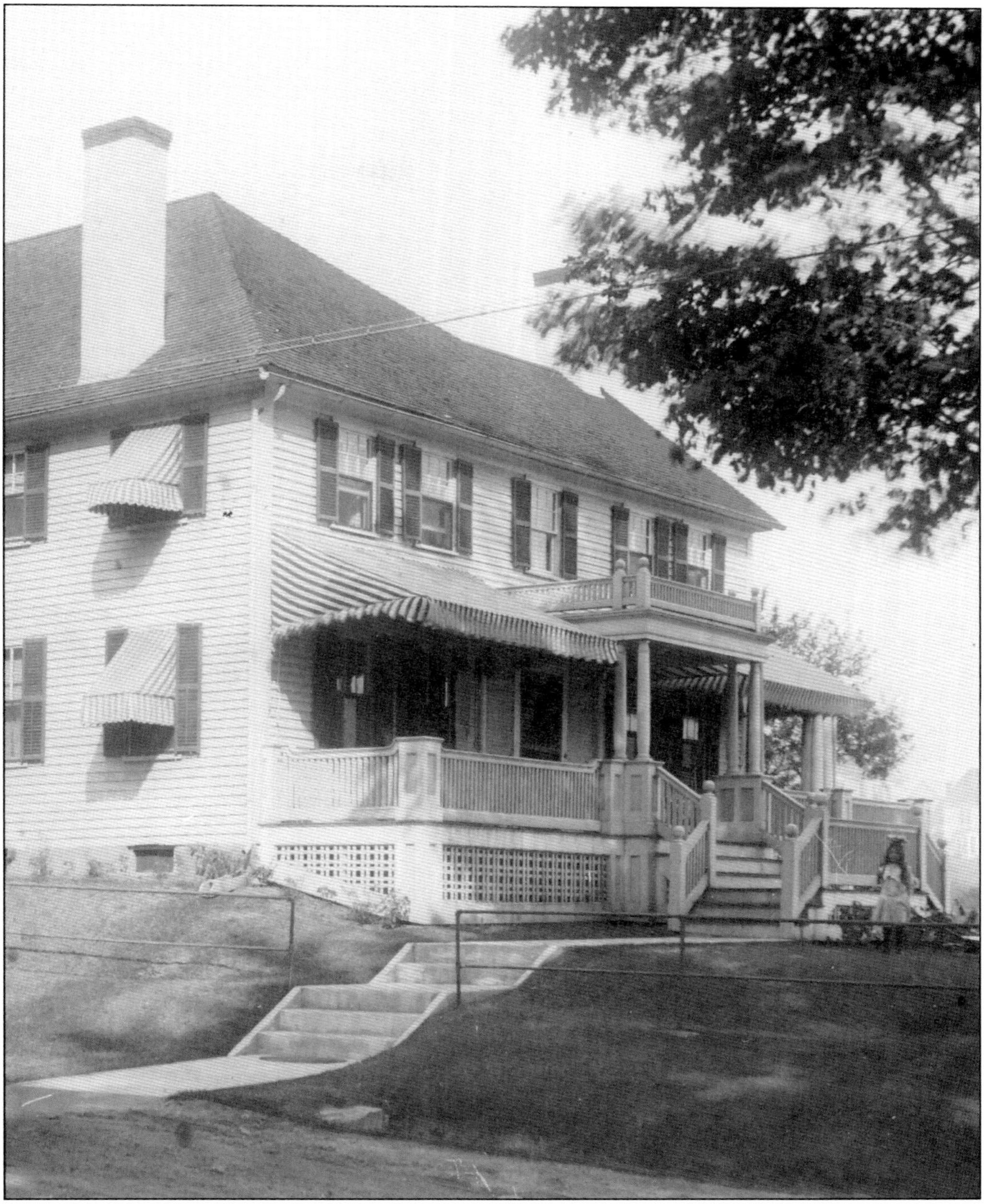

This home, located on Sullivan Street, was originally known as the Wedgewood Tavern. It was built by Millet Wedgewood in 1823, during a time of increasing economic activity within the town. The property was purchased by Winslow T. Ricker in 1854, and ownership eventually passed to Carolyn (Ricker) Goodrich and Stanley Goodrich. It then went on to house the Goodrich Insurance Company from the middle of the 20th century and into the 21st century.

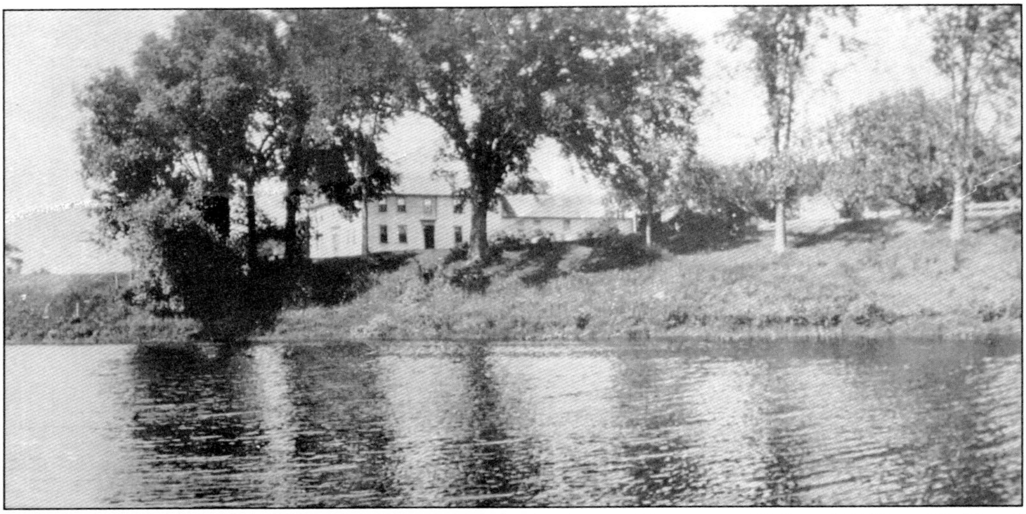

This postcard shows the old Hubbard homestead, which stood between 1806 and 1919 on Hubbard Road. The back of the postcard reads: "This was built (or begun) in 1806 to take the place of a log cabin built in 1771. It was burned by incendiary in 1919 while unoccupied."

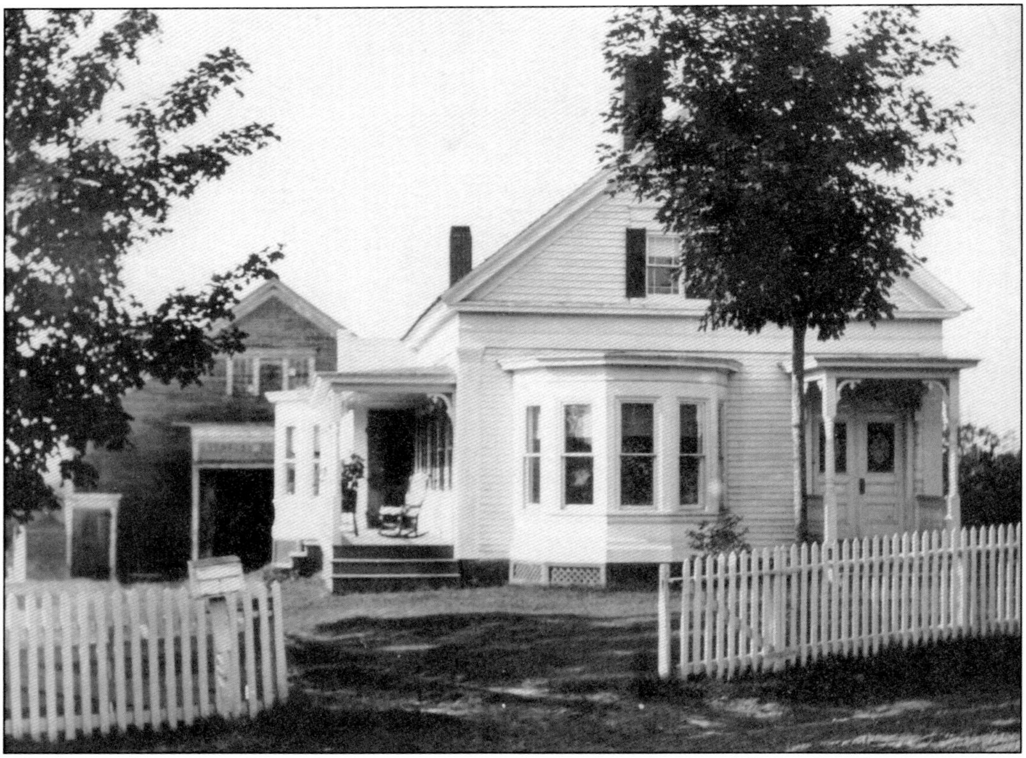

This house, located on Berwick Street, was once the home to the Randall family. The descendants of the well-known, upper-class family can no longer be found in Berwick. The style of this house was typical of Berwick homes built during the second half of the 19th century.

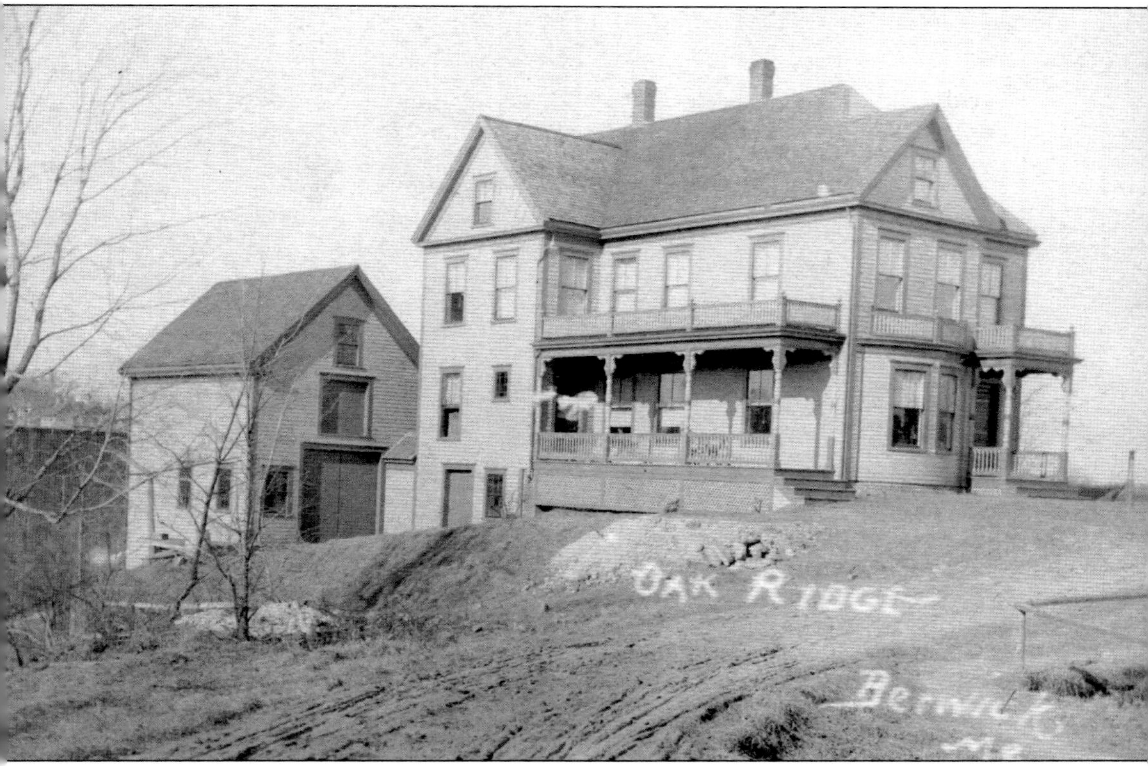

This home is located on First Street. The back of this early-20th-century postcard reads: "This is our new home, just back of the house is the Salmon Falls river and across the river is the city of Somersworth. So we have the city within a stones throw with the river between us."

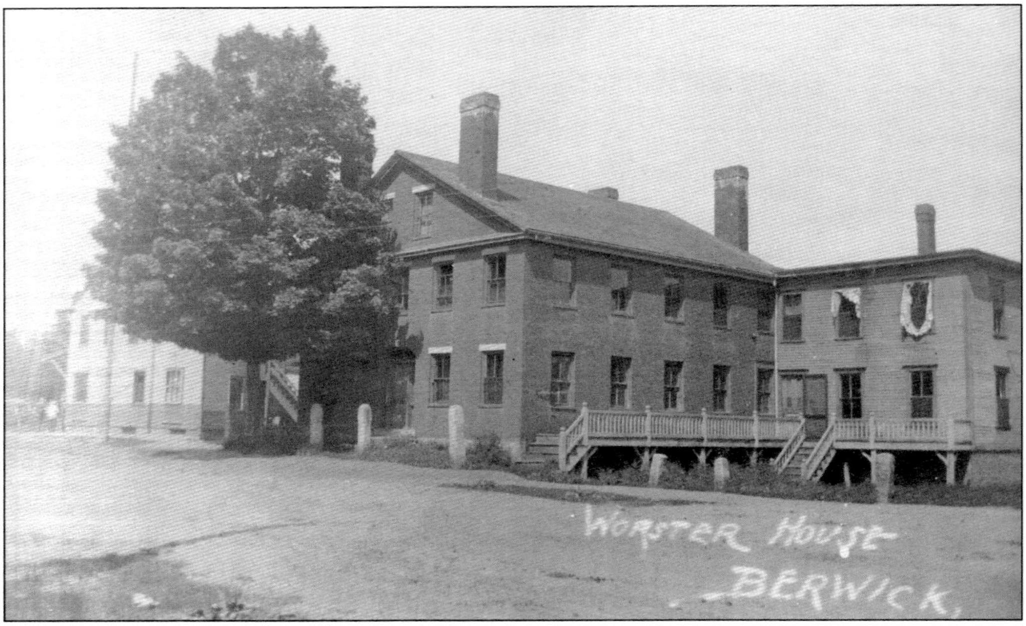

The Worster House was once located in Sullivan Square. The site was home to a number of different businesses, including a meat market operated by Arthur Randell. In 1913, it became a hardware store and was operated by Jason Tibbetts for 17 years. The structure was home to Bell's Hardware in 1930 when it was purchased by John A. Bell. He owned and operated the business for 33 years.

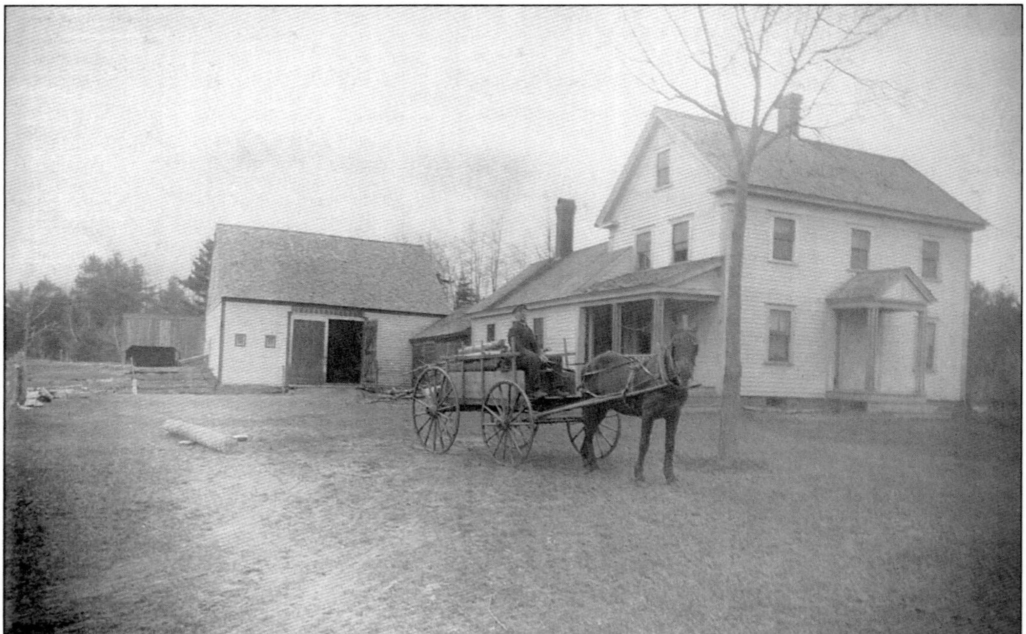

Harrison Webster, sitting in a horse-drawn wagon, hauls freshly cleared wood that will likely be used to heat his home. The Webster farm, once located on Hubbard Road, had two wood-burning fireplaces. (Courtesy of Ann Smith.)

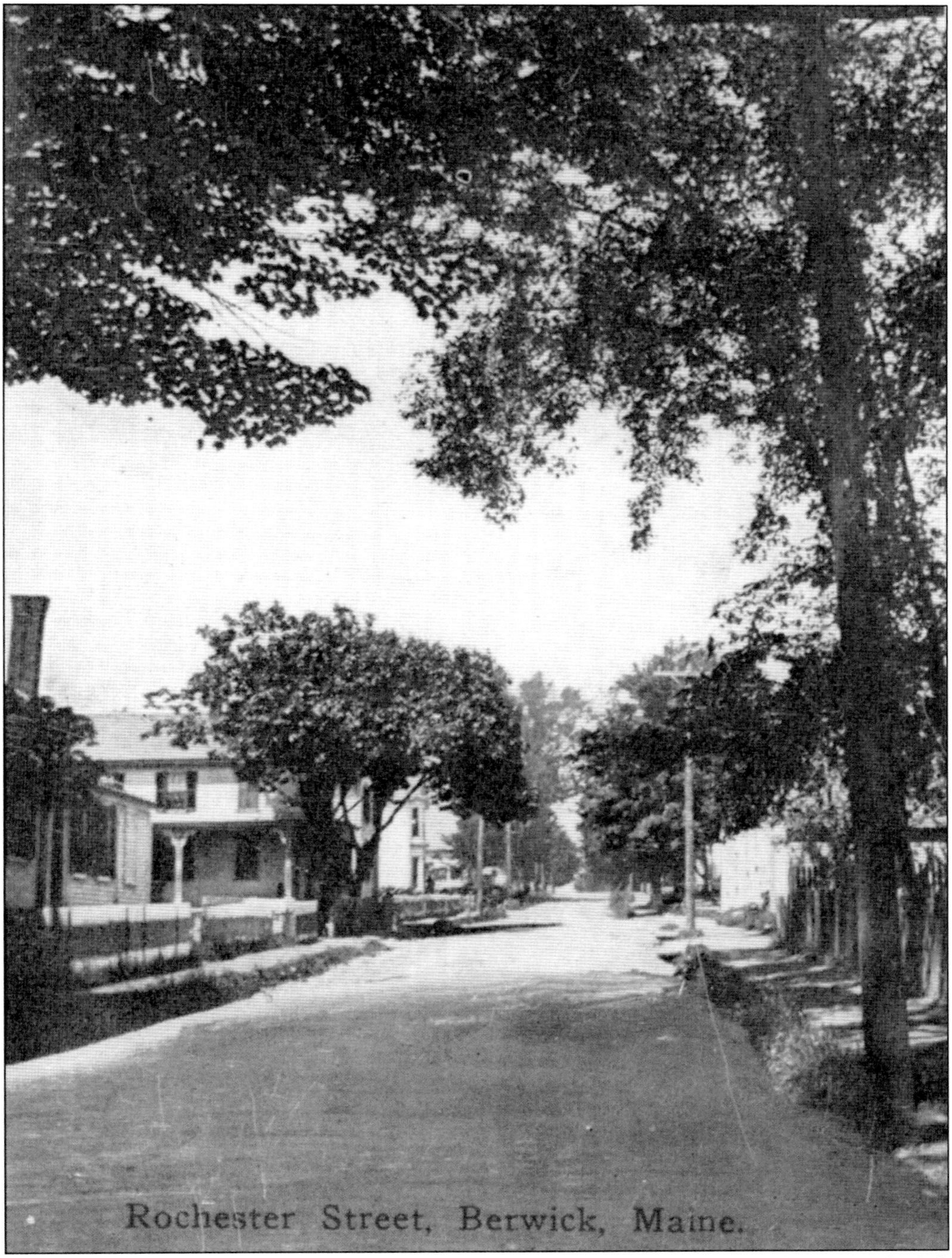

This postcard, dated July 6, 1915, shows Rochester Street in Berwick. The first house on the left is now a barbershop. The Goodwin family once lived in the second house on the left. The empty space on the right is where town hall is now located.

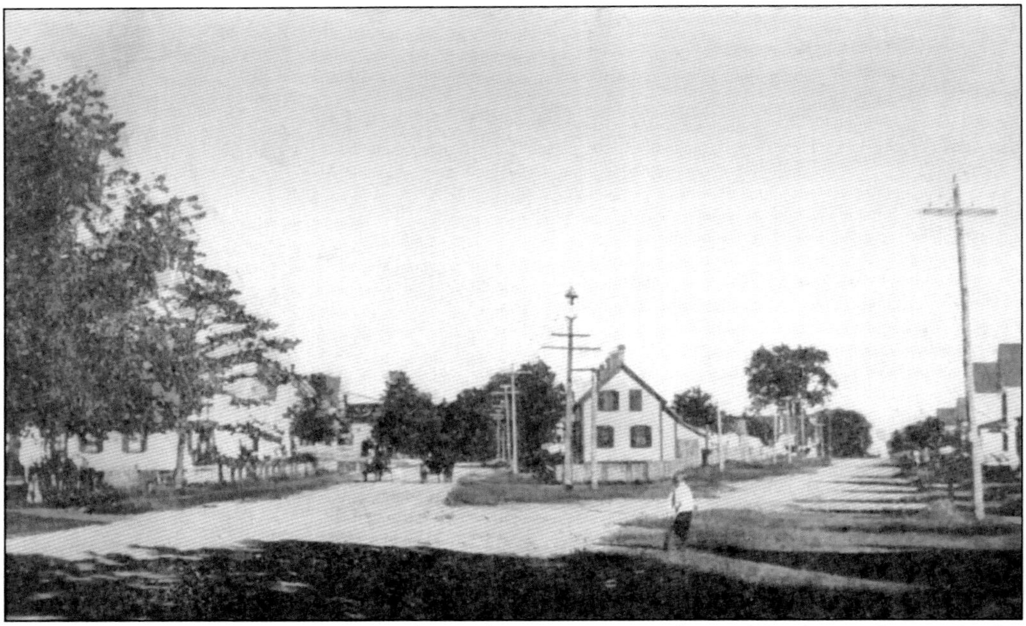

This postcard, dated August 26, 1911, shows the junction at Bridge and Rochester Streets. In the late 19th century, soap was manufactured on Rochester Street. Brackett & Shaw started a meat market on Bridge Street in 1892.

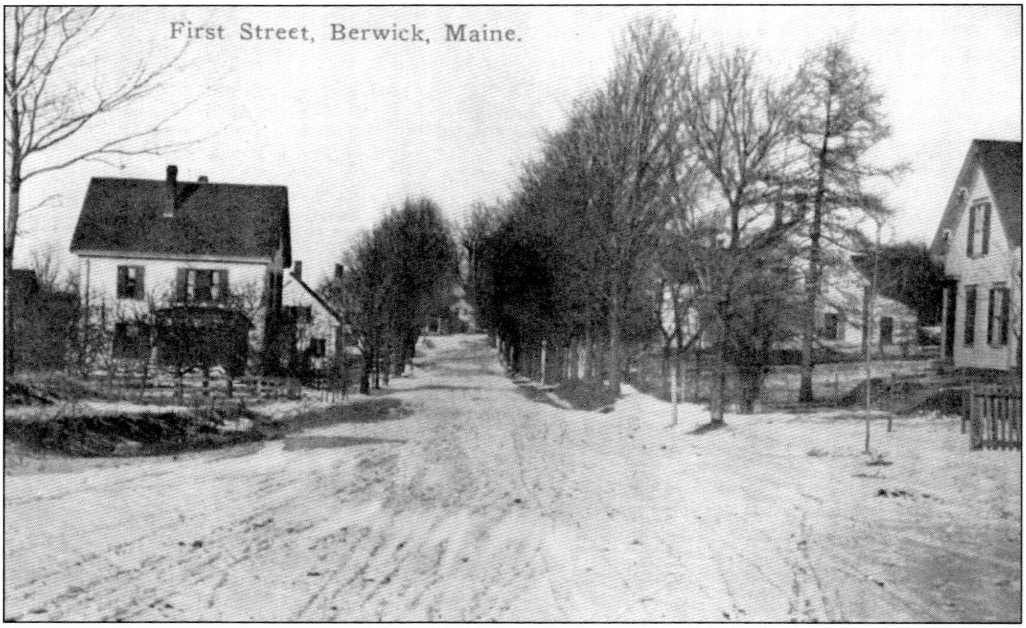

This postcard of First Street was sent to Edgar Leighton in August 1915. Marion Hamilton used to live in the first house on the left. She was the daughter of Dean Butler, who was a prominent businessman in Berwick.

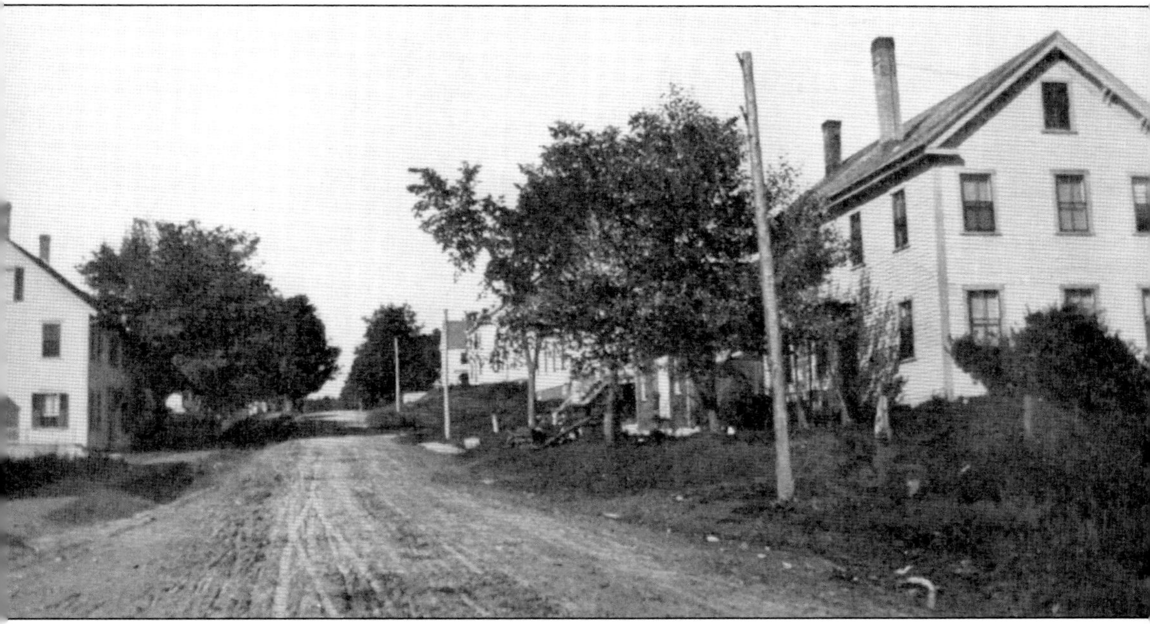

This postcard depicts Lower School Street in Berwick, Maine. The Bernier house is the first building on the right. A laundry service was once run out of this building. Over the years, School Street has accommodated many businesses, including beauty shops, barbershops, restaurants, car dealerships, and construction businesses.

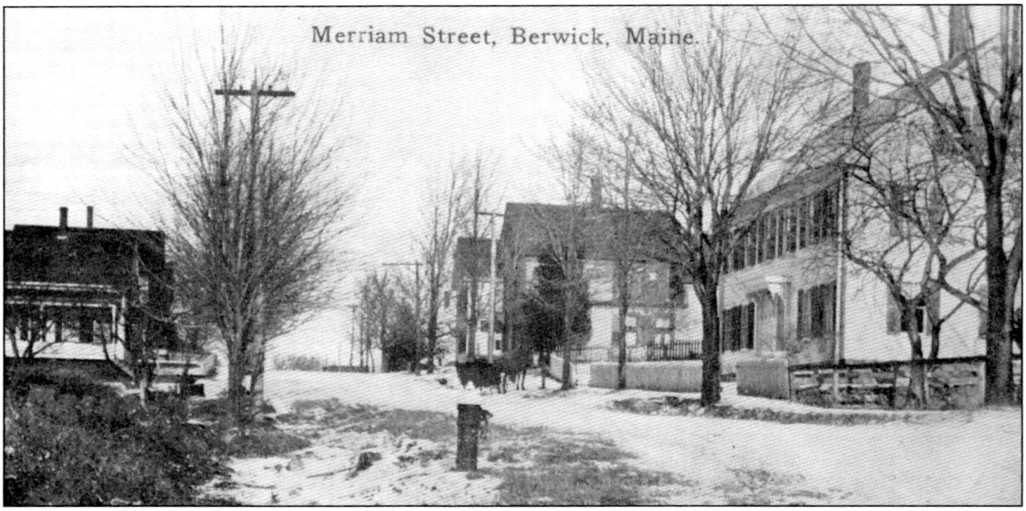

This postcard, from the early 20th century, depicts Merriam Street. The first house on the right was a duplex. One side was the home of the Gallop family, and the other side was occupied by the Eliots. The first two houses on the left side of the street used to be occupied by the Lord family. The Hall Brothers Roofing Company, first known as Samuel Hall & Sons, started on Merriam Street in the 1920s.

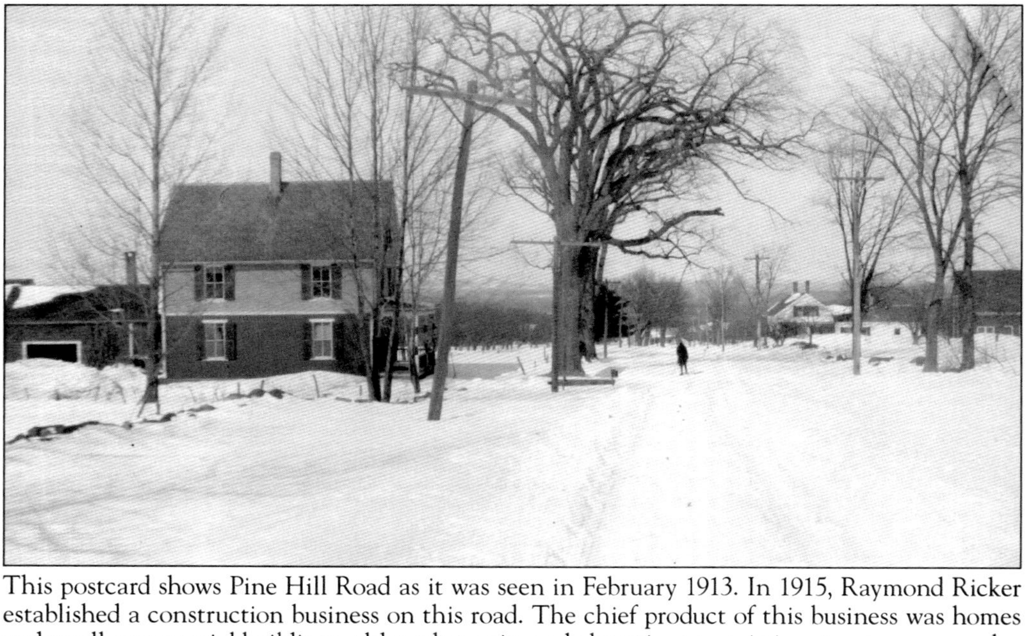

This postcard shows Pine Hill Road as it was seen in February 1913. In 1915, Raymond Ricker established a construction business on this road. The chief product of this business was homes and small commercial buildings, although repairs and alterations to existing structures were also performed. In 1946, Ernest Ricker joined the firm to work alongside his father.

Eight

People to See and Places to Go

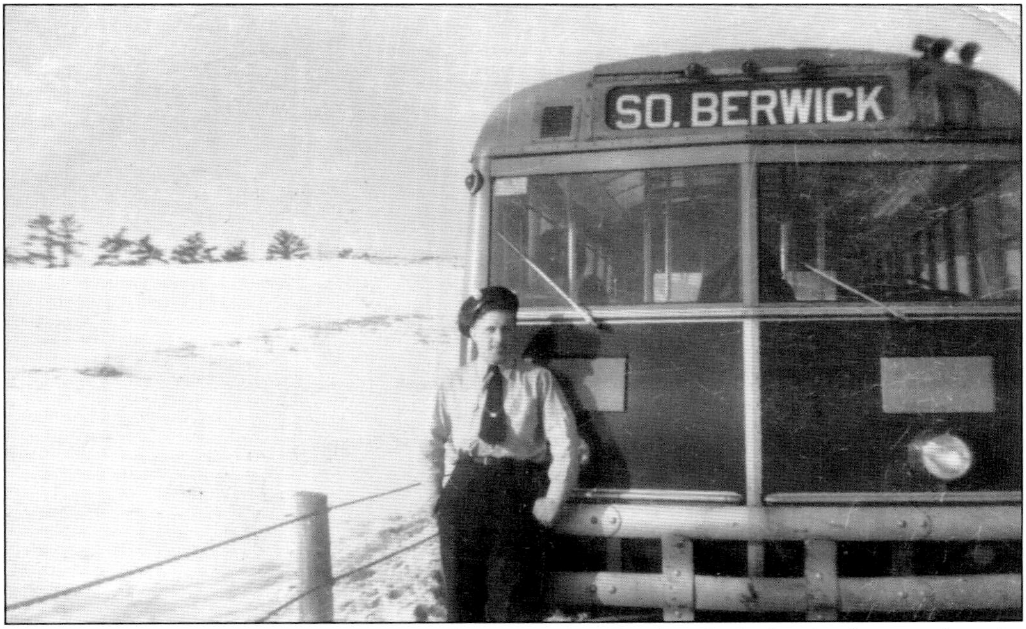

Raymond Worster stands outside on Cranberry Meadow Road with the bus he drove within the seacoast area. Worster also drove a school bus in Berwick when he was just 16 years old. He was known for driving a bit recklessly, but he was never involved in any vehicular accidents. (Courtesy of Dawn Milbury.)

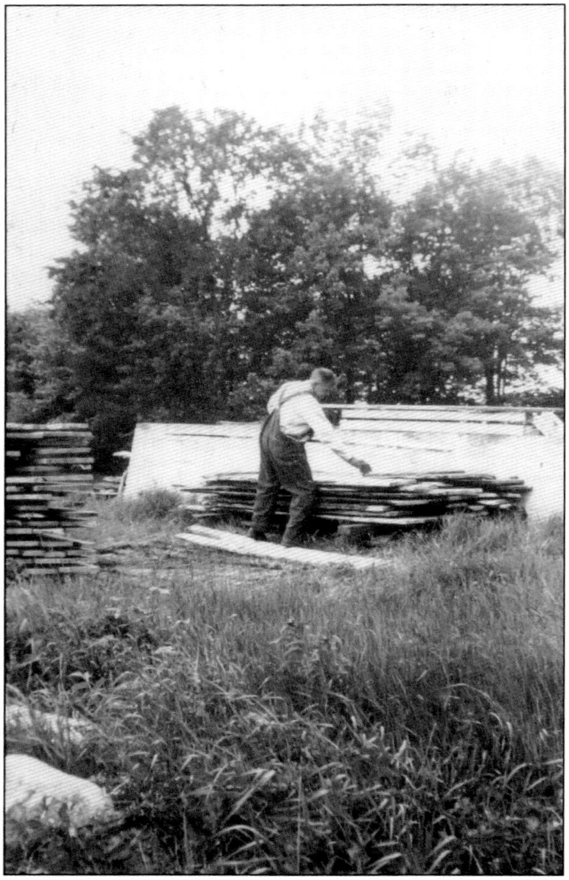

Arthur Worster, father of Raymond Worster, can be seen here building the home that now stands at 253 Cranberry Meadow. He worked at a lumberyard, so materials were sold to him at a discounted rate. (Courtesy of Dawn Milbury.)

Ethel Worster stands beside the family car outside her Berwick residence. She was known for the work she did writing for the *Rochester Currier* newspaper. For many years, Worster wrote the Berwick community events page for the paper. The car she is standing next to is a Ford Mercury. (Courtesy of Dawn Milbury.)

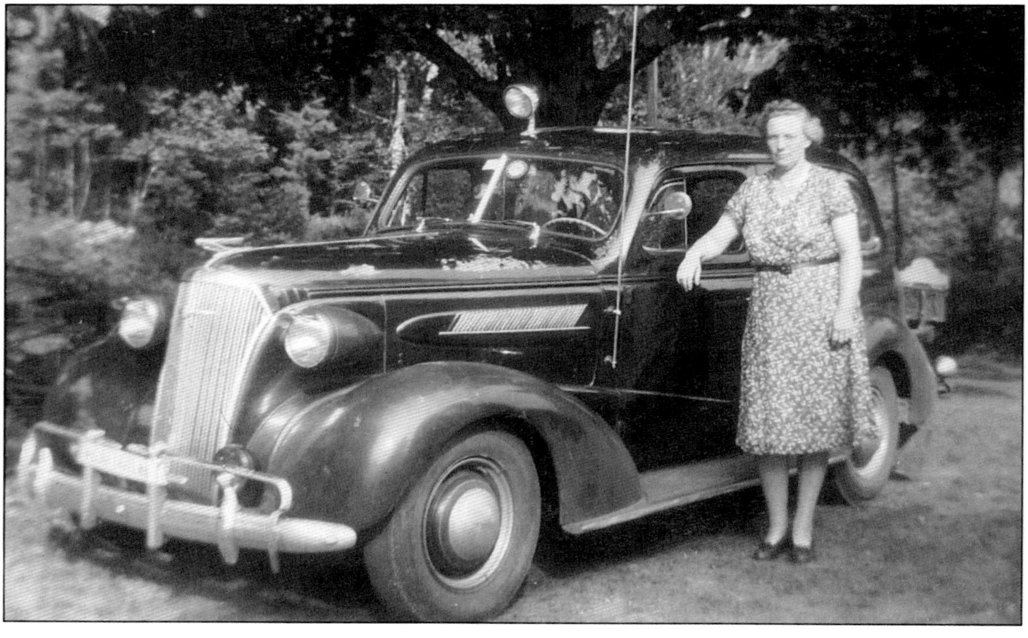

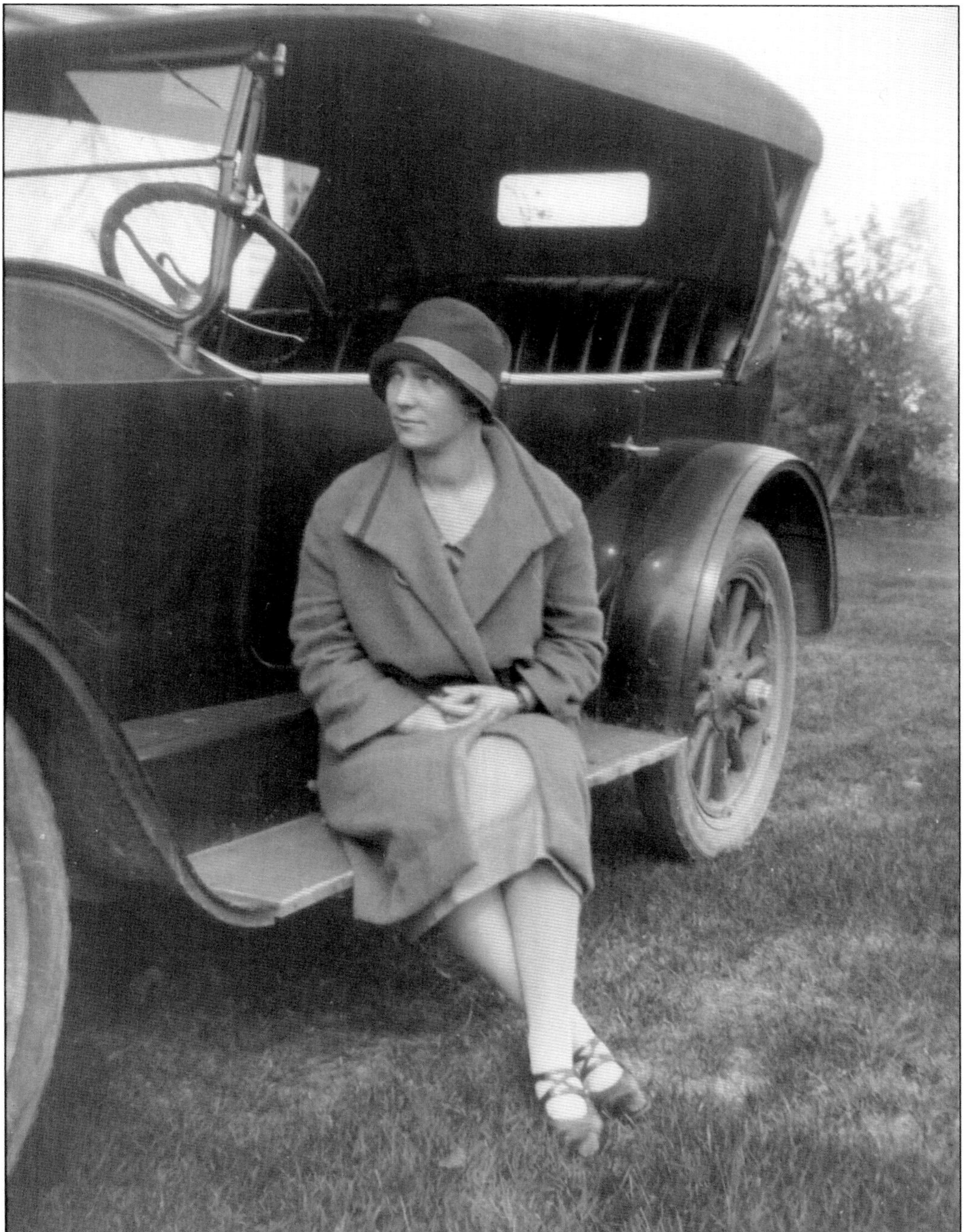

Ethel Worster poses on the side step of a vehicle outside her Berwick home. Worster was known for her work throughout the community. In the 1940s, she was the first woman to serve on the board of selectmen in Berwick. It was a very contentious act for a woman to serve in politics during that time. However, she prevailed, despite initially facing strong opposition. (Courtesy of Dawn Milbury.)

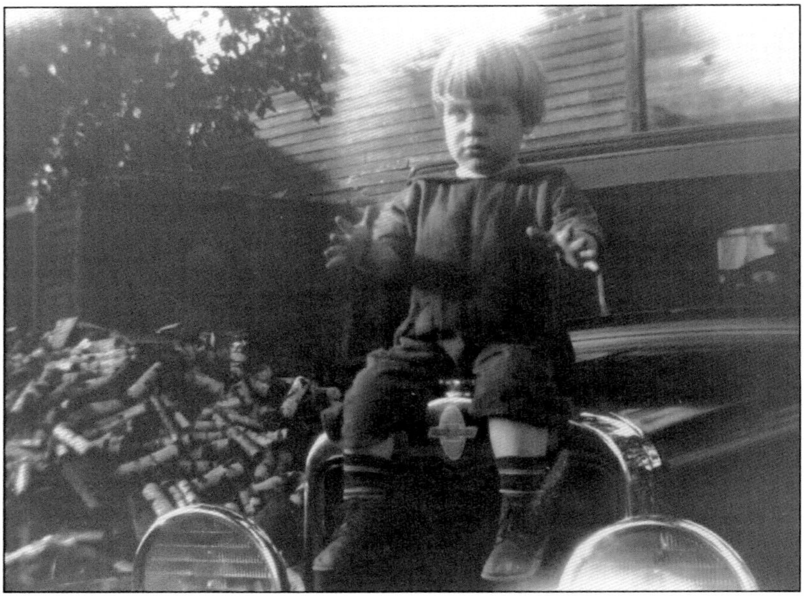

This photograph shows Raymond Worster sitting on the hood of an early-1920s Chevrolet. A large pile of freshly chopped wood that would be used to heat the Worster farm can be seen in the background. (Courtesy of Dawn Milbury.)

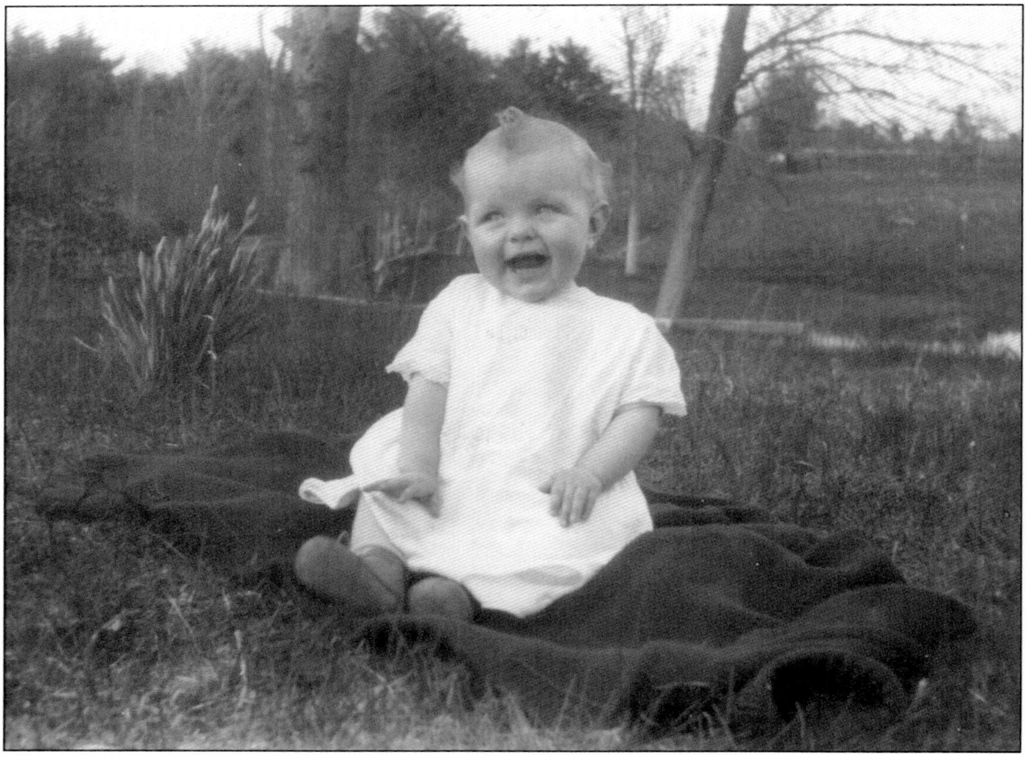

This is the earliest photograph of Raymond Worster, as he sits in a field outside the Worster farm. It was not uncommon for little boys to wear gowns in this era. (Courtesy of Dawn Milbury.)

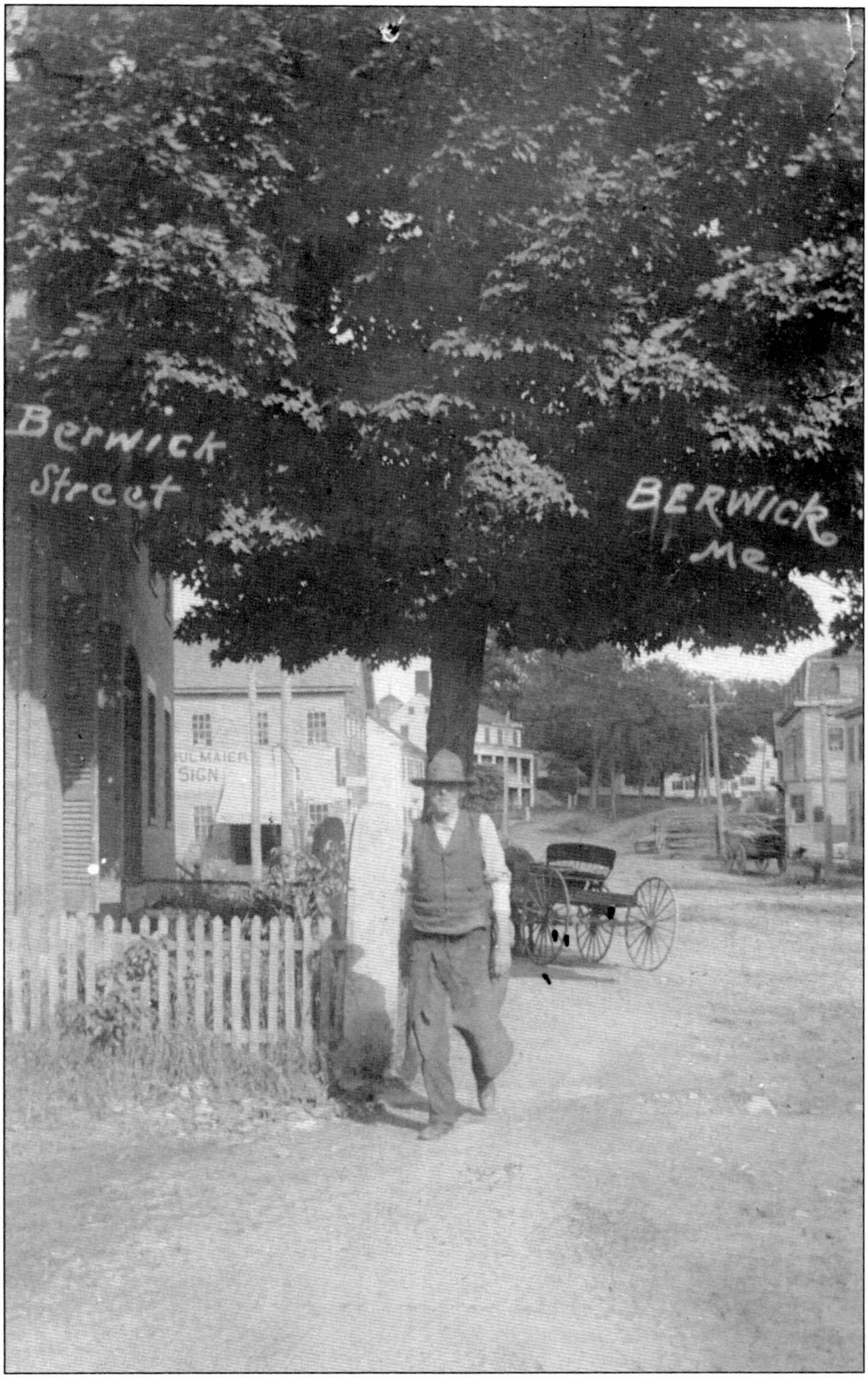

Joe Mathews stands in front of Schulmaier Carriages & Signs on the corner of School and Berwick Streets. Joe Mathews was one of six boys who were brought up on the Mathews farm, located on Cranberry Meadow Road. Joe married Annie Roberts in Somersworth, New Hampshire. They had a son who would later become known for opening Spencer & Mathews Insurance Company.

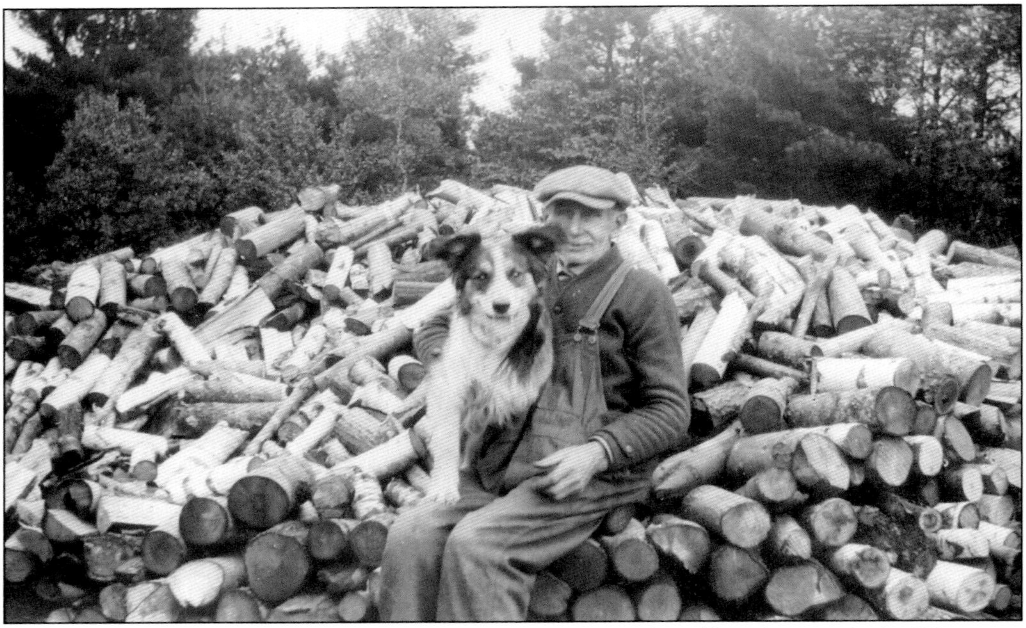

A hired hand sits with the Worster family dog on a woodpile outside the Worster farm. This photograph was taken during the Great Depression, when many area farms survived by hiring local teenagers to complete chores for very little money. (Courtesy of Dawn Milbury.)

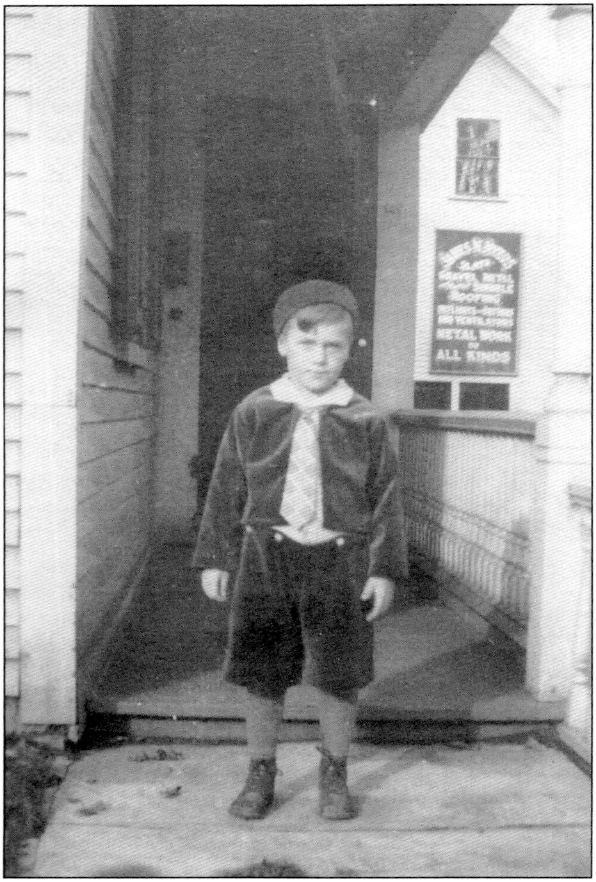

This postcard shows a young boy standing on the porch of James M. Myers Slate. This was a metal shop in Berwick specializing in roofing, gutters, and ventilation. (Courtesy of Dawn Milbury.)

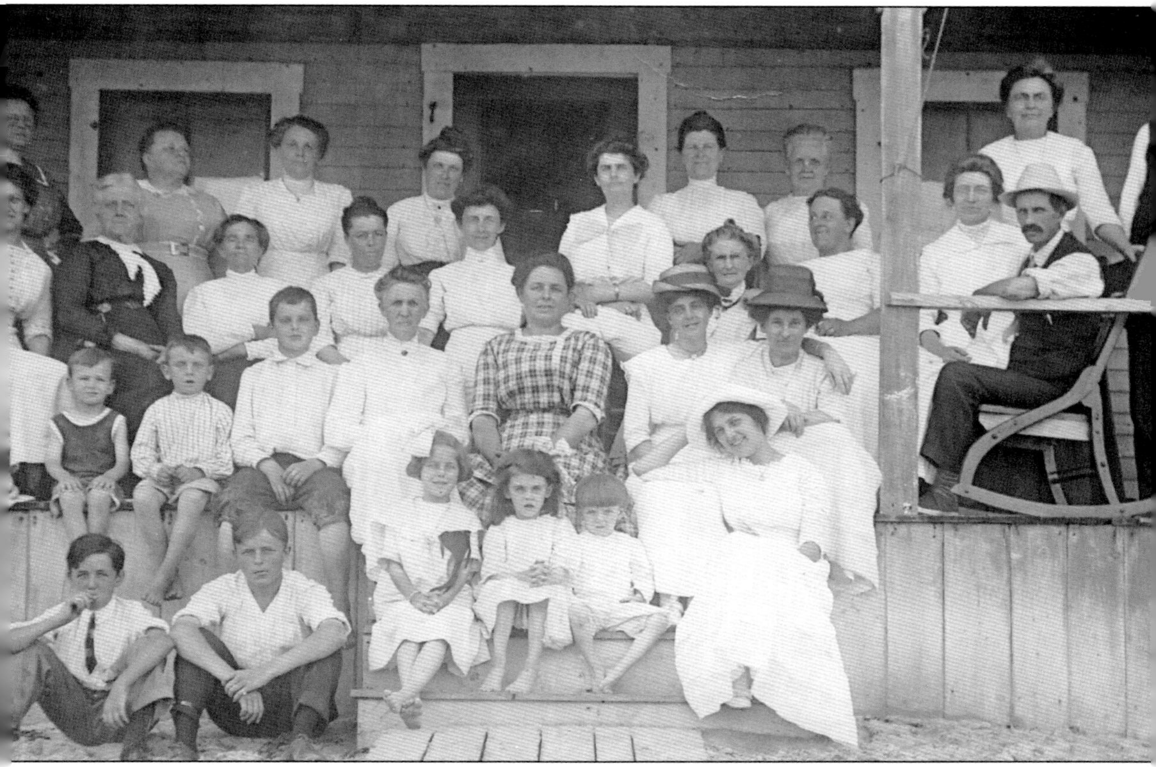

Many of the children in this photograph attended the Rochester Street School in Berwick. Shown here are, from left to right, (first row) Eugene Hatch, Burton Day, Lura Wallace, two unidentified, and Evelyn Spence; (second row) two unidentified children, Clifford Andrews, Harold Audrey, a Mrs. Horne, Alice Andrews, Catherine Johnson, and Edith Spence; (third row) Mattie Matthews, Julia Chesley, a Mrs. Winn, Sadie Brackett, Lucy Hatch, Ella Davis, Anna Andrews, Bernice Wallace, and Rev. C.W. Wallace; (fourth row) Lutie Day, Ada Bryant, unidentified, Nellie Brooks, Carnie Tibbetts, Ella Lord, unidentified, Mrs. Henry Downs, and Henry Downs.

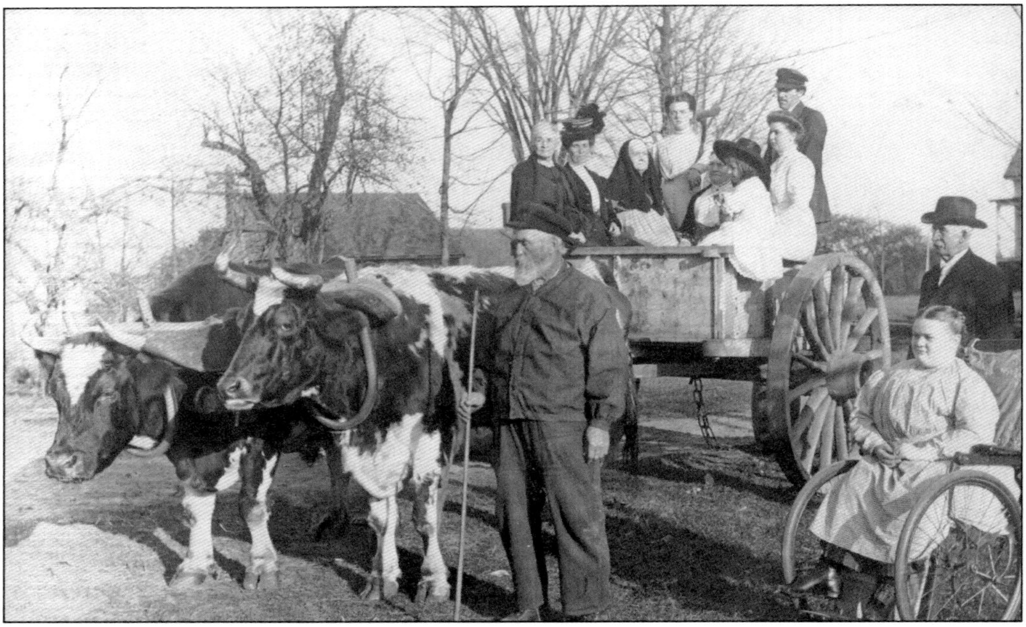

The Webster family prepares for an outing outside the Webster farm. The woman in the back of the wagon is carrying an axe. This farm was once located on Hubbard Road. (Courtesy of Ann Smith.)

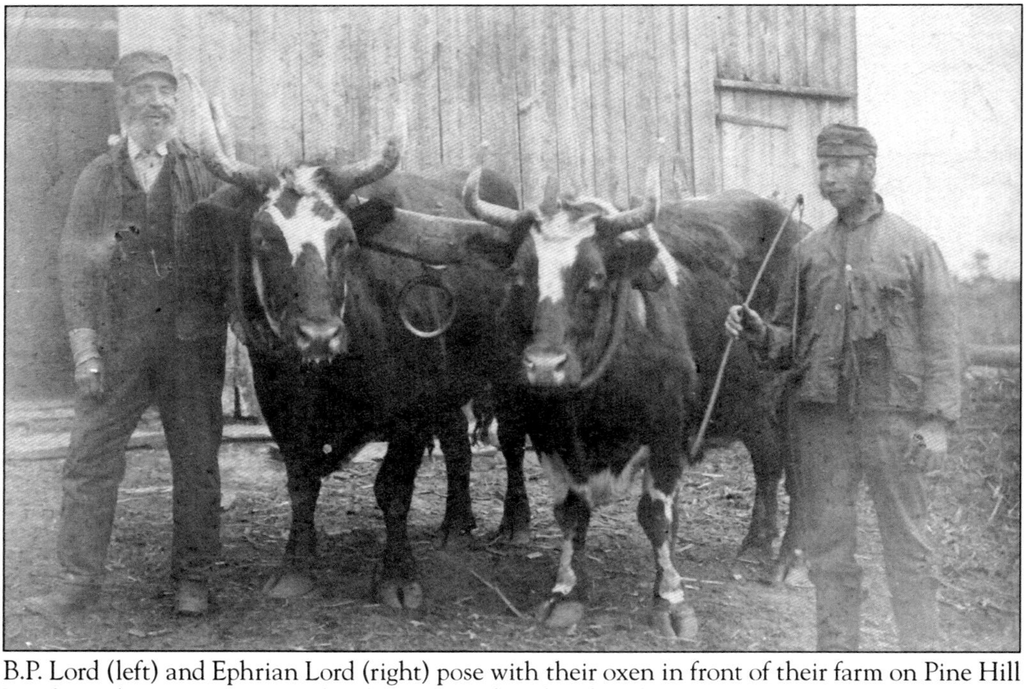

B.P. Lord (left) and Ephrian Lord (right) pose with their oxen in front of their farm on Pine Hill Road. Lord was a prominent family in town that dated back to the early days of Berwick. The Lord cemetery is the oldest burial ground in Berwick. The oldest grave within dates to 1753 and belongs to Ebenezer Lord.

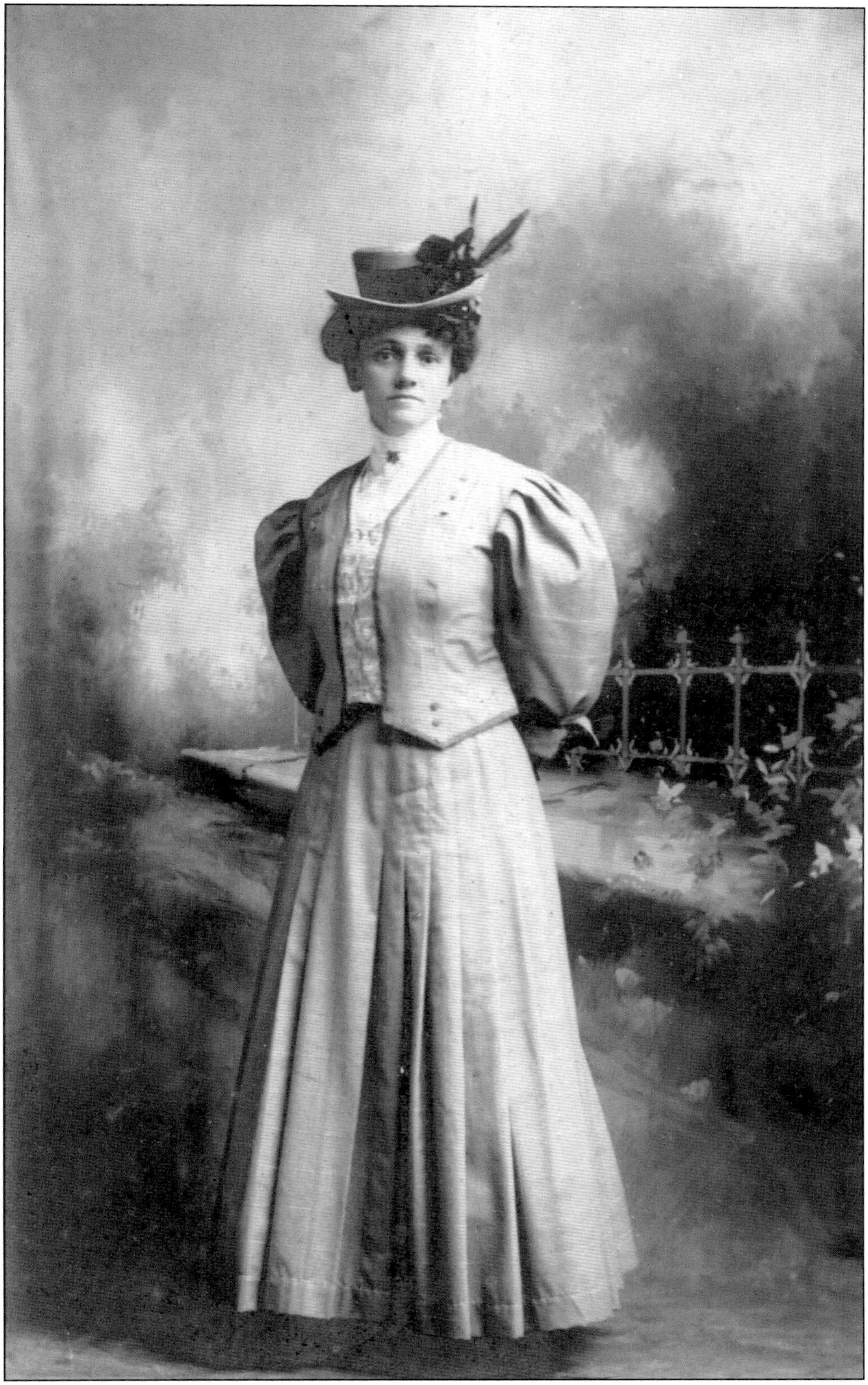

This postcard depicts one of the members of the Littlefield family in the late 19th century. The Littlefield family once lived on Bridge Street.

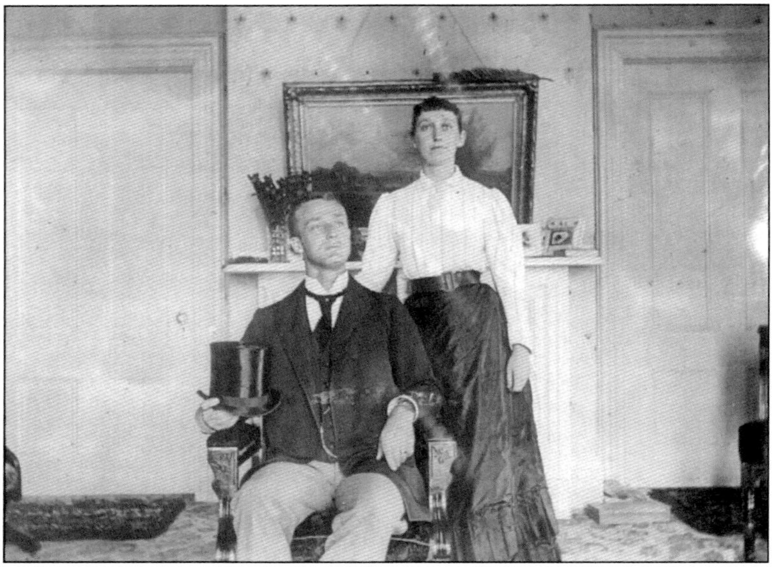

John Russell Perkins and Effie Perkins pose inside the Perkin farm property on Blackberry Hill Road in 1892. During that time, Maine farms were producing a mixture of crops, ranging from hay, potatoes, apples, sweet corn, and blueberries to poultry, eggs, milk, and butter. (Courtesy of Patricia J. Fulton and Nancy W. Fulton.)

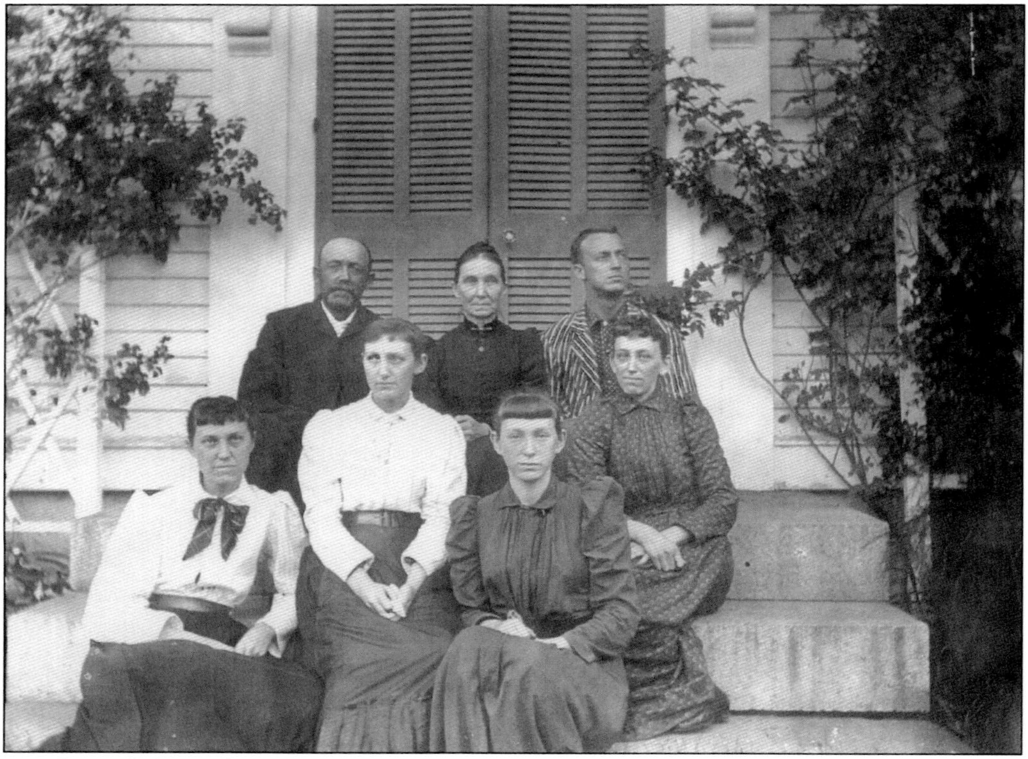

Members of the Perkins family pose for this 1892 photograph taken in front of the Perkins farmhouse located on Blackberry Hill Road. Shown here are, from left to right, (first row) Clara Perkins, Effie Perkins, and Anne Perkins; (second row) Abigail Perkins sits alone on the middle step; (third row) Samuel Perkins, Sarah Allen Perkins, and John Perkins. Anne Perkins would later go on to become a doctor. This was quite unusual for women during this time. (Courtesy of Patricia J. Fulton and Nancy W. Fulton.)

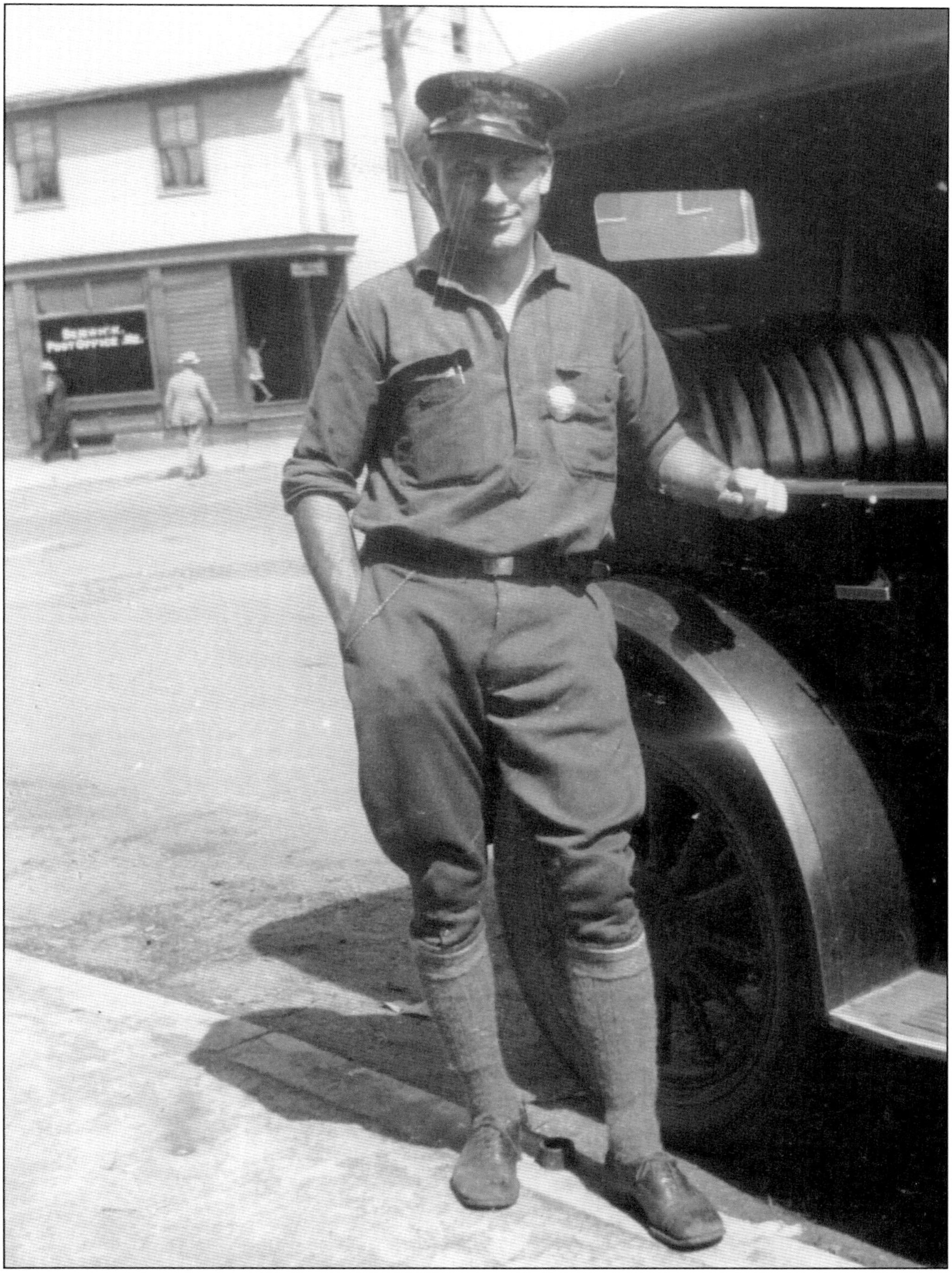

The State of Maine postal inspector stands in front of the old post office in Berwick; it was located on Sullivan Street. The inspectors served as the post office's law enforcement. Their job was to investigate crimes of fraud against the US mail, postal system, or the post office's employees. The inspectors could also audit the post office and all the mail that passed through it. (Courtesy of Dawn Milbury.)

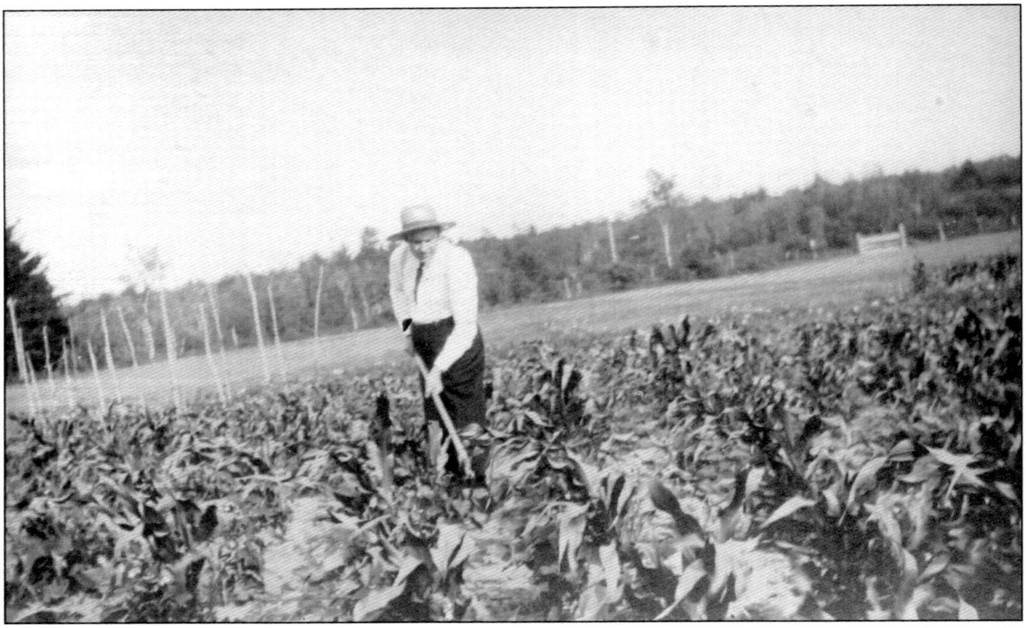

Harry Webster tends to the growing corn crops, which would later be used to feed the livestock. The Webster Farm was once located on Hubbard Road. (Courtesy of Ann Smith)

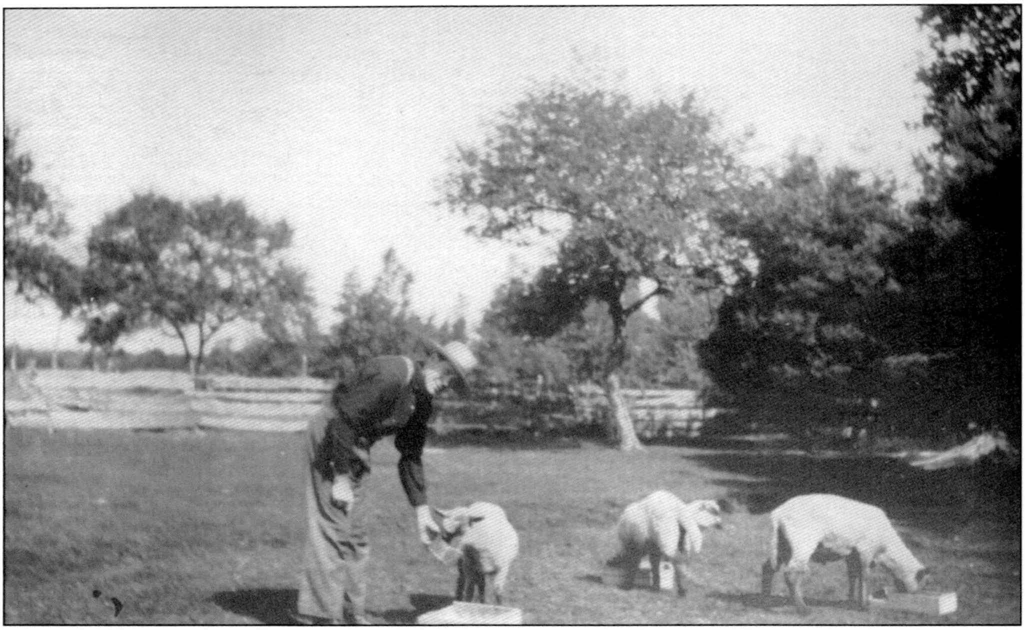

Harry Webster tends to sheep on the Webster Farm. During that time, sheep were raised primarily for wool, which was spun into blankets and clothing. This farm was once located on Hubbard Road, but it not longer stands today. (Courtesy of Ann Smith.)

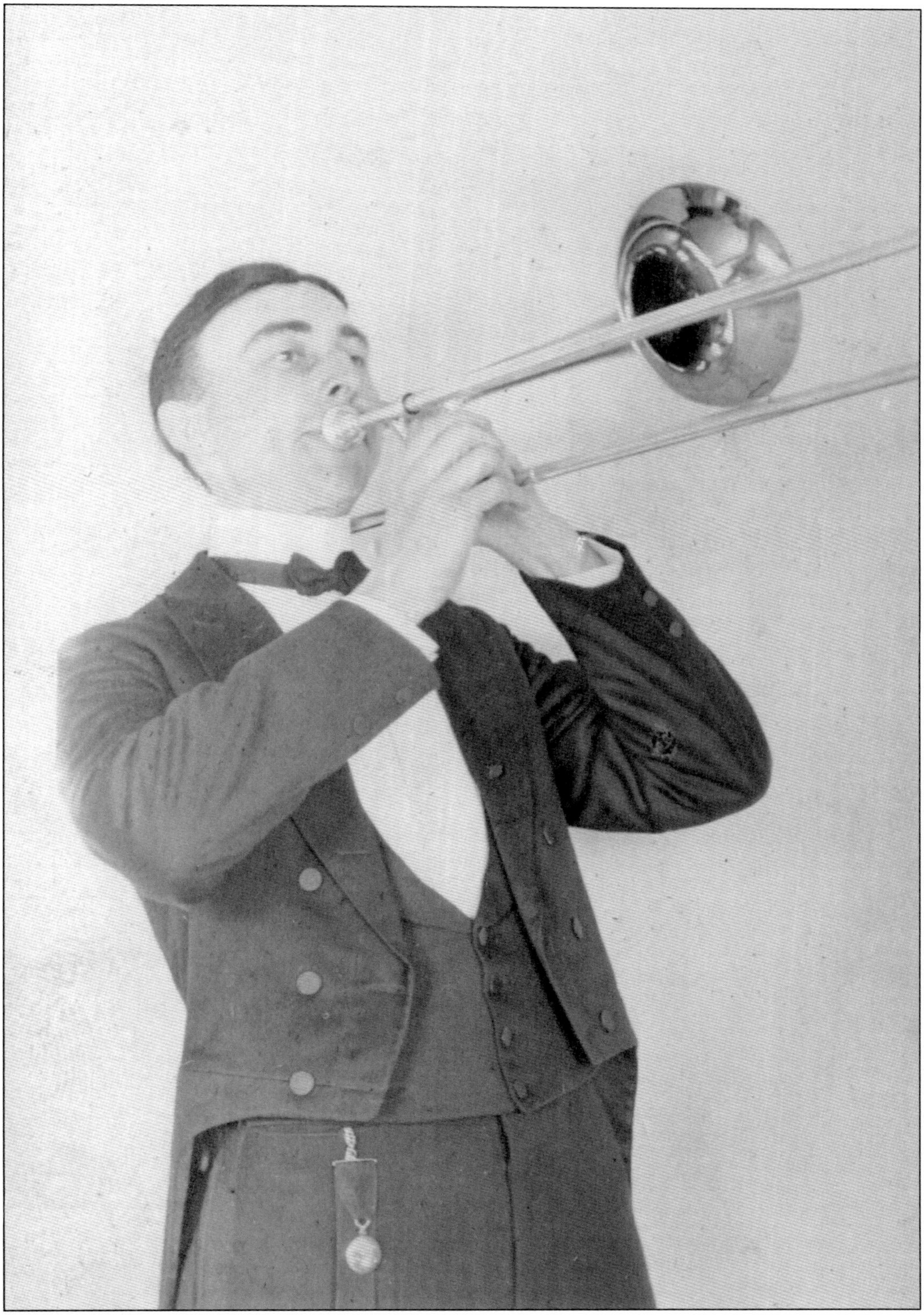

This is a photograph of Arthur Webster playing the trombone. He grew up on the Webster farm, once located on Hubbard Road. (Courtesy of Ann Smith.)

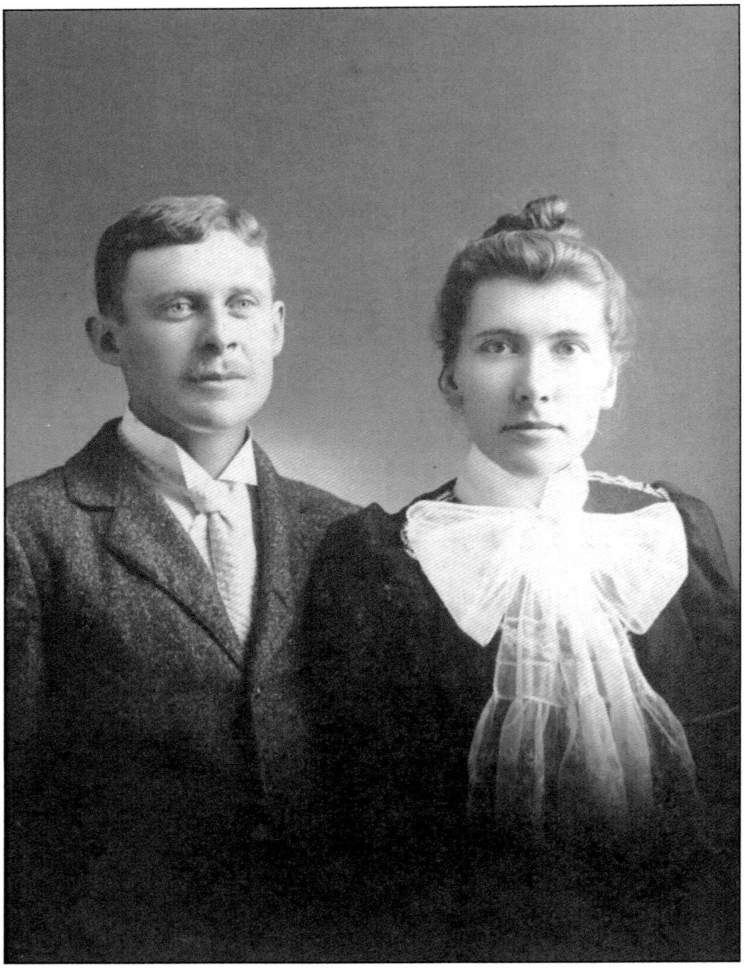

This is a photograph of Harry Webster and his wife, Hattie. Harry Webster, the son of Harrison Webster, served as a postman in the Rural Free Delivery (RFD) service. (Courtesy of Ann Smith.)

George Snow and his son ride in a horse-drawn wagon. George Snow was known for the time he worked as a teacher at Sullivan High Grammar School in 1898. (Courtesy of Ann Smith.)

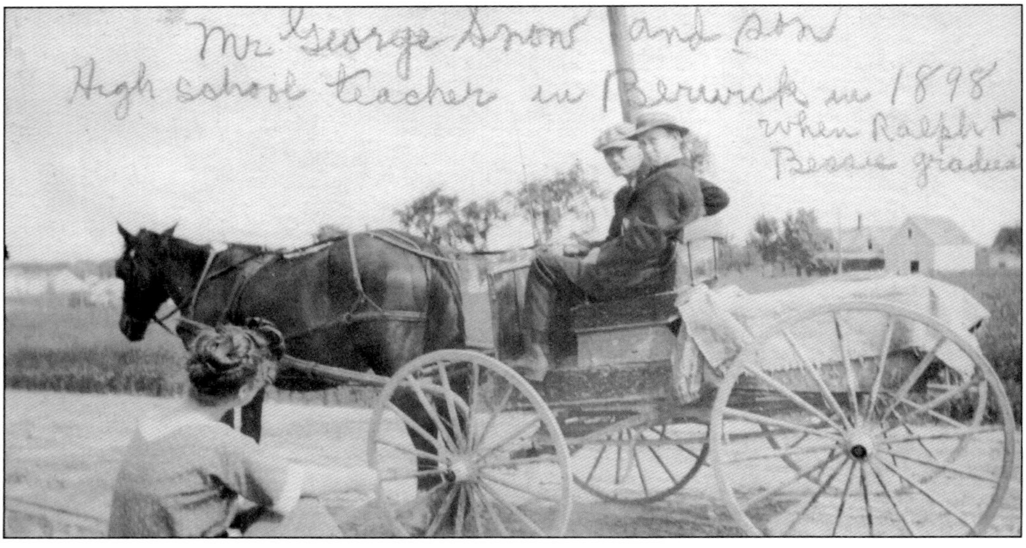

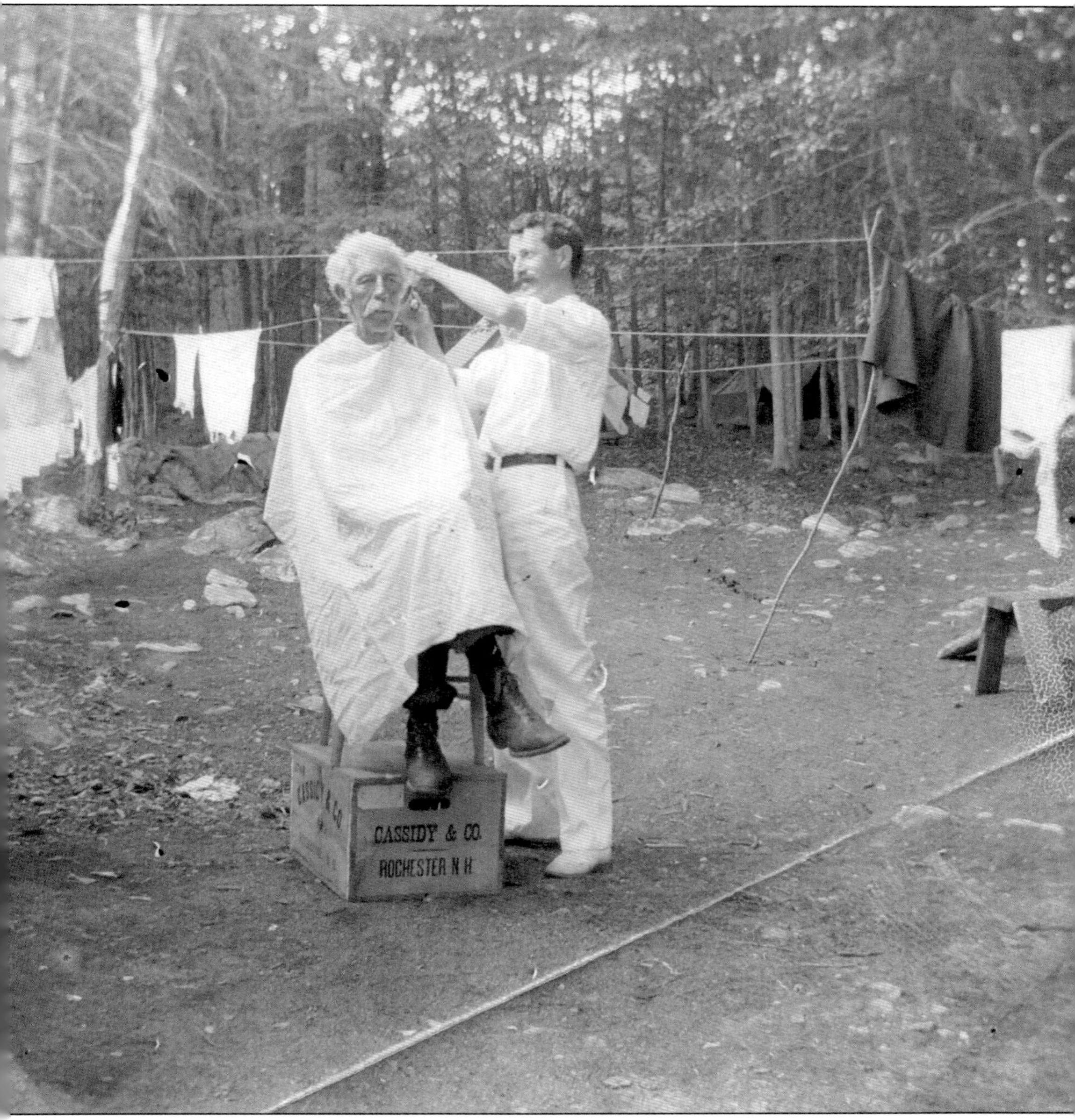

Here, a man receives barber services in true Maine fashion—while camping out! The men are in the process of building a house and have camped out at the work site, located on Cranberry Meadow Road, until the project was complete. (Courtesy of Dawn Milbury.)

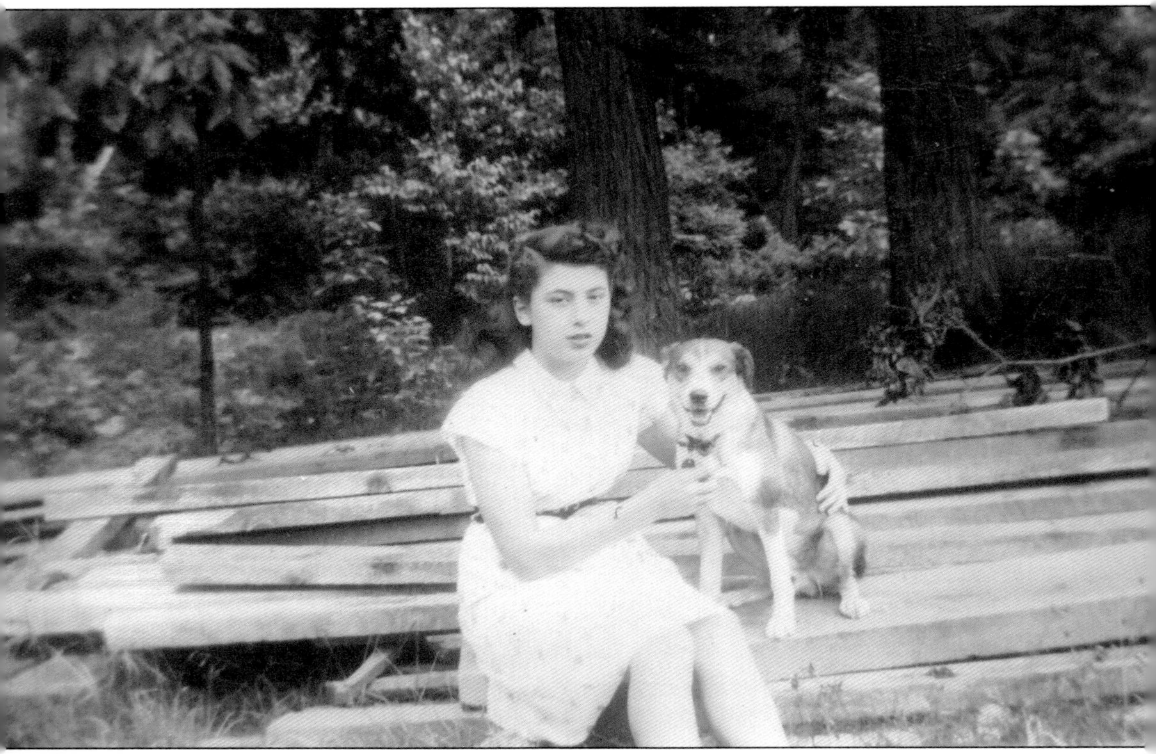

Here, a young lady sits with her dog on the lumber being used to build the home at 253 Cranberry Meadow Road. (Courtesy of Dawn Milbury.)

Nine

CELEBRATIONS

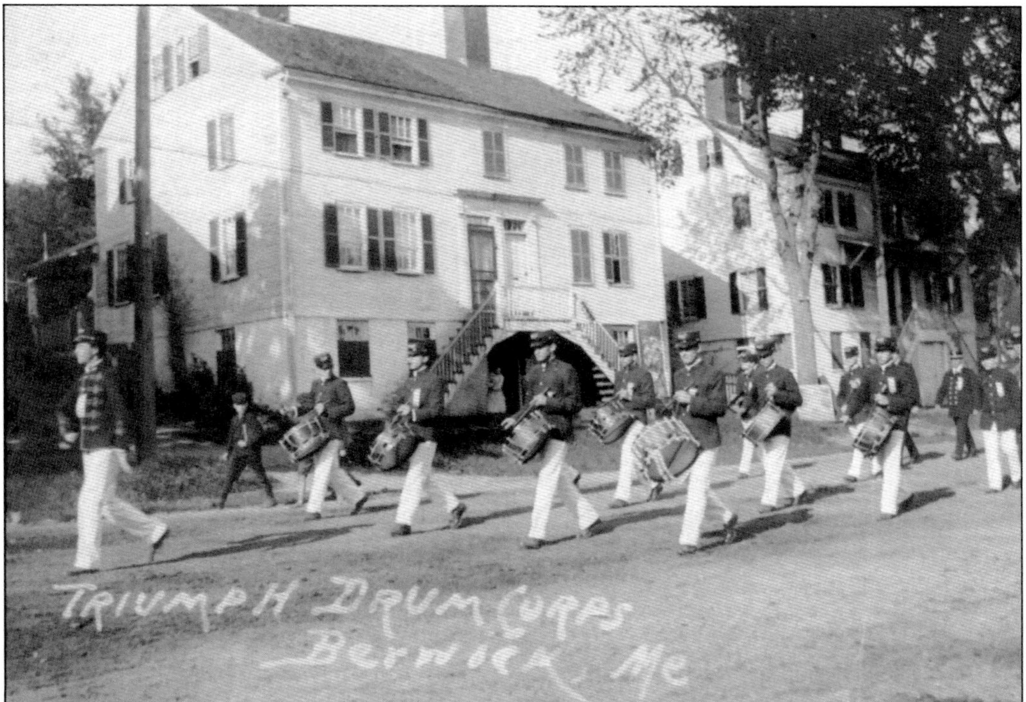

The Triumph Drum Corps, formed in the early 1900s, was affiliated with the Berwick Fire Station. In the early part of the 20th century, military drum and bugle corps were being organized to perform at military and public ceremonies. During this time, surplus military equipment was sold to veteran and civilian organizations. Organizations such as the American Legion and Boy Scout Associations purchased this equipment and formed drum and bugle corps youth activities.

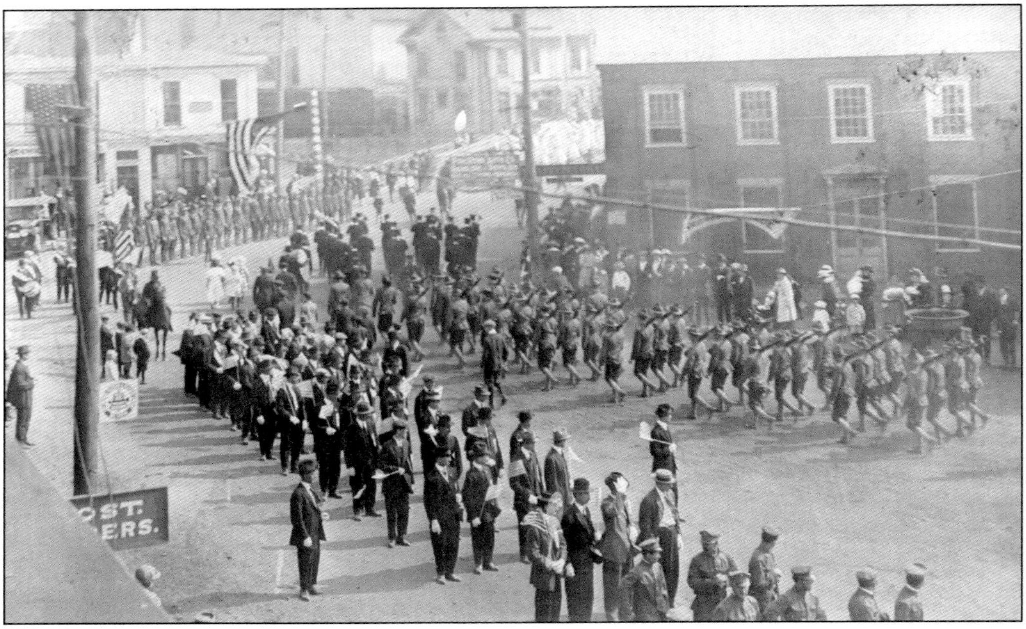

These postcards depict the Sullivan Square Preparedness Parade on May 20, 1917. In 1915, a strong "preparedness movement" emerged to strengthen the military of the United States after the outbreak of World War I. These parades were organized countrywide as part of the preparedness movement, also referred to as the "preparedness controversy." This campaign was led by Gen. Leonard Wood and Theodore Roosevelt; Pres. Woodrow Wilson was initially against it. He believed the United States should be in a position of armed neutrality. However, Wood and Roosevelt stood strong on the argument that the United States needed to immediately build up naval and land forces for defensive purposes. There was an unspoken assumption that the nation would fight sooner or later.

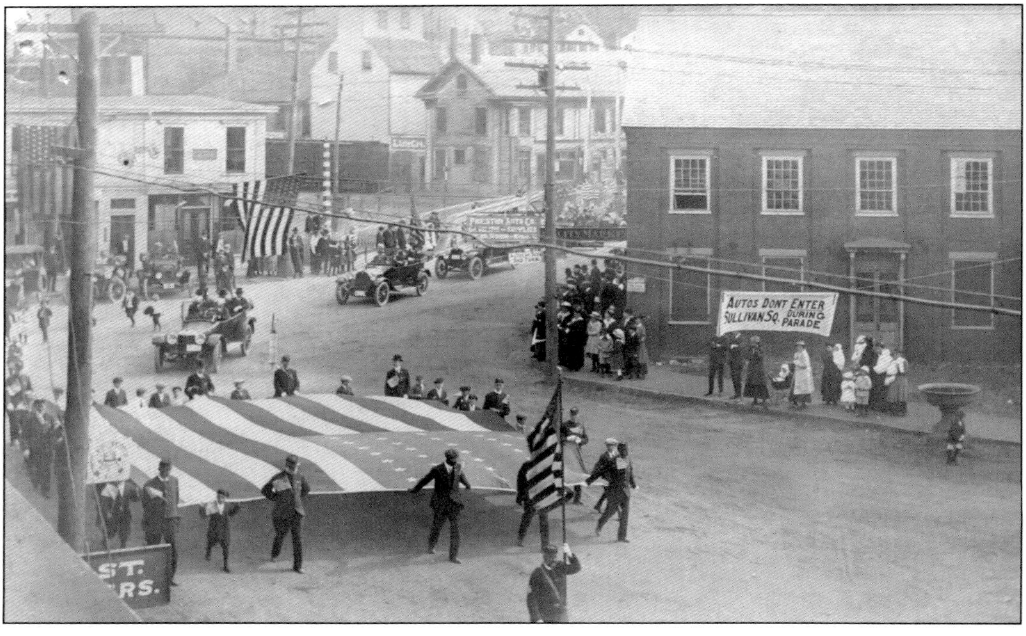

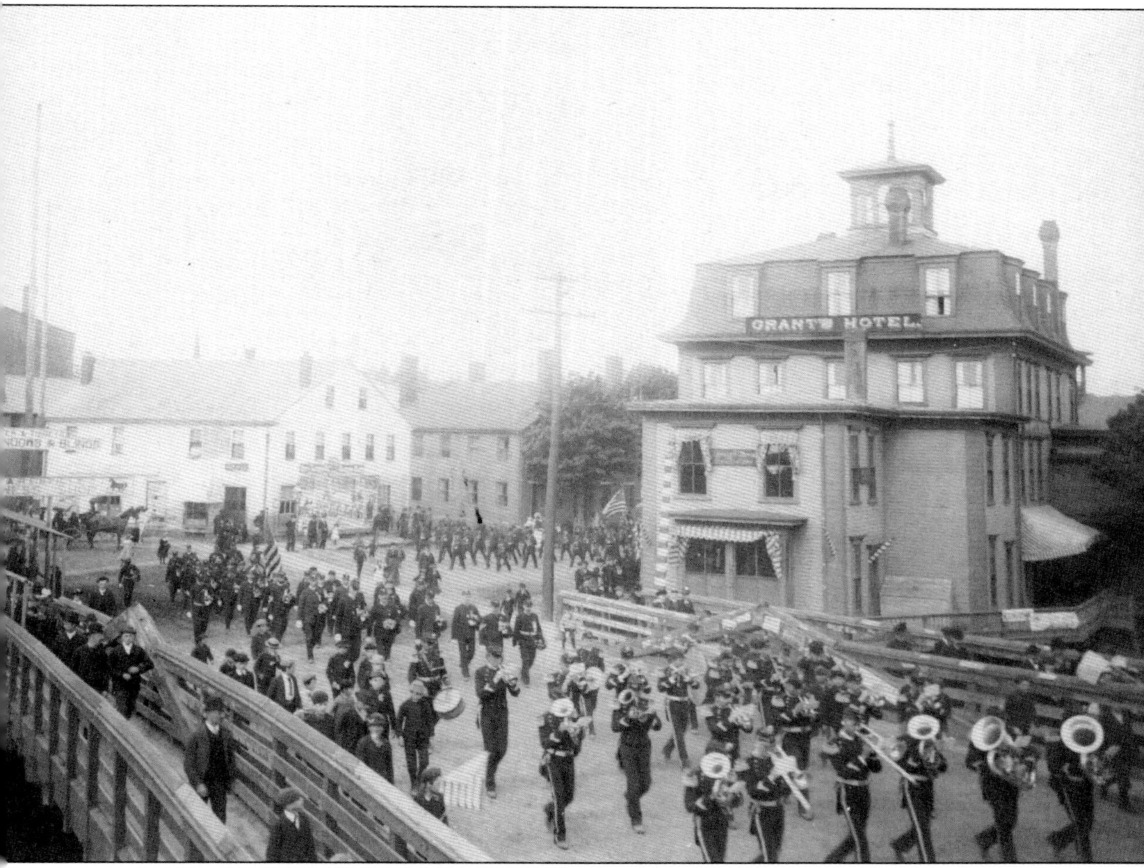

This Berwick Preparedness Parade includes a marching band crossing over the bridge from Berwick into Somersworth, New Hampshire. Drum and bugle corps started forming across the country in the beginning of the 20th century. With the invention of radio, bugles became solely used for the purpose of signaling soldiers. The Grant's Hotel can be seen on the right. The location is currently occupied by Gateway Gas.

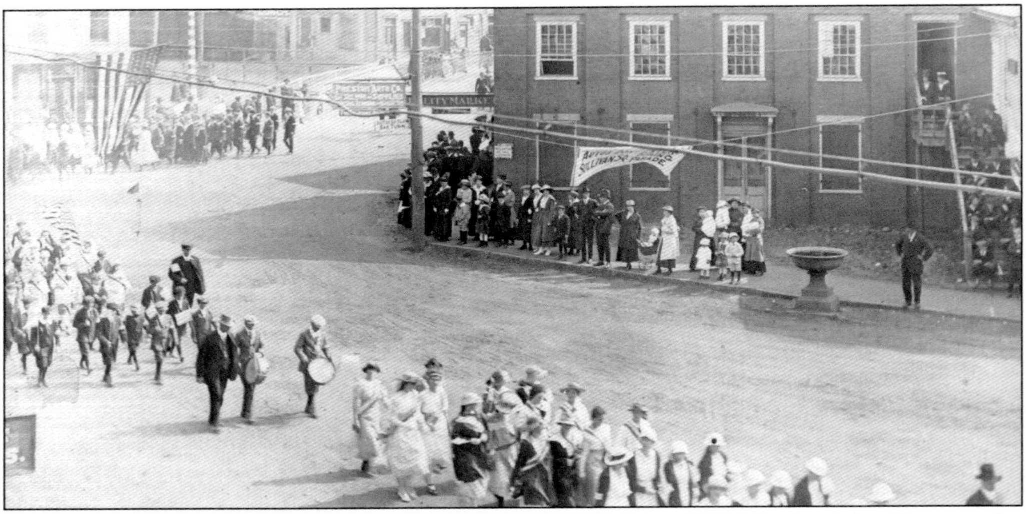

This postcard depicts Sullivan Square Preparedness Parade in 1917. The brick building on the right is the current location of the Summit Church, at 1 Sullivan Square. However, the front part of the building has since been removed. The Grant's Hotel can be seen in the upper left corner. This building later went on to house an insurance agency, restaurant, and barbershop in turn, but it was destroyed by fire in the late 1930s.

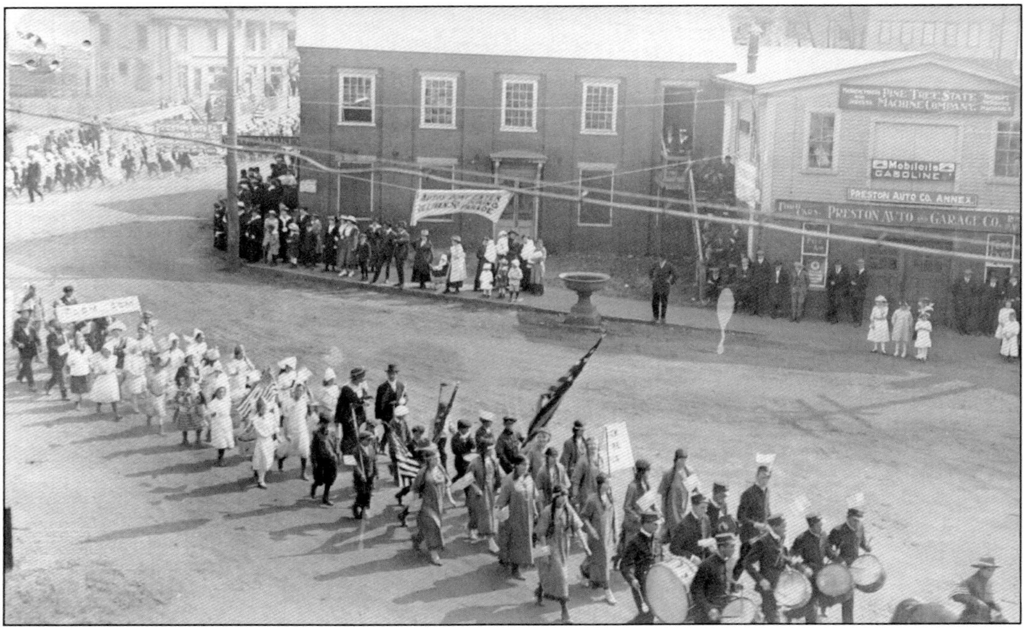

This postcard depicts the Sullivan Square Preparedness Parade in 1917. Here, the Triumph Drum Corps lead Berwick schoolchildren dressed as pilgrims and Indians down Sullivan Street.

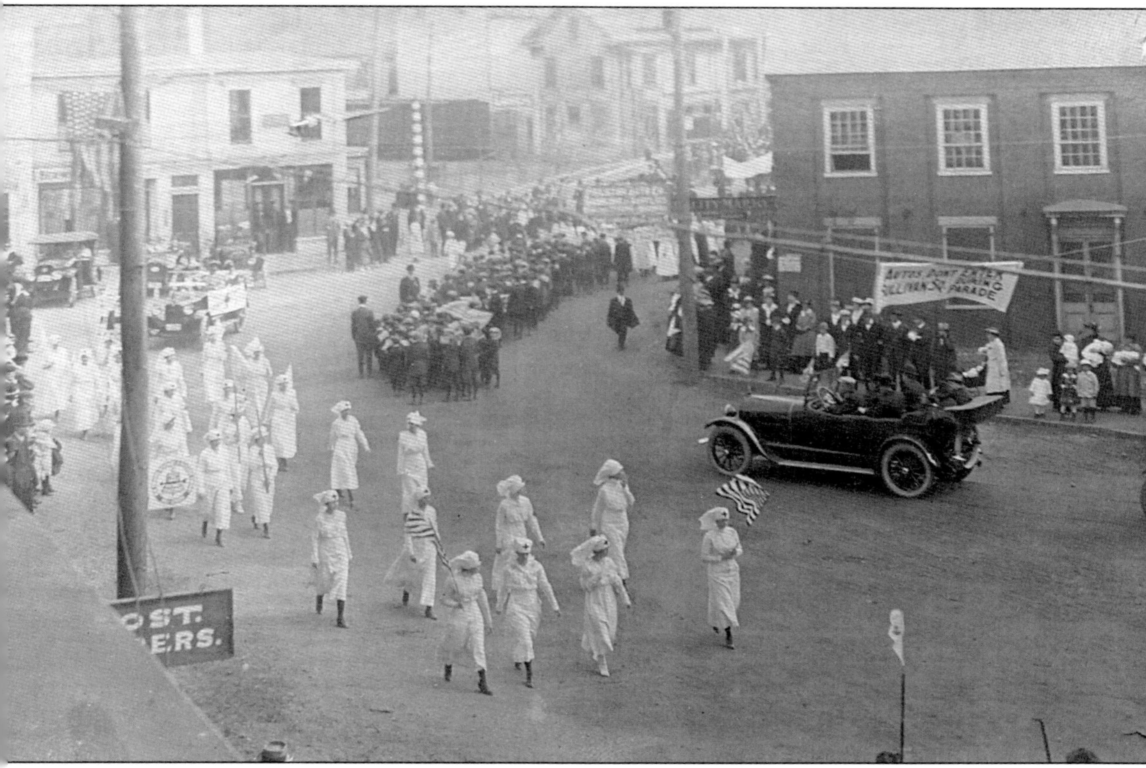

Shown here is the Sullivan Square Preparedness Parade in 1917. The women marching in white uniforms are members of the Women's Relief Corps, founded in the early 1900s. These women worked to provide assistance to needy veterans and their dependants. They were also known for their efforts at teaching patriotism in local schools.

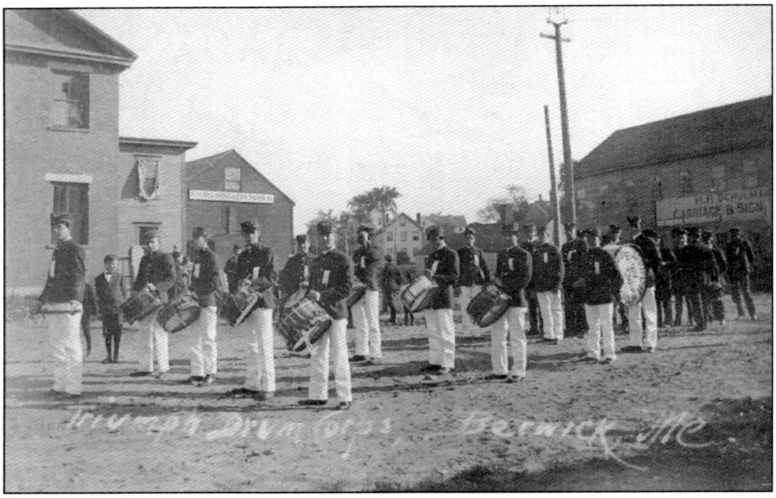

The Triumph Drum Corps gathers downtown as it prepares to march into Somersworth, New Hampshire. Visible in the background are Bachelors Livery Stable (left of center) and H.R. Schulmaier Carriage & Sign (right). The livery stable was owned and operated by Moses Weeks.

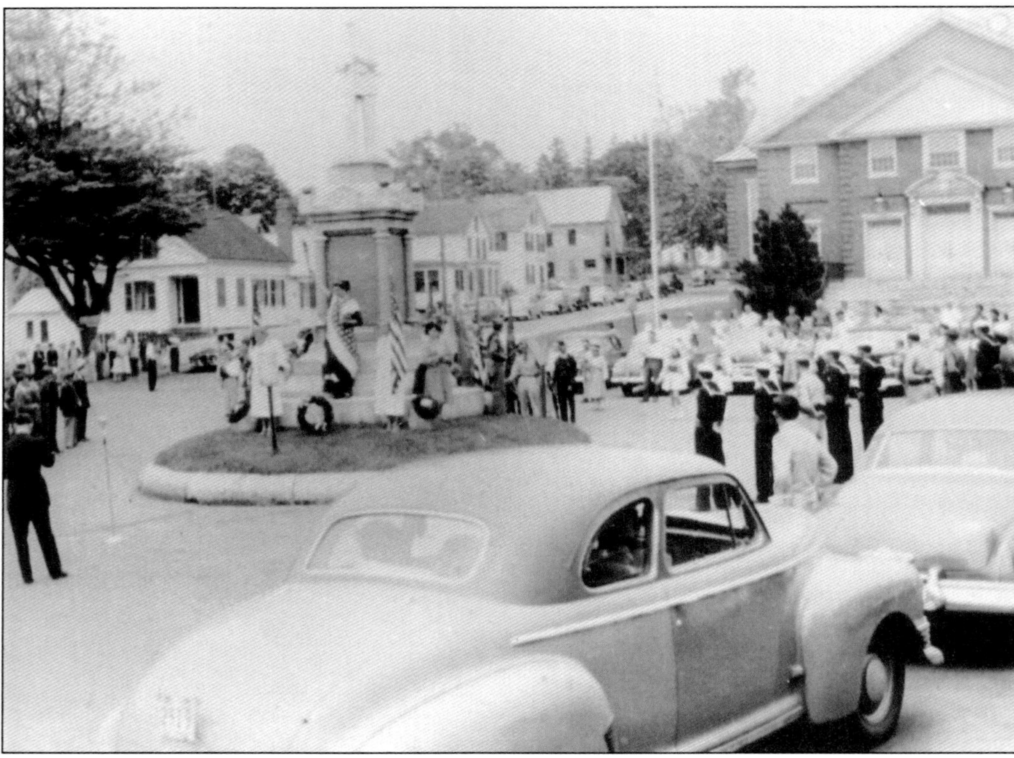

Berwick citizens gather for a Memorial Day celebration in Sullivan Square shortly after World War II. Berwick's men have bravely set forth to defend the freedom of their country in times of war and conflict. Freetly Spencer is one of the first Berwick residents documented to have served in battle. He is known as Berwick's only resident to fight with the Americans at Bunker Hill in the Revolutionary War. (Courtesy of Dawn Milbury.)

Citizens gather to celebrate the Berwick Firemen's Muster. The view is looking from Berwick in Somersworth. The Queensbury Mill can be seen in the background. In the late 1800s, the Queensbury Mill was known as a planing mill, where doors and sashes were manufactured. It later became a cotton mill. (Courtesy of Dawn Milbury.)

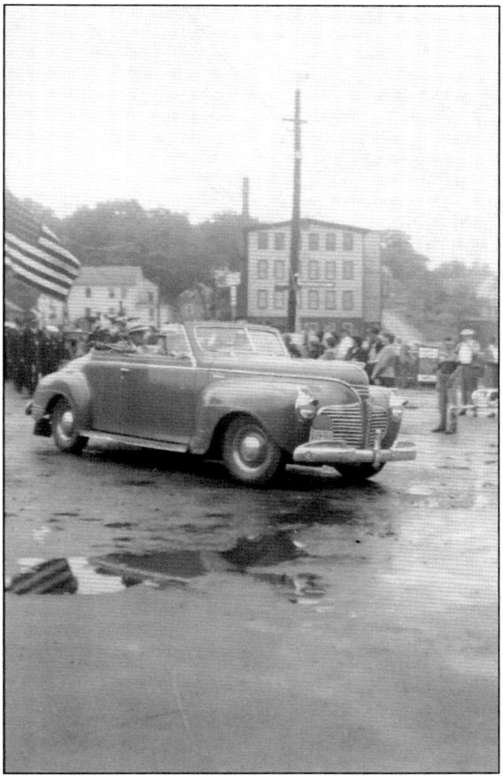

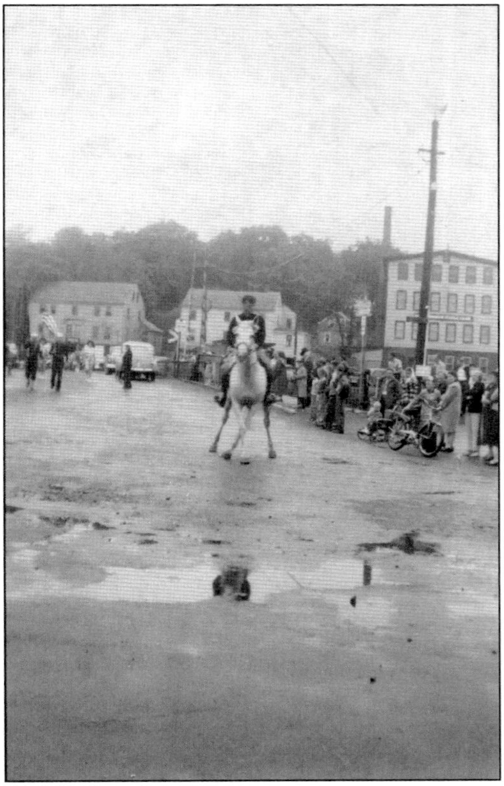

People gather for the Berwick Firemen's Muster. The view is looking over the bridge from Berwick into Somersworth, New Hampshire. Larry Preutice can be seen on the horse. The Queensbury Mill is the large building to the right in the background.

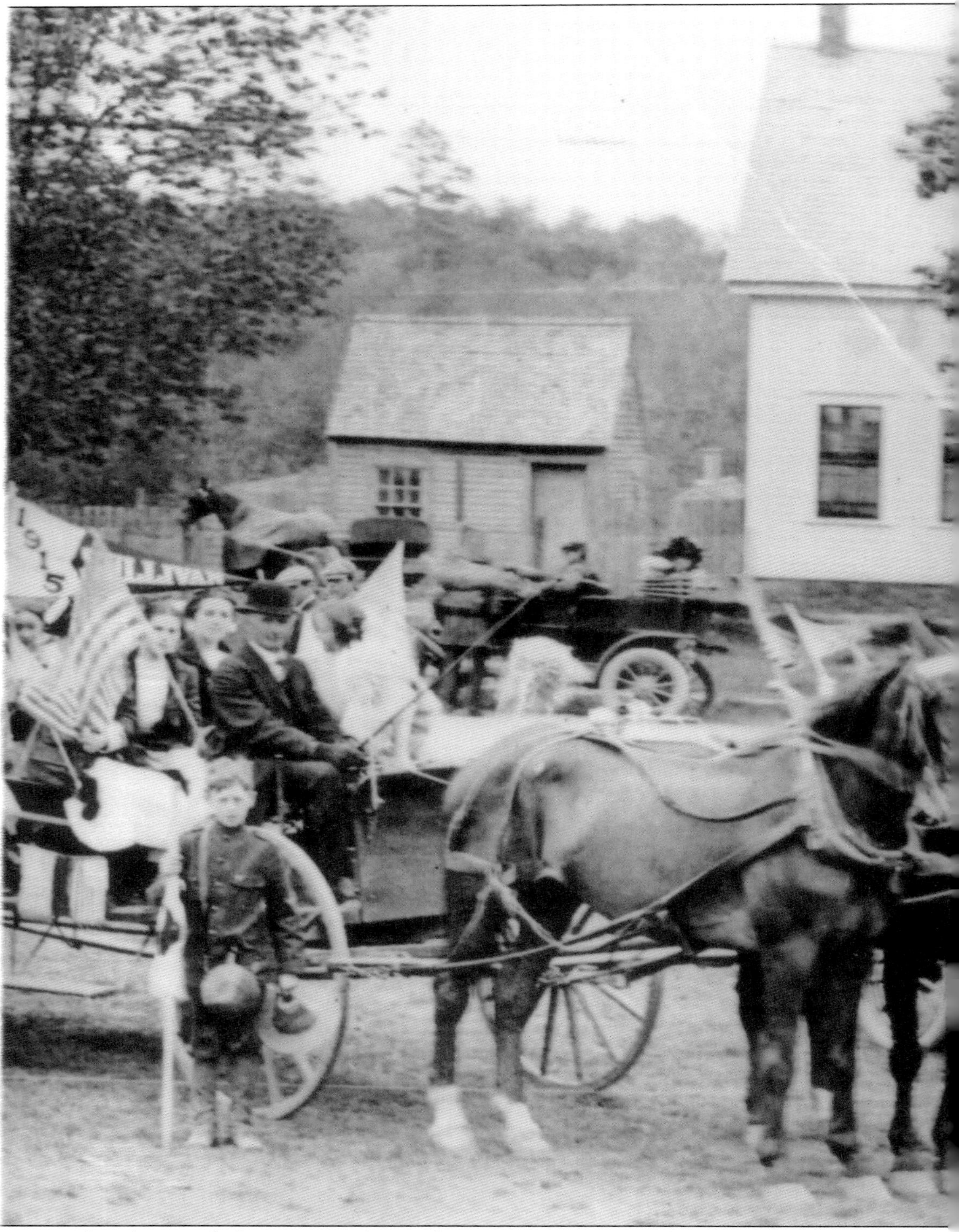

This photograph depicts Berwick's 200th anniversary, just after the turn of the 20th century. Berwick residents wave flags and cheer with hometown pride as they celebrate the anniversary

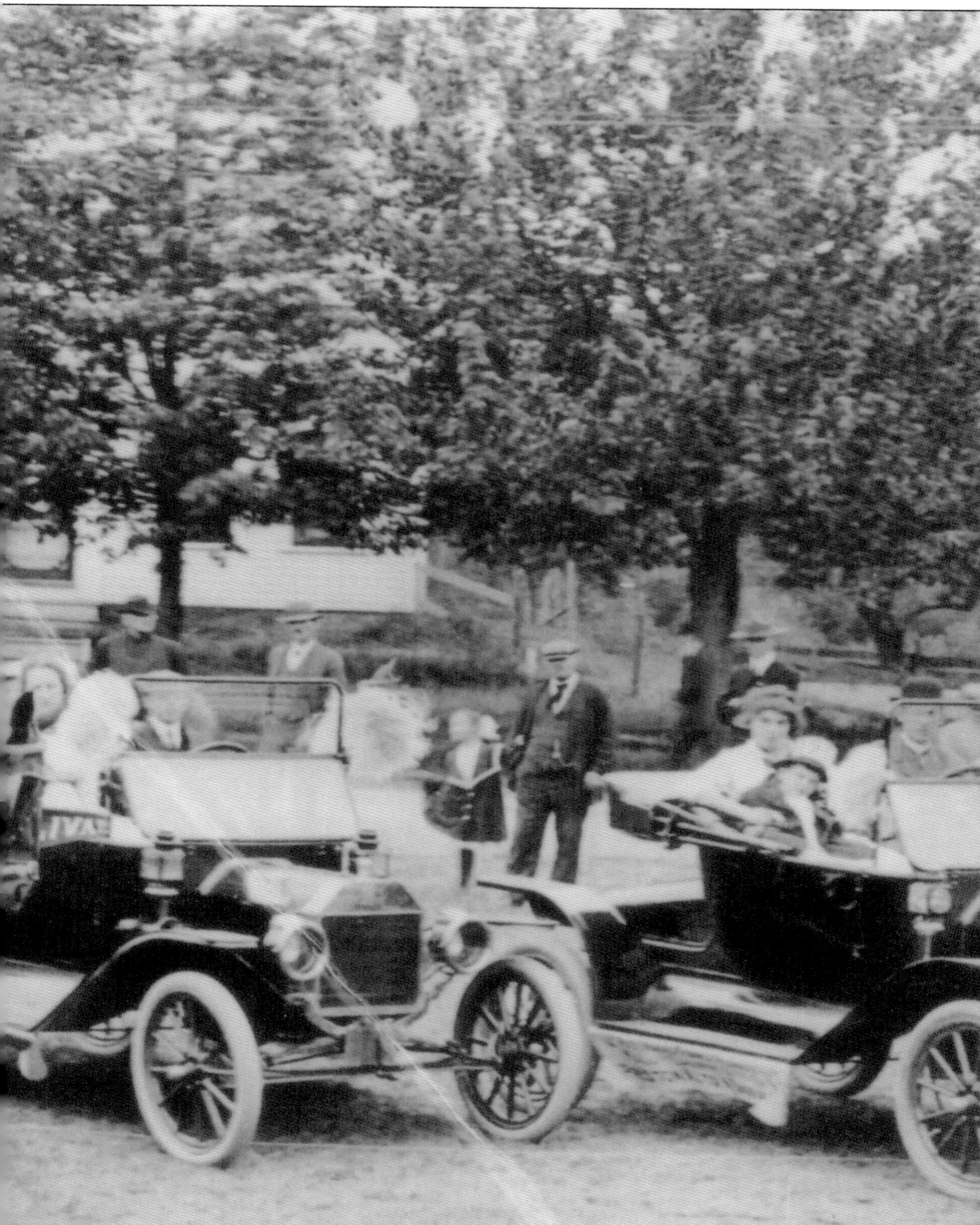

of their town on School Street.